THE MAN

IN THE DUGOUT

by DONALD HONIG

*Fifteen big league managers
speak their minds*

University of Nebraska Press
Lincoln and London

First Bison Book printing: 1995
Most recent printing indicated by the last digit below:
10   9   8   7   6   5   4   3   2   1

Library of Congress Cataloging-in-Publication Data
Honig, Donald.
The man in the dugout: fifteen big league managers speak their minds / by
Donald Honig.
p.   cm.
Originally published: Chicago: Follett Pub. Co., c1977.
Includes index.
ISBN 0-8032-7270-7 (pbk.: alk. paper)
1. Baseball managers—United States—Biography.   I. Title.
GV865.A1H619   1995
796.357′092′2—dc20
[B]
94-42714
CIP

Reprinted by arrangement with Donald Honig. Statistics on major league
managing careers have been added in an appendix to this Bison Book
edition.

For Bill Henderson

CONTENTS

ILLUSTRATIONS

ACKNOWLEDGMENTS

The author would like to express his gratitude to the following: Joan and Theron Raines, Stanley Honig, David Markson, Larry Ritter, Alan J. Grotheer, Edward Bartley, Joel Oppenheimer, Frank Rollins, and Roland Johnson, whose contributions were generous and valuable.

Above all, the author wishes to express his heartfelt thanks to the big league managers who so generously and good-naturedly shared their memories with him and allowed him to use pictures from their personal albums.

THE MAN
IN THE DUGOUT

INTRODUCTION

Baseball fans are probably the most informed of all sports fans. Their knowledge of the game and their recognition and appreciation of talent are always in evidence. Most fans, however, would be unable to evaluate a manager fairly. Fans know when to remove a pitcher, and many know when and whom to pinch-hit. But not many think of the manager's contribution when they see the well-executed relay from the outfield, the successful pickoff, or the carefully engineered rundown on the base paths. The positioning of the men in the relay, the timing of the pickoff, and the teamwork in the rundown are all the handiwork of a manager who has drilled his players constantly and thoroughly for these eventualities.

It is universally agreed that no matter how skilled a manager is, he cannot win unless he has the talent on the ball club. It is also agreed that sometimes the most talented ball club does not win the pennant, and when this happens, the fault generally lies with the manager. So while a "good" manager cannot by himself win a pennant, a "bad" manager can lose a pennant.

The fifteen men herein interviewed all have one thing in common—each at one time or another managed in the big leagues. They range from Bob Shawkey, who managed the New York Yankees for one year, and Burleigh Grimes, who managed the Brooklyn Dodgers for two years, to Joe McCarthy, who managed for twenty-four years, and Walter Alston, who spent twenty-three years as manager of the Dodgers. They range from Ossie Bluege, who almost won a pennant with a wartime collection of retreads, to Mayo Smith, whose team scored one of the great comeback victories in World Series history. They range

3

from Jimmy Dykes, who managed for twenty-one years and never finished higher than third, to Dick Williams, who won a pennant in his managerial debut.

Managers, as Bobby Bragan puts it, are "hired to be fired." And Dick Williams says about the job, "It's the most insecure position in the organization." Both statements are true, and what's more, there is no discernible or predictable pattern to dismissal. Jimmy Dykes managed the White Sox for thirteen years, never finishing higher than third. What kept him on the job? According to Dykes, it was an intelligent general manager, Harry Grabiner, who realized that Jimmy was consistently saddled with second-division clubs and, under the circumstances, was doing the best possible job year in and year out. Not until Grabiner left did Dykes lose his job. Eddie Sawyer, on the other hand, brought the Phillies their first pennant in 35 years and a year and a half later was fired in the middle of the season. In 1944 Luke Sewell won the only pennant the St. Louis Browns ever won—and was fired two years later.

There are as many theories as there are managers (and players and owners and fans) as to what makes a good manager. It's not one's strategy, according to Roger Peckinpaugh. There's no mystery there: "Don't I know what you're going to do, and don't you know what I'm going to do?" Rather, it's the ability to get the most out of one's players. That, it seems, is the manager's most important skill. How does a manager accomplish that? Says Peckinpaugh, "All you have to remember is not to do anything to make them hate your guts." That's not to say that managing is a popularity contest, but while managers say that all they're interested in is winning, they all recognize well the crucial element, and it is crucial, involved in the player-manager relationship—the earning and maintaining of the players' respect for the manager's judgment. Leo Durocher is a prime example of this fact. His abrasive personality irritated and offended a lot of his players, but, as Bobby Bragan, who played for Durocher, says, "He was so knowledgeable and so adept at making the right moves that he just forced you to respect him, which was all he wanted."

Billy Herman says, "I can tell you exactly where the manager makes his biggest contribution to the winning and losing of ball games—in his knowledge of the fundamentals and his insistence upon his players knowing them." Further, Herman says, "There's no way you can really measure it, but at a guess I'd say that if every man hustled on every play, it could mean an extra ten games a year for the team."

The consensus, therefore, is that winning is contingent upon successful communication with one's players. The approaches and the techniques differ with the man. Eddie Sawyer, who won a pennant with a young Philadelphia Phillie team, liked to get as close to his players as possible. He wanted to know about their families and their backgrounds. Sawyer believed that if you knew a player thoroughly off the field, you would be in a better position to guess what he might do on the field. Paul Richards, on the other hand, says, "I wanted to keep them at arm's length, but no further. The door was always open, as far as baseball was concerned. . . ." Richards, whose insistence upon his players being constantly drilled in the fundamentals is unrelenting, also says, "You learn more through the mistakes of the managers you play for than you learn through their good points," which suggests that successful managing is an unlearning as well as a learning process.

John McGraw was by many accounts a tyrant on the ball field, an absolute lord and master who would not tolerate mistakes. (By mistakes, it should be pointed out, one means errors of omission, not commission. No manager will ever criticize a player for fumbling a ball.) But McGraw was successful because he had won his players' respect and had instilled pride in them. (Read Al Lopez's comments about what a McGraw-led team looked like on the field.) Even as hard-bitten and tough-minded a veteran as Burleigh Grimes considered it a privilege to have played for McGraw.

Connie Mack, also a very successful manager, was McGraw's opposite in temperament. He was a kindly, patient man who never lost his temper or used profanity and whose disposition was just as even whether he was in first place or last. Today

venerable baseball men who played for Connie Mack, such as
Bob Shawkey, remember him with affection and respect because
"he knew how to handle men."

The job then, on the face of it, seems virtually impossible to
perform. Not only must a man be a strategist and tactician with
sophisticated knowledge of a highly detailed game and have the
capability of making snap decisions in critical moments, but he
must also maintain harmony on a squad of twenty-five men of
diverse social, economic, cultural, ethnic, and racial backgrounds
during seven months of continuous traveling and constant pressures from within and without. He must be the soother of the
delicate ego and the builder of the broken self-confidence. He
must disguise his despair and disappointment, temper his elation,
and maintain his optimism. He must deal daily with an inquiring
press, be polite to countless strangers, and reassure his employ-
ers, who have placed the heart of a multimillion-dollar franchise
in his care. He schemes and scrambles to keep it all going, to
somehow get more spring into a man's legs and snap into his
swing. And if he is a realist—and they all are—he knows that
one day the general manager will call him into the office or
appear suddenly at the hotel in the middle of a road trip and tell
him that "for the best interests of the club we have decided. . . ."

DONALD HONIG

1

BOBBY BRAGAN

ROBERT RANDALL BRAGAN
Born: October 30, 1917, Birmingham, Alabama
Managerial career: Pittsburgh Pirates, 1956–57; Cleveland
    Indians, 1958; Milwaukee-Atlanta Braves, 1963–66

Versatile as a ballplayer, Bobby Bragan was colorful and innovative as a manager. After a playing career that saw service with the Philadelphia Phillies and the Brooklyn Dodgers, Bragan went on to manage three major league clubs. He later became president of the Texas League and is now president of the National Association.

I was with the Dodgers in 1947 when Jackie Robinson was promoted from Montreal. This was a big moment—the first black player in the big leagues. Branch Rickey had laid an awful lot of groundwork in getting ready for it. He'd spent countless hours with Jackie, readying him to accept all the abuse and name-calling that he knew was going to come Jackie's way.

In spring training there were newspaper stories about some of the southern boys on the Dodgers not wanting to play on the same team with a black man. So Mr. Rickey asked several of them to come to his quarters to talk, one at a time. I was one of them. I was born and raised in Birmingham, Alabama, which I suppose is just about as southern as you can get. When I walked into the room, the only other person present besides Mr. Rickey was Arthur Mann, a writer and a very good friend of his. Mr. Rickey came right to the point.

"I understand that there's a conspiracy going on around here to get Robinson off the club and that you're part of it."

"I'm not part of any conspiracy," I said. "And if there is one going on, I don't know anything about it. But I do know there's some resentment."

He lifted those big bushy eyebrows and said, "Oh, is there?" pretending to be surprised.

"Yes, sir," I said. I'd made up my mind that I was going to be as honest with him as I could.

"Well, I'm going to tell you this," he said. "I don't care if a man's got pink skin or green skin or black skin. If he can go farther to his left or farther to his right than the man who's out there now, he's going to play. Do you understand that?"

"Yes, sir. I understand it."

"So if you'd rather be on another club, if you want to be traded, we'll accommodate you."

"That's fine with me," I said. "I'd just as soon be traded. I don't want a big fuss made of it, but I'd just as soon be on another team."

He stared at me for a while, very thoughtfully, and said, "I appreciate your honesty, Bobby."

And that was the start of a great friendship between Mr. Rickey and me. That's right. He didn't take offense at what I'd said because he knew I was born and raised in Alabama. He knew that I'd grown up surrounded by a way of thinking that had been there long before I came on the scene and that I couldn't help but have it imparted to me. He understood that for me it was going to be a tremendous adjustment to play alongside a black man. He took it all into account; he took *everything* into account. He was a great student of human nature, that man, a great psychologist.

A few days later Arthur Mann came to me and said, "Bobby, Mr. Rickey really appreciated what you told him in there. You were honest with him."

Of course, a month or so later any resentment that anybody had left them because it soon became apparent that there wasn't any way we were going to win without Jackie. The guys who had been reluctant to sit down with him in a dining car were sitting down now. I wasn't traded; I stayed with the club all year, and we won the pennant and got into the World Series.

Bobby Bragan in 1940

And I'll tell you, Jackie won the respect of everybody by sheer
guts and ability. Nobody ever came into the big leagues under
less favorable circumstances, and he handled himself beautifully
and he played like a demon. He was one of the greatest ballplayers ever to come down the pike.

Being Jackie Robinson's teammate was one of the best breaks I
ever got. Watching what he had to go through helped me. It
helped make me a better, more enlightened man, and it helped me
to have a future in baseball as a manager because later on I was
going to have to manage fellows like Felipe Alou, Maury Wills,
Henry Aaron, and plenty of other black players. If I hadn't had
that experience with Jackie, I don't think I could have done it. It
was a breakthrough for me, a great experience that I learned from
and built upon later in life.

Jackie and I became good friends. Side by side we mourned our
great loss in the same pew at Mr. Rickey's funeral. The respect
and admiration that we shared for our mutual "father" served to
cement our friendship.

Branch Rickey was the greatest man I ever met. I don't know
who's in second place, but there's quite a gap between them. You
can't praise that man enough for his achievements. You can't give
him enough credit. And I know that, above everything else, he
was proudest of having had a hand in breaking down the color
barrier in baseball.

You want to know why the National League is the stronger
league? why it's dominated for so many years? why it draws more
fans? Branch Rickey. He's the answer. Pure and simple. He
signed Robinson. Then he signed Campanella and Newcombe.
Then the other teams in the league started to get the message, and
here come Willie Mays and Monte Irvin and Frank Robinson and
Ernie Banks and Henry Aaron, and so on. All in the National
League. All due to Mr. Rickey's leadership. The American League
was left holding the sack for a long, long time, and it's going to be
a long, long time before they catch up.

When you're managing, you always want to improve your
ballplayers. I suppose every manager thinks he can do that. But
you can't always do it, and you shouldn't always want to try it.

That's something I learned from Mr. Rickey. He'd have us all together at meetings in Vero Beach, all the minor league managers and coaches and scouts. He'd have these big meetings, with charts and blackboards. One day he was talking about a kid hitter in camp. "This fellow's got an unusual batting stance. Boys, I don't want you to fool with a man who's got an unusual batting stance." Then he turned and wrote on the blackboard *In extremis.* "How many of you fellows know what that means?" he asked. "That's Latin for 'extreme circumstances.' " Then he went on to tell a story. He was always illustrating his points with stories.

"I had an uncle," he said. "An avowed atheist. Never believed in a supreme being. In his eighty-third year he took ill and his doctor said to him, 'It grieves me to tell you this, but for you it's just a matter of a few hours.' My uncle looked up at the ceiling and said, 'God help me.' First time in his life he'd ever uttered those words." Then Mr. Rickey gave us all a very stern look and said, "Mr. Manager, when that hitter comes to you and says 'Would you help me?' that's when I want you to experiment with his stance and his approach to hitting. And not until then. Otherwise *the finger of guilt will point at you the rest of your career.*"

So after you've heard that and you go back and take over your club and a guy goes 0 for 14, you don't get too excited about it.

Time and time again he'd drive his point home with a story. One night, not long before we broke camp and scattered around the country, he told us, "You managers are all going to different cities, some of you for the first time. First time you've been in Pueblo, first time you've been in Valdosta," and so on down the list. "Now, I want you to go in there and be part of that community. All it takes is a little bit of the right kind of effort." And then came the story.

"There used to be an old boy who'd sit in the railroad station and wait for the trains to come in. Once in a while a man would get off, put his bag down, and say to the old boy 'What kind of town is this?' Invariably the old boy would say 'What kind of town did you come from?' 'Oh,' the man might say, 'everybody cutthroat—hooray for me, the hell with you.' 'That's the kind of town this is,' the old boy would say. A few days later another train would stop and another man get off. He'd see the old boy sitting there and ask him the same question, 'What kind of town is this?' The old boy would give him the same answer: 'What kind of town did you come from?' 'Oh,' the man might say, 'very cooperative. Everybody helping one another.' 'That's the kind of town this is,' the old boy would say."

That was Mr. Rickey's way of telling us that if we went into those towns with positive, cooperative attitudes, we'd find positive, cooperative people. Managing to him was more than strategy and developing ballplayers; it was becoming part of a community and getting a community to become part of a team.

UPI PHOTO

Branch Rickey
"The greatest man
I ever met."

I came up to the big leagues as a shortstop with the Phillies in 1940. That was fortunate for me because we had the worst team in the National League. If I had gone to St. Louis, where they had Marty Marion, or to Brooklyn, where they had Pee Wee Reese, or with most any other team, I would have been sent right back to the minors. But the Phillies needed a lot of help, and Doc Prothro, who was managing, opened the door for me to play short. Sometimes there's an advantage to being on a bad ball club. Later on, when our catchers were injured, I volunteered to go behind the plate. Being able to catch helped keep me in the big leagues a few more years.

It was different for a manager in those days. All he had to do was walk in to the dugout and say "Sic 'em," and we'd take off for our positions hell-bent for leather. If the manager asked you to run through the wall, why you'd run through the wall. Blind loyalty. The kind that doesn't exist anymore. No question in my mind about it. How do I account for it? Change of times. Everything has changed, not just baseball. The whole social fabric—all the attitudes, perspectives, what have you. I suspect that today there's less concern for the team as a whole; individual accomplishment supersedes everything else. But it's no different from any other business.

It's a different breed of player today, and consequently a different breed of manager. There was a time when the manager didn't give a damn if anybody in the clubhouse liked him or not. He'd dress you down in front of everybody else or call you into the office and take a thousand dollars from you for loafing on the field and not really be concerned about repercussions or feelings. Today, you take a guy's money for loafing or for not showing, you get a call from the Players Association the next morning or from the general manager wanting to see you in his office to thrash it out. It makes running the club more difficult.

After Prothro left, Hans Lobert took over. He was an old-timer from the McGraw era. Lobert was unique in one respect—he had a different sign for every ballplayer in the lineup. My bunt sign might be somebody else's hit-and-run sign. He had four or five different signs for each player and remembered what each one of

them was. He was the only manager I ever played for who had
that particular system. He had to have a hell of a memory.

Lobert was a wonderful fellow, with a fine sense of humor. But
I saw him do something one day I'll never forget. He was
coaching third, and one of those raucous fans in Philadelphia got
on him and stayed on him the whole game. Wouldn't let up. With
the small crowd we had, everybody in the ball park could hear
this loudmouth giving it to Hans. Inning after inning Hans came
back to the bench and never said a word. Here's the mark of a real
veteran, I thought, somebody who's been around long enough to
ignore the vituperation. Calm, cool, above it all. But as soon as
that last out was made, Hans took off. He must have been over
sixty years old at the time, but he went over the railing like a kid
and went tearing up the steps to the upper deck where that guy
was. He grabbed him by the collar and was really going to work
on him, but a couple of ballplayers who had gone up after him
interceded. So I guess you might say that those fires never went
out in Hans Lobert.

That couldn't happen today—at least it's very unlikely—
because the manager is seldom out there on the coaching lines
anymore. Managing has become a specialized field. A lot of
things have become specialized. The manager used to be out
there coaching third base himself because that's the most important coach you've got, that fellow at third. He can't afford to make
mistakes. He knows the contours of the fence in every park; he
knows which outfielders have got the good arms and which ones
you can run on; he knows his own runners, which ones he can
send home and which ones he'd better stop, given the circumstances. It's a science all in itself, and to put the extra responsibility on yourself, if you're managing, takes away from your efficiency.

That's one way the game has become more sophisticated today.
You've got all these specialists—on the lines, in the dugout, in the
bull pen. In the old days all you had was one or two coaches. It
made managing a bit more difficult, but a guy who's equipped to
manage a big league ball club has got to be knowledgeable in
every facet of the game, whether it's baserunning or throwing a

curveball or breaking up a double play. He really doesn't need a coach to impart all that.

I was traded to Brooklyn in 1943. Durocher was managing there then. Best manager I ever played for. Never heard a ballplayer second-guess him. He never missed a move. On most teams there will be a game now and then when you hear a player say "I sure wish we'd have bunted that man over," or a similar comment. I never heard those remarks when Durocher was managing. Not once. His players had implicit faith in his moves and maneuvers on the field.

Leo had an aggressive personality. He wanted to win. That came first with him, ahead of everything else. Not everybody cottoned to him. He could irritate some people. You either loved him or you didn't; there wasn't any in-between. But by and large they all respected him.

We had some great ballplayers on the '43 Dodgers—fellows like Dolph Camilli, Billy Herman, Arky Vaughan, Dixie Walker, Paul Waner, Joe Medwick, Whit Wyatt, Kirby Higbe, Bobo Newsom, Johnny Allen. That's quite a cluster of veteran ballplayers, some of them real individuals. But there was only one master on that ball club, and they all knew who he was. In the clubhouse the manager is king, and nobody was ever more so than Leo Durocher. He was so knowledgeable and so adept at making the right moves that he just forced you to respect him, which was all he wanted. Didn't mean a damn to him whether you liked him or not.

We had a kid join the team that year—in '43—who could throw the hell out of the ball. Rex Barney. There's an awful lot of guys who will tell you Rex Barney was the fastest pitcher they ever saw. Speed to burn. Now and then somebody will ask me what happened to him, what went wrong, why a boy with an arm like that never became a star. Well, I don't know. I've seen him down at Vero Beach in what they called the string area. Mr. Rickey had devised this area where he had strings constructed to form the strike zone. If the pitcher threw the ball between those strings, you knew he was throwing strikes. Well, one day Leo tells me to

*Dixie Walker, Joe
Medwick, Dolph
Camilli, Pete Rei-
ser of the 1941
Brooklyn Dodgers*

go over there and warm up Barney because he might use him in
the eighth or ninth inning of this game we're playing.

I went over with Rex and began warming him up. Every pitch
he threw went right through those strings. Fastballs and curves.
Then Leo calls him in. Rex promptly walks two men on eight
pitches. Seeing a batter up there with a bat in his hand made a
difference.

Then another time, we're playing the Giants in the Polo
Grounds. This is in 1947, when Burt Shotton was managing.
Barney is pitching for us, and the score is either tied or we're a
run ahead. There's a runner at second and Sid Gordon is the
hitter. Shotton sends Clyde Sukeforth, one of our coaches, out to
the mound with a message: "Throw the fastball. Stay with the
fastball." Sukeforth does that and then comes back and sits down
next to Shotton. The next pitch Barney throws is a curve that
bounces on home plate and goes over the catcher's head, and the
guy scores from second.

After the game, when we got in the clubhouse, Shotton called
Barney over and said, "What did Sukeforth tell you when he came

Rex Barney
"He probably threw as hard
as any man who ever lived."

to the mound?" Barney looked at him and said, "Sukey? He didn't come to the mound." He hadn't even been aware that Sukeforth had been out there to talk to him. That's hard to believe, isn't it? But that's probably one of the things that kept him from being a great pitcher—his mind wandered while he was working, and the ball wandered with it. It was heartbreaking because he probably threw as hard as any man who ever lived. And a nice fellow, too. Very likable.

After I'd played for about four or five years, I started to think about managing. When I was with the Dodgers, I used to spend as much off-time as I could talking baseball with Clyde Sukeforth and with Gene Mauch, who was just a rookie then but always a keen student of the game. One time Mickey Owen, Eddie Stanky, and I were having a baseball confab in the club car of a train going to Indianapolis, where we were going to stop off to play an exhibition game before going on to Chicago. Well, we got so engrossed that when the train stopped at Indianapolis and the team got off, we went right on with our baseball strategy session, not taking any notice at all, and rode on to the next stop. That's how deep some of that talk got.

There's an awful lot of thinking that goes along with the job, and a lot of discussion and theorizing. I remember one time down at Vero Beach, when I was managing in the Dodger organization, there was a difference of opinion among some of the managers as to how to make the double steal with men on first and third. Some had the opinion that if you're on third you can wait until the catcher's peg got by the pitcher on its way to second before you headed home. We went out and disproved that. In other words, that runner on third has got to have a good lead and he's got to run as soon as the catcher releases the ball; otherwise two throws back and forth will nail him every time. What happens if the pitcher cuts it off? You lose.

Some of the old, acquired wisdom has to be tested, too, occasionally. When I was making the transition from shortstop to catcher, one of the things they used to teach in that situation was to look the runner back to third before you threw to second. Well, if I've looked down there a thousand times, I still haven't seen anything. I look, all right, but as far as seeing if he's got a twenty-foot lead or a ten-foot lead or if he's standing on the bag, I would never see it because if you look long enough to actually see what's there, there's no way you're going to throw the man out at second.

Now, these things are very fine slices out of a ball game, but they can make the difference between winning and losing. You can keep refining this game until it becomes very, very subtle. Sometimes you wait all season to pull a certain play. For instance, with a man on first and the count two and two on the hitter, the next pitch eludes the catcher and the runner goes to second. You might want to walk the batter to set up the double play, or you might *pretend* you want to. You have two different signs to give the catcher. You get his attention and hold up four fingers—that means you want the batter put on. Or you point to first base—that means you want him to pretend the fourth ball is coming up and you want the pitcher to throw a good hard strike to surprise the batter.

I got away with that a few times. You might strike out a guy
once or twice a season that way, but when you do it, it can mean a
ball game. I pulled it on Minnie Minoso once, when I was
managing in Cuba. The situation came up and I made a big
production out of yelling "Put him on. Put him on." The catcher
moved out and in this case the pitcher, Billy O'Dell, threw a
change of pace up there, a little lollipop that floated right over the
plate. Minoso didn't even see it. He had his head turned and was
in conversation with the umpire. In the middle of the conversation the umpire said, "Minnie, I'm afraid you're out."

How did I become a manager? In June of '48, Mr. Rickey came
up to me one day and said, "Burt Shotton has spoken highly of
you, Bobby. We both think you've got managerial possibilities. If
a job comes up in the organization, would you like to try it?"
"Yes, sir," I said.
Later in the month they let the manager at Fort Worth go. Mr.
Rickey offered me the job and I took it. I stayed at Fort Worth for
five years and then went on to manage Hollywood in the Pacific
Coast League. Again it was through Mr. Rickey. Hollywood was a
Pirate affiliate, and by that time Mr. Rickey had left Brooklyn and
taken over at Pittsburgh. Then in '56 I got the Pittsburgh job.
When I arrived there, Mr. Rickey was moving out of his office to
make room for Joe Brown; his last official act had been to bring
me in to manage the club. Looking back now, I suppose I should
have appreciated Joe Brown, since he was taking over as the new
general manager, but my allegiance and my loyalty and my
respect were for Mr. Rickey. I even invited him down to spring
training to get the benefit of his advice. Politically, that probably
wasn't the smartest thing to do.
The Pirates were a last-place club when I took over, but there
was some potential there. We had Dale Long, Dick Groat, Bob
Skinner, Bill Mazeroski, Roberto Clemente, and a few good
pitchers, like Bob Friend, Vern Law, and Roy Face.
Clemente was just a kid then, his second year up. He was a real
introvert. Very quiet, morose almost. But he performed; man, did
he perform! And he had tremendous pride. But I learned one

Roberto Clemente

thing about him early on—if he didn't feel like playing, you'd better let him sit. Wherever I managed, two hours before the game started, that lineup was posted on the board. I always wanted a man to know if he was starting. Now and then Clemente would come to me and say, "I don't feel like playing." If it had been somebody else, I would have asked him what the hell he was talking about. But not Clemente. When he didn't want to play, he wouldn't play, and that's all there was to it. It didn't happen very often, but it happened. It was usually a backache that he complained about. How serious it was, I don't know, but I do know that he believed it was serious and that he was sincere about it. Remember, this was before he was a great star, so you had to believe he was sincere about his aches and pains and not trying to take advantage of his status.

I tried to innovate when I was managing. For instance, I had a theory that your best hitter should lead off, your second best should bat second, and so on. I discussed this with Mr. Rickey and he said, "A manager cannot be faulted for batting his best hitter first. There's no way you can fault him for that." You see, the first inning is the only time a manager controls who will hit. So if one batter on your ball club is going to go to bat five times and the rest of them are going to go four, I'd rather have DiMaggio go for me, or Ted Williams, than, say, Dick Groat or Eddie Stanky or Maury Wills because I may be one run behind when he's up there for that fifth time. And on the other hand, if DiMaggio or Williams is leading off the game for me, I may suddenly be one run ahead.

Then the argument comes up, What about the pitcher? Your best hitter is always batting behind the pitcher. But you can take care of that by moving the pitcher up to the seventh spot and dropping your normal two leadoff men down to the eighth and ninth spots, so your big hitter is still batting behind them. You see, you bat your big hitter third, not fourth, to insure he's going to come up in the first inning; otherwise he's liable to be leading off the second inning for you. So why not hit him first? For one thing, it's a deterrent against intentional walks—that's 162 times you know he's going to be pitched to.

Based on the 154-game schedule, which I operated under, the leadoff man would go to bat 17 times more than the number two man. And the number two man would go 17 times more than the number three man. Same thing for numbers three and four. So that's 51 more at bats than if he's hitting fourth. That can be four or five more home runs, which can mean four or five ball games for you.

I tried it out at Pittsburgh for about 65 games. What happened? We continued to lose. It was a last-place club any way you wrote out the lineup. But we had some fun with it. Frank Thomas was my leadoff man. Dick Groat was normally the second hitter, but under the new lineup it meant he was hitting ninth. He was a sensitive man and very proud. I must have had fifteen guys standing around waiting for Groat to come in and read his name in the ninth hole. He came in and took a look—wanted to know what the hell was going on. It went on, all right. I still think it's a good idea if you've got the right horses.

I had another theory—hitting and running with a man on third. You've got to have the right man up at the plate, of course. Take a Groat or an Alvin Dark or a Billy Herman—guys that you know can hit the ball and get a piece of it. If the man on third is running, he'll score on a ground ball. If it's a fly ball, there's still time to go back and tag up. So you've got two shots at getting the run home. Sure, it's a gambling play. You need a man who can lay the bat on the ball and who's not going to hit a line drive down third and decapitate your runner. We tried it a few times—that particular situation doesn't come up that often, of course—and more times than not it worked.

We had another play all primed when I was with Pittsburgh—men on first and third, less than two out, and a pop foul hit down the line to either the first baseman or the third baseman. I want that runner from first to break for second after the catch. If he draws a throw, the runner on third will score. But I'll be damned, the play never came up.

I was let out in Pittsburgh in the middle of '57, after a year and a half. I don't know if it was because I was Rickey's man or not. Anyway, Joe Brown gave me the word in Chicago. I'll tell you

Leo Durocher
"You either loved him or
you didn't. There wasn't
any in-between."

what happened the night before, in Milwaukee. I had been thrown out of five games and all five times by the same umpiring crew. In this particular game in Milwaukee, Groat thought that a runner had missed touching second base going from first to third, and he made an appeal play to the umpire, Stan Landis. Well, as soon as Landis disallowed it, he took about four steps toward me in the dugout and said, "He's safe, Bobby. What do you think of that?"

I held my nose and then said, "That's what I think of it, right there."

He took a few more steps and gave me the old "Get out of here." He's throwing me out of the game for that! So I came running out and said, "This is five times you guys have thrown me out. I don't know why this crew always gives me trouble, but I'm going to find out. And I'm going to be comfortable while I'm finding out. I'll be right back."

I went back to the dugout and told Danny Murtaugh—he was one of my coaches—to get me a hot dog and a cold drink. All they could rustle up was an orange drink with a straw in it, and I took that and went back out there.

"Now let's talk about it," I said to Landis. "What have you guys got against me? Would you like a sip of orange drink while we discuss it?"

He got provoked and told me to get out. Eventually I did, of course, but I thought I'd made my point. Warren Giles, the league president, fined me a hundred or two, but that was all right.

The next day is an off-day in Chicago and Joe Brown flies in. He came up to my room and gave me the word. He was upset about it, but I told him not to shed any tears for me. There's the old saying about managers—you've heard it a thousand times— "Hired to be fired." Sure, it hurts your pride, but you know it's inevitable.

Did the orange juice have anything to do with it? Well, it was something to hang it on. The pot had been boiling, and that made it boil over. A cup of cold orange juice.

I guess I've pulled a few antics on the ball field as manager. One time when I was managing in the Pacific Coast League, I had a little run-in with an umpire. I thought a pitched ball had struck the hitter's bat. The umpire said no, that it had hit the man's hand, and awarded him first base. I went out to him and said, "Would you ask the other umpire if he heard a wood sound?"

"I don't need to ask anybody," he said. "I know what it hit."

"Oh," I said, "you've got all the answers, is that right? You know everything, is that it?"

"That's right," he said. "I'm in charge out here."

"You are, are you?" I said. "Well, I'm going to show you how much respect I've got for your authority. I'm going to lay down here and go to sleep. What do you think of that?"

And I did that. Stretched right out on the grass. He was

flabbergasted. Then the other umpire came over, looked down at me, and said, "Bobby, he's thrown you out of the game."

"That's right," I said. "But I'm not ready to go just yet."

So I got the reputation for doing the unorthodox thing. I wouldn't say that that reputation was unjustified. Another time I sent my batboy out to coach third base. This was out in Hollywood. Ed Runge was umpiring behind the plate—this is before he went up to the American League. We had a disagreement about something and I was ejected. I went into the dugout and said to the batboy, "Hey, go coach third base." So the kid takes off for third base. He's about thirteen years old. Runge stops him. "Listen," he says to the kid, "don't let Bragan make a fool out of you." "Oh, he's not," the kid says. "This is great." And he runs up to the third-base coaching box and starts clapping his hands to get a rally going, whereupon Runge runs him right back to the dugout.

Then one night we're playing extra innings in Hollywood against Oakland. And I mean extra innings—we're in the bottom of the 21st. Allen Gettel pitched all the way for Oakland. Now, you can't start an inning after five minutes to one, and there are two clocks on the wall indicating two minutes to one. So I use a pinch hitter for my pitcher, Bob Hall, who's been pitching a hell of a ball game, figuring this is the last inning. We don't score, and when the inning is over, it's one o'clock by the clocks on the wall. But the umpire behind the plate shows me his watch and says, "This is the official time, and I've got six minutes to one. Start another inning."

I didn't even have a pitcher warmed up, so I had to do that in a hurry, after letting the umpire know what I thought of his watch. Well, we lose the game in the 22nd inning. Oakland gets four runs.

So the next night I sent my coach, Gordie Maltzberger, up to home plate with the lineup cards, and he's got wristwatches running up and down both arms and an alarm clock around his neck. The umpire pretended not to notice.

That was my way of getting to them. I never believed in going out there and calling them all kinds of names. Had my own

approach. Another time in the Coast League we lost the first game
of a doubleheader on what I felt were a couple of questionable
calls. Late in the second game we're losing big, around 12–1, and
another dispute comes up. I went out to talk to the plate umpire.

"Listen," I said, "you guys are making a farce of the game, do
you know that? Now if you really want to make it a farce, I'll
show you how to operate."

Lee Walls was the batter. I took him back to the dugout with me
and sent up a pinch hitter, Mel Queen, a pitcher. I gave him
instructions. "Don't stay up there long enough for the pitcher to
throw you a ball." He's announced, gets into the box, and then
steps back out. Time. I send up a pinch hitter for him. Same
instructions. Kept doing that. Sent up eight pinch hitters in the
same slot and didn't let any of them look at a pitch. Just having a
little fun, trying to get under the umpire's skin.

I don't want to sound like a wise guy. I really do have great
respect for authority. When I was managing Fort Worth, Mr.
Rickey decided to economize a little. Instead of the managers
wiring in their reports, he told us to airmail them. A little while
later he sends me a telegram: "Do you need a shortstop or can you
go with your present infield?" So in order to save money, I wired
him back a one-word telegram—"Yes." He wires me back, "Yes
what?" And I wire him back, "Yes, sir."

In the winter of '57 I was managing in Cuba, and Hank
Greenberg came down and hired me to manage the Indians. A
few weeks later Hank left the job and there I was, again working
for a man who hadn't hired me. This time it was Frank Lane. He
was an unusual fellow. Nice guy, but impetuous. He was inclined
to second-guessing. Out loud. One day we're getting beat 2–1 by
the Orioles in the bottom of the ninth with two out. Billy O'Dell
is pitching for them and Russ Nixon is scheduled to hit. That's
lefty against lefty, so I bring in J. W. Porter to hit for Nixon.

Lane is sitting in the press box and he says, "Who's that coming
up to hit?"

"J. W. Porter," somebody says.

"Automatic strikeout," Lane says.

Porter steps in and the first pitch is around his cap bill and he swings at it. Strike one. Next pitch is neck high and he swings at it for strike two. The next pitch is right down the middle and he takes it, but the umpire calls it a ball. That started a big furor which saw Paul Richards, the Orioles' manager, get ejected. After things quieted down, J. W. hit the next one out of sight, over the left center-field fence.

Lane starts yelling in the press box, "That's my boy, J. W. Porter. I signed him. Signed him to his first contract."

Somebody says to him, "But, Frank, you said he was going to strike out."

Lane looks at him and says, "Dammit, he did. The umpire didn't call it, that's all."

Isn't that beautiful? What do you do with a guy like that?

Another time I'm sitting beside Lane in spring training and Minnie Minoso walks up to hit. The count goes to three balls. Lane yells, "Atta boy, Minnie, that's the way to watch that ball." Strike one called. "That's all right, Minnie, you're still way out in front." Strike two called. "Don't take too many now, Minnie." Strike three called. Lane stands up and yells, "You look like a big bag of shit with a cherry on top!" Prerogatives of the general manager.

So I knew how unpredictable he was. I was out of there by the middle of July. But we're good buddies today. Frank Lane is Frank Lane, that's all.

In '63 I took over the Braves. They were still in Milwaukee then. I managed them right through their first year in Atlanta. Had Henry Aaron on my club. What kind of player was he to manage? A dream. Just a dream—on and off the field. I made only one contribution to Henry Aaron as a manager. In my second year there I said to him one day, "Henry, you're making about seventy thousand dollars and Willie Mays is making a hundred and twenty. There isn't a thing he does that you can't. The only difference is he runs. From now on you've got the green light whenever you want to run." He went out and stole something like 31 bases out of 37 attempts. Later on, in evaluating the managers

GEORGE BRACE PHOTO

Henry Aaron
with the Jacksonville Braves in 1953

that he'd played for, he said, "Bobby was the one that made me a complete player." That was very nice to hear. But that was the only contribution I ever made. He made plenty of contributions to me—kept me in business for almost four years.

After the All-Star Game in 1966, I started to hear the rumors again. In fact, I went to John McHale, the general manager, and told him I knew that the owners were putting some pressure on him and that if it would make it more comfortable for him, I would be glad to step aside. He told me to sit tight. But the string was running out, and I was fired before the end of the season.

I'll tell you frankly, I wasn't that brokenhearted. It was around that time that things were starting to change. The demands were starting to come in. There were complaints that the temperature inside the bus wasn't 72 degrees and that the ride to the airport was too long. Transistor radios blared music on the bus. Hair dryers started showing up in the clubhouse. More and more demands for this and that. It seemed that the fun was going out of it—at least it was for me. Times had changed and baseball was changing along with them. I found I didn't have the patience to go along with it.

"Hired to be fired." You've always got to remember that. That's one part of this game you've got to be realistic about. If you're a player, no matter how great, you're going to slow down one day and be released. If you're a manager, you're going to lose your job. It's basic—part of the whole pattern.

One night, when I was managing the Braves in Atlanta, I was attending a banquet honoring Gale Sayers and Henry Aaron. I was sitting at the front table next to the president of a southern university. Midway through the evening he leaned over to me and said, "Mr. Bragan. That job you have as manager of the Braves, it's a very precarious job, isn't it?"

"Yes, it is," I said. "But like they've said before, 'Managers are hired to be fired.' "

He said, "You know, there's a lot of philosophy in that statement. I'll tell you, a lady made a statement to me not too long ago that had a lot of the same philosophy in it."

"What was that?" I asked.

"She said, 'If you come into this world, you will leave it.' "

BURLEIGH ARLAND GRIMES
1916—1934

ONE OF THE GREAT SPITBALL PITCHERS.
WON 270 GAMES, LOST 212 FOR 7 MAJOR
LEAGUE CLUBS. FIVE 20 VICTORY SEASONS.
WON 13 IN ROW FOR GIANTS IN 1927.
MANAGED DODGERS IN 1937 AND 1938.
LIFETIME E.R.A. 3.52.

30

2

BURLEIGH GRIMES

They used to call me Ol' Stubblebeard. That's because I'd let my beard grow the day before I was going to pitch. Did that deliberately. Some people thought I wanted to give myself a mean look out there, but that wasn't the reason. You see, I never used resin because it would smart my skin. All the other fellows used it though, and it was on all the towels. I perspired a lot when I pitched, and I hated picking up a towel that had resin on it because it would burn my face. So I let my whiskers grow to give my skin a little protection.

I was the last of the spitball pitchers—the legal ones. I always threw that pitch. I brought it into pro ball with me. I had an uncle who was a cattle buyer, you see, and one time he let me ride down with him to St. Paul, to the stockyards. This was in 1903. I was ten years old then. First time in the big city. Hell, I'd never even seen a streetcar before. After transacting his business, my uncle took me to a ball game with him, at old Lexington Park. Toledo and St. Paul were playing. The pitcher for St. Paul kept going to his face all the time. I'd never seen that before, and I asked my uncle what he was doing.

"He's loading it up," he said.

"Loading what up?" I asked.

"The ball. He's throwing spitballs."

That was the first I'd heard of that. When I got back to the farm, up in Wisconsin, I talked to an old catcher about it. Then I tried throwing it. About the second or third one I threw did something. He got all excited and told me to try some more, and I did, and that's how I got started throwing that thing.

I used to chew slippery elm—the bark, right off the tree. Come spring the bark would get nice and loose and you could slice it free without any trouble. What I chewed was the fiber from inside, and that's what I put on the ball. That's what they called the foreign substance. That ball would break like hell, away from right-handed hitters and in on lefties.

It wasn't necessarily my number one pitch—the fastball generally was. The spitter was always a threat. When I got into trouble, then they started looking for it, and when I knew they were looking for it, I'd give them something else. But you get a reputation and what can you do about it? People meet me today and they say, "Oh, Burleigh Grimes? You were the spitball pitcher." Well, hell, I threw a fastball, curve, slider, change, screwball. One time I pitched 18 innings against the Cubs, beating Hippo Vaughan 3–2, and I threw only three slow spitters in the ball game. The rest were all fastballs.

I was always interested in baseball. So was my father. He played a little amateur ball around here in Wisconsin back in the 1890s. One day they were playing over near New Richmond and this pitcher threw a curveball to him. Right then and there he quit. He said, "When they get so they can start a-curvin' that thing, I'm through." He retired, and I'll tell you, bud, that curveball has retired a hell of a lot of guys. It's like the fellow said, whoever invented that thing took all the fun out of the game.

We had a kid team called the Redjackets. We played baseball because we loved it, that was all. I was ten or twelve years old at the time, so this was around 1905. No, I didn't have any idols as a kid. Hell, I hadn't heard of anybody yet. I knew there was such a thing as big league baseball, but I'd never heard of Honus Wagner or John McGraw or Christy Mathewson or any of those fellows. The news hadn't got through the timber yet.

I played some semipro ball around home and then decided to take a crack at the pros. This was in 1912. There was a team down in Eau Claire. My dad gave me fifteen bucks, and I went to Eau Claire and asked the manager if I could work out with the team if I paid my own expenses. He said I could. I had fifteen bucks for three weeks—five bucks a week to live on. You could do that in those days, even if you didn't enjoy it a hell of a lot.

After three weeks they came to where they were going to cut

Christy Mathewson
"I'd never heard of
Christy Mathewson
or any of those fellows."

down. They were going to send me away. So I went to the manager.

"Mr. Bailey," I said, "I paid my own expenses. You ought to give me at least one shot anyway."

He said all right and took me along with them. I pitched batting practice and did one thing and another for a while. Still hadn't signed a contract though. Then we were playing in Rochester, Minnesota, and I was on the gate. Taking the tickets, you see. I was the visiting player assigned to the gate. That's how good they thought I was. In the first inning one of the guys comes running around and says Bailey wants me. So I went inside and he told me to warm up.

I came in with the bases full and nobody out. First pitch I make is belted and two runs come in. And that was the last hit they got for the rest of the game. After it's over, the catcher comes out to shake my hand and he says, "Kid, he's going to offer you sixty dollars. Get eighty out of him." I reach the dugout and Bailey is all smiles. He tells me to come into the clubhouse with him.

"I'm signing you up," he says. "Sixty a month."

"I think I ought to get eighty," I said.

His smile went away. "Somebody told you that," he says.
"That's right."
"All right," he says. "I'll give you eighty."
That was my first contract.

I stayed in the minors for four years and in 1916 the Pirates
bought me from Birmingham. I came up in the latter part of the
season. Honus Wagner was still playing ball, though near the end
now. Yeah, by that time I'd heard of him. He was forty-two years
old then and was still something to watch out there at shortstop.
To look at him, you'd have thought he was anything but a
ballplayer. Bowlegged as all get-out. But then you saw him move
on a ball field and you just sat there and watched him with plain
old awe.

He was a cutey too. One day he was batting against a young
pitcher who had just come into the league. The catcher was a kid,
too. A rookie battery. The pitcher threw Honus a curveball, and
he swung at it and missed and fell down on one knee. Looked
helpless as a robin. I was kind of surprised, but the guy sitting
next to me on the bench poked me in the ribs and said, "Watch
this next one." Those kids figured they had the old boy's
weakness, you see, and served him up the same dish—as he knew
they would. Well, Honus hit a line drive so hard the fence in left
field went back and forth for five minutes.

Then I was pitching against the Dodgers in Ebbets Field. This
is 1916 and they're fighting for the pennant. It's late in the game,
the score is 1–1, I've got a man on first, and there's one out.
Wagner walks in from shortstop.

"Hey, kid," he says. "Make this guy hit it to me and I'll get you
a double play."

"Okay," I said. Now, of all things, in those days I certainly
couldn't make a guy hit a ball in any particular direction. So I
threw it in there and darn if it doesn't go down to shortstop. Boy, I
was pleased as hell with myself! Figured I'd impressed old
Honus. He comes in and the ball hits his shoe and goes off into
right center field, the runner scores, and the batter goes to third.

After the ball came back into the infield, here's Honus walking

Grover Cleveland Alexander
"If anybody was ever a better
pitcher than that guy, I wouldn't
know what his name was."

it back to the mound. I can see him to this day—pounding it into his glove, staring at it as he came over, never looking at me. I was wondering what he was going to say.

"Those goddamn big feet were always in my way," he said.

Babe Adams was on that club. Real fine pitcher. Quiet fellow. Never talked much. But he was one of the best pitchers the Pittsburgh ball club ever had. Wilbur Cooper was another one. A left-hander with a good fastball. And they had Max Carey in center field. Hell of a ballplayer.

The year I came into the league, Grover Cleveland Alexander won 33. The year before he'd won 31; the year after, 30. That's who he was. If anybody was ever a better pitcher than that guy, I wouldn't know what his name was. It was just a pleasure to watch him work, even though he was beating your brains out most of the time. Smooth and easy—always smooth and easy. I used more effort winding up than he did in pitching nine innings. He threw a sinker and a curve. Always kept them down. He was fast, too. I'll say he was! That thing would come zooming in and then kick in about three inches on a right-handed hitter. He'd throw you that fastball and that curve, and you couldn't tell which was which because they didn't do anything until they were right on top of you. And once they showed you what they were going to do and where they were going to do it, your bat was someplace else. Yeah, he's my pitcher, Alex.

In 1918 I was traded over to Brooklyn in a deal that sent Stengel to the Pirates. I liked playing in Brooklyn, and I liked managing there. Those fans were all right—a little peculiar at times, but all right. They'd tear the hide right off of you, but just let a stranger come in and say one wrong word to you and they'd throw him out. Boily. That's who I was. "Hey, Boily," they'd yell. "Throw harder. We don't hear you gruntin'." When I was managing there, I had Waite Hoyt, and one day it's in the papers he's got an injury. The next day I go out on the field and some guy yells at me, "Hey, Boily, I hear Hert's hoit."

Had a few good ballplayers there in 1918. Zack Wheat. He won more ball games for me than any other individual. He was just terrific. A great hitter in the pinch, particularly after the seventh inning.

We had Jake Daubert at first base. Gentleman Jake, they called

Jake Daubert

him. Why? Well, he was a gentleman. Conducted himself very nicely. And quite a good hitter—he led the league in batting twice. But they traded him soon after I got there. You see, when the Federal League started up in 1914, Gentleman Jake told Mr. Ebbets that he was going to jump unless the Dodgers gave him a five-year contract at $9,000 a year. Ebbets had no choice but to pay and hated Daubert for it. Traded him first chance he got. Was nine thousand a lot of money in those days? I wouldn't say it was a lot; I'd say it was *all* of it. Christ, I was paid around eighteen hundred my first year in Brooklyn.

I played there for Wilbert Robinson. Uncle Robbie. Great old fellow. I sure liked him. He's the guy that made a pitcher out of me. I'd been just a throw-in in the Stengel deal; hell, I was 3 and 16 for the Pirates the year before. Nobody was interested in Grimes. But I turned right around and won 19 for Uncle Robbie. Somebody asked him, "What'd you do to that guy?" "Hell," he said, "all I did was just give him the ball." Some managers would have filled a billboard telling all that they had done for me, but not Robbie. What he said was what he did—he simply gave me the chance to pitch, and that's all I needed. There was no baloney with him.

How did he handle his players? Well, I think they handled him more than he handled them. It was his clubs, you know, that got called Daffy Dodgers. We had Ivy Olson. Shortstop. He wanted to make a hit in every ball game. Very laudable. But the problem was he never wanted to bunt. Uncle Robbie always sat in back of that concrete post we had in the dugout. When Olson was up and he knew a bunt was in order, he'd keep moving around in the batter's box to keep that post between him and Robbie so Robbie couldn't flash him the sign. We'd watch Robbie move in one direction, Olson in the other. The bunt sign was a clenched fist, and here's Robbie sliding around on the bench with that fist clenched, looking like he wanted to punch somebody, and there's Olson up at the plate ducking around to keep that post between them. Finally Robbie would say, "Ah, the hell with it."

Then we had Chick Fewster. Second baseman. One day he made the double play backwards. Instead of crossing the bag and going to his right while he threw to first, he took the throw from the shortstop and spun all the way around, making a complete circle, and did it that way. When he came into the dugout, Uncle Robbie said, "I've been in baseball for forty years, and I want to ask you a question. What the hell kind of a way is that to make a double play?"

"How'd you like it?" Fewster asked.

"I didn't," Robbie said.

Then there's that famous story about Uncle Robbie trying to catch a ball dropped from an airplane. This happened in Daytona Beach, during spring training in 1916. I was with the Birmingham club then and by chance we were in Daytona that day. We heard some talk in the morning about Ruth Law, who somebody said was the only woman aviator of the day. It seems that some damn fool idle talk had built up as to whether a man could catch a baseball that had been dropped from an airplane. Uncle Robbie said he could do it. He had been a good catcher in his day, you know, and took a lot of pride in that.

So they set it up. Ruth Law would take the plane up and a fellow named Kelly, the Dodgers' trainer, would go with her. He was going to drop the ball. Naturally everybody went out to see it. There was Uncle Robbie, with his catcher's mitt, very serious about the whole thing. Well, the way I heard it, this fellow Kelly thought it would be funny if he traded the baseball for a grapefruit. The plane took off and sailed overhead and this thing dropped out. Robbie went running for it, holding out his mitt, and he caught it all right and was knocked right over with the impact. Of course, the moment the grapefruit hit his glove, it broke and the juice covered his face, and he yelled, "Jesus Christ, I'm all blood!" Then he had a look at what the hell he had caught and everybody was laughing. When he found out who'd done it, he fired him. Fired Kelly's ass right off the Dodger club.

Nineteen twenty was a hell of a year. We won the pennant and had some real fun along the way doing it. That was the year we played that 26-inning 1–1 game with the Braves. That's one of the most famous games in baseball history. And one of the things people like to talk about is the fact that the two starting pitchers went all the way—Joe Oeschger for them and Leon Cadore for us. And most everybody else played all the way, too—that's what people forget. So here's my theory on that. While everybody marvels at the stamina of those two pitchers, they forget that those guys were pitching to two very, very tired ball clubs. You never saw so many lazy bats; they couldn't get a ball out of the infield. Oeschger and Cadore were just throwing that thing right in there. Toward the end of that game Jeff Pfeffer, Sherry Smith, and myself—all pitchers—were agitating Uncle Robbie to put us in the outfield. We were all pretty good hitters, and we were fresh. And by the end of the game Oeschger was throwing just our speed. But Robbie wouldn't do it. So we played until it got dark and nobody won.

You want to hear the payoff on it all? The next day I pitch 13 innings against the Phillies and lose. The day after that we're playing the Braves again and we go 19 innings and lose that one. Christ, there's 58 innings of baseball in three days, and we don't win a game.

We had some other lovely experiences in the World Series that year, against the Indians. I pitched a shutout in the second game, beat them 3–0. I should have stayed in bed after that. You know, after I pitched that shutout, Tris Speaker, who was playing and managing for the Indians, told a newspaperman, "Grimes won't win another game in the Series." What's cooking now? I wondered. That was a hell of a statement for Speaker to make, particularly since he wasn't a pop-off sort of guy. But he was right because he knew something I didn't, and I'll tell you what happened and then I'll tell you how it happened.

I start the fifth game and goddamn it in the first inning they get four runs. Elmer Smith hit a grand slammer off of me, first one ever hit in a World Series. I've got that distinction. They were taking my spitters, you see—taking real good tight pitches. So I came in there with a fast one and he whaled it. Four runs. You know what else happened in that game? I was out by then, but that's the game where Bill Wambsganss pulled the unassisted triple play on us. Only time *that* ever happened in a World Series.

Now get this. We had a fellow named Pete Kilduff playing

Wilbert Robinson
"He's the guy that made
a pitcher out of me."

second base. He's out there and he can see the catcher's signs. Before each pitch he's picking up some sand and putting it in his glove. If it's not a spitter, he drops the sand. If it's going to be a spitter, he keeps it in his glove. He's doing that, you see, so if the ball is hit to him, he'll get some of the wet off of it so it won't slip when he throws it. Christ, I don't know why the hell he had to do that—fellows were throwing it from short, from third. Anyway, it didn't take long for somebody to pick that up and all the hitters had to do was watch Kilduff. We found out about it after the Series. I had some words with Kilduff. He denied doing it, but he never cared a hell of a lot for me after that.

Dazzy Vance joined us in 1922. I've never seen anybody who could throw harder. Bob Feller, Van Mungo, Vance—all out of the same barrel. If you could have measured their speed, you wouldn't have found too much of a separation to make a difference.

A funny thing about that Vance. He'd been knocking around for years with all that great stuff. Hell, he was thirty-one years old when he joined us and finally put it all together. He'd never been able to find that missing link. But I've always believed he found it all at once one day in Pittsburgh. You see, he had that tremendous stuff, but when he pitched to a hitter, he'd hold back just a little. I don't know why—maybe afraid of killing somebody. It's not unusual to see that. The sight of a guy standing up there with a bat in his hand has taken the bloom off many a pitcher.

On this day in Pittsburgh, it was his turn to pitch, and because of a rain delay or something, he went down to warm up in front of the Pittsburgh clubhouse. Some of the Pirates came out to watch him, and he made their eyes pop. You never saw a ball do such tricks. Not only did he have that blazer, but he had a curveball that came in there like a scared snake. One of the Pirates said, "For Christ's sakes, if you threw that way in a game, nobody could touch you." Vance believed him, I guess, because from then on he went and became a great pitcher. Finally made it to shore.

I was traded over to the Giants in '27. I wasn't at all unhappy about it. I always wanted to play for McGraw. I think most everybody in the league wanted to play for McGraw. Sure, he was a strict disciplinarian, but he played the best baseball. He was the smartest man I ever played for. He showed me one simple thing that made me a better pitcher. You see, the way my spitter broke to right-handed batters, they'd hit it to right field in a majority of cases. That's the way I'd been pitching for ten years, and with pretty good success. When I joined McGraw, he said to me, "Burleigh, how's your curveball?"

"Mediocre," I said.

"Pitch it over the middle of the plate and down," he said. "Make them pull the ball to left field. Don't let them hit behind the runner all the time."

You see, if somebody gets a base hit to right field with a man on first, you've got runners on first and third. But if the same guy hits it to left field, you've got runners on first and second. So instead of throwing that spitter all the time and having them snub it into right field on me, I threw the curve over the plate when I had a

John McGraw

man on base and made them hit it in front of the runner. My chances of getting the double play were better, and the base hit didn't hurt me as much.

So I pitched that way and had a fine year, 19–8. Then I went over to Pittsburgh the next year and kept pitching that way and won 25 games, something I'd never done before. I ended up winning 270, but I could've won 300 if I'd learned how to pitch sooner keeping those right-handed hitters out of right field. McGraw proved he knew what he was talking about, which didn't surprise me at all.

He used to have a saying. If you'd made a bad play he'd say, "Son, come over here and sit down by me." You'd do that and he would say, "Now, why did you make that play that way?" Usually the fellow would say, "I thought—" and McGraw would interrupt and say, "What with? You just do the playing. I'll do the thinking for this club." Bill Terry tipped me off about that when I joined the club. "Don't ever say 'I thought' to him," he warned me. I never did. I did my share of thinking, but I never told McGraw about it.

You had to sign in in the mornings, you know. He had an alarm clock in the clubhouse at the Polo Grounds. You had to be there by ten o'clock—and in those days a game started around three or three-thirty. At ten o'clock that alarm went off, and if your name wasn't on that list, it cost you. That's the way he ran things. But he was a great guy.

He had this reputation for being rough on his players—for chewing them out unmercifully. I asked him about that once, how he accounted for it.

"Burleigh," he said, "I pay the highest price for players in baseball. When I get them here to New York and they have two or three good games, the newspapers blow it all up. So then everybody in this town gets interested, all the sharpies and chorus girls. If I can save that guy from himself for two years, I've got me a ballplayer." That come pretty close to answering it? He puts the knuckle on them and lets them know it's going to cost them. His philosophy was to put a little scare into a guy and get a better ballplayer. He knew there was no place like New York, and he tried to put himself between the city and his ballplayers.

McGraw was a great manager because he had his kind of team, and he had his kind of team because he'd been given time on the job to put it together and prove himself. That's what I tried to do when I took over the Dodgers, put together my kind of team. If you can do that, get the boys to play the way you want to manage, then you're a good manager. But you don't do that overnight. It takes time. The average ballplayer who comes along can only play his type of baseball. So on the short term you've got to play what he can play, which limits your game as a manager.

McGraw's was an aggressive game. He was a slasher. He'd run on you, play hit-and-run, suck you in for the bunt, and then hit by you. He liked those guys who'd hustle and break their necks to win a game, like Frisch and Ross Youngs—guys who could do the unexpected and get away with it, who were daring, daring but never reckless. He was that kind of manager, and when that kind of manager gets his kind of players, you can't beat him.

He was secure in his job, you see, so he wasn't afraid of the newspapers' second-guessing him, and he wasn't afraid of making himself look bad. You can avoid ever making yourself look bad by playing a book game. Bunt when the book says to, take when the book says to, and so on. But if you hit in a bunt situation and you're successful, you've just broken it wide open. On the other hand, if you ram into a double play, you've just blown your ball game. Either way it's the manager who makes the first guess and takes the responsibility. And McGraw, more than any other manager who I ever saw or heard about, wasn't afraid of taking on responsibility.

This is not to say you can't win as a book manager. Bill McKechnie was that way. I never saw anyone like him. He always played it the same way, whether he had a good ball club or a horseshit ball club. Always by the book. And he was pretty successful; he won four pennants. Bill was a long-run manager. You knew he was going to be around a long time because he played pure, conservative baseball. Steady. Those kind of guys always have a job, and they'll win for you now and then. Nothing wrong with them.

I stayed with McGraw only a year. I didn't want to leave, but they wouldn't pay me what I wanted. They offered me $15,000, and I wanted more. I would liked to have stayed, but you've got to go where the money is, don't you?

So I was traded to Pittsburgh. That's where I had the pitcher's best friend playing behind me at third base—Pie Traynor. He was a miraculous fielder. Now more than ever it made sense to get them to hit it to the left side. He was always in front of it. One day he dusted me off. Somebody hit a shot down there, and I knew it was a base hit—hell, I'd been around long enough. I was so disgusted I didn't even look around. Next thing I know somebody is yelling at me. Traynor had come up with it and was firing across to first. I ducked just in time; otherwise that ball would have flattened me. That had never happened behind me before.

Burleigh Grimes and George Earnshaw
Opposing pitchers in the 1930 World Series

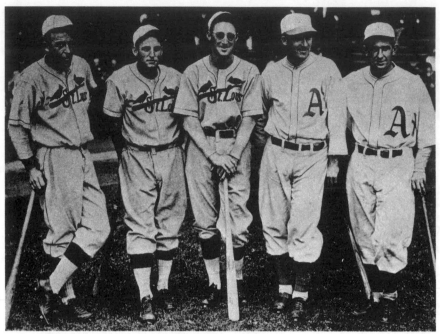

Five participants in the 1931 World Series
Jim Bottomley, Pepper Martin, Chick Hafey of the Cardinals; Al
Simmons and Mickey Cochrane of the Athletics

Yes sir, he was that good. There was a line I heard once: "Hornsby doubled twice down the line and Traynor threw him out each time." You can believe it, too.

I was traded over to the Cardinals in the middle of 1930, and that was the best thing that could have happened to me, since they were going to take pennants that year and the next. Had some good ballplayers—Frisch, Jim Bottomley, Chick Hafey, Taylor Douthit, Jimmie Wilson. Hell of a ball club. In 1930 all eight regulars hit over .300. Today a guy hits .300, they cover him with roses.

We got into the Series both times against the Athletics. Oh, Connie Mack had sweet teams in those years. We'd heard about Lefty Grove, how hard he could throw. But I'll tell you, the guy we thought threw the hardest was Earnshaw. Big George Earnshaw. But Grove could throw hard, no doubt about that. He beat me in the opening game and then again later on, in relief. That game was a heartbreaker. It was 0–0 to the top of the ninth. I walked Cochrane on a 3–2 spitter with two out. Geez, that pitch didn't miss by much. It was just a little tight. Then I threw Jimmie Foxx a curveball, and he knocked the concrete loose in the center-field bleachers. He hit it so hard I couldn't feel sorry for myself.

We got hunk with them the next year, beat them in seven games. That's the one they call the Pepper Martin World Series. Pepper went hog-wild, got 12 hits and stole a passel of bases. They blamed Cochrane for it, but the truth was he was running on Grove and Earnshaw because neither of them knew how to

Pepper Martin scoring in the second game of the 1931 Series

hold a man on. Cochrane never had a chance. Every time poor
Mickey looked up, there was Pepper sliding around to one base or
another. I beat Earnshaw in the seventh game, and we had
ourselves a World Championship. It'd been a long time coming.

Then the next year I'm traded again—to the Cubs—and get into
another World Series. This was getting to be a nice habit. Rogers
Hornsby was the manager up until August, when he had some
sort of dispute with ownership and they let him go. Charlie
Grimm took over.

I got along all right with Hornsby. He spoke his mind and I'd
do the same. One day I'm pitching and there are men on second
and third. I hear from behind me, "Grimes." I turn around and
here's Hornsby walking over from second base with some advice.

"Don't give him anything good, but don't walk him."

I looked him in the eye and said, "How the hell do you want
him pitched to? Do you want him pitched to, or do you want him
walked?"

He turned around and went back to second base.

But Hornsby was all right. Blunt as hell, but he never gave you
any bullshit. You might not have liked what he had on his mind,
but you always knew what it was.

That Cub team was a good one. We had Billy Herman—just a
kid then—Billy Jurges, Grimm, Kiki Cuyler, Gabby Hartnett,
Riggs Stephenson. Stephenson was the best hitter on the club. We
had some good pitchers, too, and mean ones—Lon Warneke, Guy
Bush, Pat Malone, Charlie Root. They'd saw you off. Yours truly
wasn't too shy about those things either. Look, this was for the
bread and butter. Either he got it or you got it, and if you wanted
it, you had to be tough. I think that anybody who doesn't help his
own cause is foolish. You have to be careful though. Got to know
what you're doing. Bill Terry, for instance. He had trouble getting
out of the way. He used to fall out of the box instead of going
down. I was always afraid of hitting him. So I'd throw at his feet,
make him skip a little rope. I liked Bill a lot, but what the hell,
he'd hit .400. Wasn't that enough?

You know who we had that year, who pitched one inning for

us? Bobo Newsom. Normally you don't remember a guy who comes in and pitches just one inning, but you have to remember Bobo. Just a kid. Could run like a deer. Outran every man on the club except Cuyler, who could fly, and Cuyler wouldn't run him. Then a few years later a mule gave Bobo a kick and broke his leg, and he couldn't run so good after that.

We played the Yankees in the Series that year. A mean Series. Lots of bench jockeying, and some of it got pretty damned nasty. That was the one where they say Ruth called his shot. You want to know about that, huh? All right. I'll give it to you the way I saw it. I'm sitting on the bench next to Guy Bush. Charlie Root's doing the pitching, and he's got two strikes on Ruth. Our bench is on Ruth pretty heavy, with Bush leading the tirading. After the second strike Bush yells, "Now, you big ape, what are you going to do now?" So Babe holds up his finger as if to say, "I've got the big one left." He's looking right at Guy Bush. Then he hits the next one out.

The next thing you know some newspapermen are saying he'd pointed to the center-field bleachers, and people are believing it. Ruth went along with it, and why not? Just to show you how people can be led along, I had a good friend who was at the game, and he swore to me later that Ruth pointed to the bleachers. "Forget it," I'd tell him, "I don't want to hear about it."

A couple of years later I was a Yankee myself. This was in 1934, my last year as an active player. I joined Joe McCarthy's Yankees. I liked Joe. Different type of manager from McGraw. With McGraw the ball club was like a machine and you played machine-type baseball. With McCarthy you played power. Joe had it there—Ruth, Gehrig, Lazzeri, Dickey—and that's the way he played it.

Joe was a sound baseball man, and he could be strict. He had his hot spots. Didn't like pipe smokers you know. We had a few on the club, including myself, and when we wanted to do some fanning and puff on our pipes, we'd go up to Gehrig's room and smoke there. Lou was a pipe smoker and so were Ruffing and Crosetti.

McCarthy and Ruth barely spoke to one another. Babe wanted that job of managing the Yankees. He didn't particularly care for Joe. There wasn't a hell of a lot Joe could do about Ruth. Christ, the man was an institution. But Babe was at the end of the line then, and Joe just bided his time and waited for the problem to go away on its own, which it did at the end of that season when Babe went over to the National League.

I'll tell you, when I quit as an active player in '34, I wanted to go to umpiring. In fact, I had a job waiting for me in the New York–Penn League. It was Larry MacPhail and Branch Rickey who talked me out of it. They got me to go into the Cardinal farm system as a manager. I managed a couple of years in the minors and then took on the Dodger job in 1937. A few more years managing in the minors wouldn't have hurt, to tell you the truth. I don't think a fellow can be too smart.

After the season in '36, I went on up to New York for the World Series. The Yankees were playing the Giants that year. I was walking across the field after a game when somebody took hold of my arm and said, "Hey, we want to talk to you." It was somebody from the Dodger management. We talked and they offered me the job as manager. It wasn't a big money job, but I decided I would take it because it was an opportunity and because of a loyalty I felt to the Brooklyn organization.

You know who I replaced as manager, don't you? Casey Stengel. The newspapermen didn't like the idea of seeing him go. He was always a favorite with those guys, and with good reason. In fact, they didn't even invite me to their dinner that winter. They were sore at me because I'd taken Casey's job. Hell, I didn't take his job. He lost it, and somebody was going to get it. I was a different kind of a guy. After they'd had Casey in there, they figured I was too serious. Well, I can tell you, I didn't have a hell of a lot to laugh about.

First year with the Dodgers I went out to the minor league meetings in Milwaukee with Andy High and Ted McGrew—a coach and a scout for me—and all of us paid our own expenses out there. When we sat down on the train, I said, "Boys, we sure

have got a hell of a lot to look forward to." The ball club didn't
have a dime; they were in debt up to their ears. A lot of Brooklyn
bankers were sitting on the board of directors and they weren't
turning loose very many dollars. So I had a pretty good idea of
what it was going to.be like, except I underestimated it—I didn't
think it was going to be that bad. But you see, every man thinks
that he can do something that somebody else can't do when he
starts managing. I'll give you a nickel's worth of philosophy:
Don't have hope and optimism and you'll never be disappointed.

When I took over the Dodgers in 1937, Van Lingle Mungo was
the only valuable asset that I had. I don't know of anybody who

Left to right: top, *Billy Meyer, Johnny Neun, Burleigh Grimes, Steve
O'Neill;* bottom, *Bill McKechnie, Mickey Cochrane, Joe McCarthy,
Casey Stengel, Frankie Frisch, pictured in 1938. All of them managed
in the major leagues at one time or another.*

was any faster. His problem was he couldn't carry it for nine. He was like a three-quarter horse. He would come out from the first pitch firing as hard as he could, but by the sixth or seventh inning he would start to lose it. I tried to get him to spread it out a little, to throw a few changes here and there, but he couldn't do it. That's a problem with strikeout pitchers. They like to throw that fastball past everybody. But let's say it takes five pitches to whiff a guy. Isn't it better to throw one pitch and get him to ground out? The fewer pitches you make in a ball game, the better chance you have of winning. That's the way I tried to pitch and the way I tried to get my boys to go—let the batter hit it. Give him a piece of the ball. If you've got good stuff and good control, you've got nothing to worry about.

You know, I could have made a whopping good deal with the Cubs for Mungo and Buddy Hassett. We could have got five players for them—Clay Bryant, Ripper Collins, Augie Galan, Clyde Shoun, and I think Joe Marty. Now, what I was going to do was take those fellows and trade them to the Phillies for Bucky Walters and Dolph Camilli. So I could have had, in effect, Walters and Camilli for Mungo and Hassett. But the officers of the Dodgers, those bankers, turned it down. Wouldn't let me make the deal. I'd say that was quite a mistake, wouldn't you? Hassett was traded eventually anyway, while Mungo won very few games for the Dodgers after 1938. They did buy Camilli from the Phillies, but it cost them $65,000, and they never got Bucky Walters. Do you know what a fellow like Walters would have meant to the Dodgers? Just about the best damned pitcher in the league for the next few years.

We had a lot of older ballplayers on the team. They seemed to hang around longer in those days. Heinie Manush had a great year for me, hit around .330. Hustling son of a gun. And we had Waite Hoyt, and Fred Fitzsimmons, who I got from the Giants. That was a good deal. I got Lavagetto from the Pirates and traded four players to the Cardinals for Durocher, who I'd always liked.

When Larry MacPhail came in as general manager in 1938, he would occasionally sic a detective on the club, just to find out what was going on. He wouldn't tell me about it, but I'd get a tip

*Van Lingle Mungo, Dizzy Dean, Lon Warnecke, Carl Hubbell,
Curt Davis at the 1936 All-Star Game*

now and then. The detective would go around checking rooms
and then file a report to MacPhail. When I knew something was
up, I'd call some of the boys—certain ones, you know—and tell
them to be in on time because they were getting a caller tonight.
One night I knew one of my pitchers had a woman in his room
after midnight, which was against the rules. I'd been tipped off
about the detective that morning, so I got a passkey and went up
to this guy's room. I knew that if MacPhail found out what was
going on, it would cost this guy plenty.

I knocked on the door and told him I knew he had a girl in there
and to get her the hell out because it was after midnight.

"Who's that?" he said. I could tell he was stewed.

"Burleigh Grimes," I said.

"No it isn't," he said.

"Well, yes, it is," I said. I was getting sore. Here I am standing
in a hotel corridor being told through a closed door who I'm not
by some son of a bitch who's breaking half the club's rules and

regulations all at once. I rattled the key in the door and told him I was coming in.

"Hold it," he yelled. "I'm coming out."

He came out into the corridor and started to give me some baloney. I fined him five hundred bucks right on the spot and suspended him for three days. And it would have been a hell of a lot worse if MacPhail had caught him.

Well, I never figured to keep his money. I was going to hold it over him for the rest of the season to get performance out of him. I had something on him now, right?

On the fourth day, when his suspension was up, I put him in a game to relieve. He pitched good ball and in the ninth inning hit a home run to win the game. On the way back to the clubhouse, a newspaperman detained me for a few minutes to talk about one thing or another, and then I went in. I walked up to this guy and said, "Hey, come here." We put our heads together and I said, "I'm going to give you a hundred of that back." His face got all bright, and I figure I've got a good thing going with this guy for the rest of the season. He's really going to be busting his tail for me. But then later I find out that MacPhail has been there ahead of me and given him *two* hundred back. So he had three hundred back already, and I didn't have much more to use on him.

I guess I got thrown out of my share of games when I was managing—maybe more than my share. There were some umpires who would run me out for saying hello to them. One time I was suspended by the league for three days for having a to-do with a man in blue, and Ford Frick called me up to his office. He was president of the National League at that time.

"How come," I asked him, "that some managers in this league can say the same thing that I do and get away with it?"

"Well," he said, "I guess it's the way you say it."

I said, "Boy, I must have awfully good diction."

Of course, managing a second-division club doesn't help your disposition any. There are a lot of things you don't realize or think about when you take over a bad club until you start going through the season with them. You're playing a good team and they've got nine positions all filled with good ballplayers. The best you can put on the field is maybe five pretty fair ones. So, as a fellow says, you've got to get a well-pitched ball game, and the ball can't be hit to your poor fielders, though it usually is. So there you go. And those losses start piling up, and under that pile are all the high hopes of spring. You've got just so much to work with and that's all there is; there isn't any more.

You may be the nicest and softest guy in the world, but when you're out there managing, you've got to be absolutely ruthless about putting in your best men and winning. Otherwise you're going to second-guess yourself, and you don't need that. Was I second-guessed much? No, I don't think so. They couldn't second-guess me too much because with what I had to work with, I was lucky to be able to get in my one guess.

It's a hell of a job. Even if you're playing .500 ball, winning 77 and losing 77, that's still 77 nights you're eating your heart out. And what about a club that loses 90 or 100 games a season? Of course when you have a ball club like that, your worries don't last too long, since nobody is too shy about canning a manager. Very often the fault lies with the team's general manager. What the hell, he's the one who's supplying you with the players. But how often do you hear of a general manager getting fired? The manager is the one who gets it in the neck because he's visible, he's out there, and the fans know him.

Listen, there are so many things that enter into this game of baseball. Physical condition. Mental condition. Mental condition—that's very important. If you're the manager, you've got to take that into consideration. If a man isn't eating and sleeping well, it's going to affect him physically. But if he isn't eating and sleeping well, then something's bothering him mentally. He's got problems. Maybe he's got family trouble or money trouble. This is a high-tension profession—this baseball—and when you mix it in with a man's personal problems, anything can pop. A manager's got to know a hell of a lot about his players. Some of them can handle themselves better than others, and you've got to make that leash tighter or looser, depending on the man and your knowledge of him.

A lot of it comes down to this: Can you handle individuals or can't you? A good manager can. That's all there is to it. Don't ask me how or why some men can do it and others can't. It's just something a man has inside of him or he doesn't.

A sense of humor doesn't hurt either. Sometimes that'll do more for you than a three hundred and fifty hitter. We were down in spring training one year and I'm coaching first base. The steal sign—when we were fortunate enough to get a man on base—was a wink of the eye. Not very elaborate, but friendly. In the middle of the game, I had to leave the field for a few minutes and I said, "Put somebody in to coach first." I didn't know Max Butcher was going to run out there. Max had an affliction, I think they called it St. Vitus dance—his eyes were always blinking, always blinking away.

When I come back on the field, there's a baserunner, Gibby Brack, running like a bastard for second, with nobody out, and we're behind in the game. Jesus, he's thrown out from here to

Burleigh Grimes

Canarsie. When they came in off the field later, I asked Brack, "What the hell kind of a play was that? Who sent you?"

He jerked his thumb at Butcher. "He did," he said.

"Max," I said, "what the hell did you give him the go sign for?"

"I didn't give him the go sign," Max said, blinking away.

"You're giving it to me right now," Brack yelled.

Another time Brack is on third base, Manush is on first, and my good hitter, Babe Phelps, is up there. This is during the season now. I'm one run behind, and the next hitter behind Phelps can't hit anything. So I decide I'm going to run Manush and open up a hole for Phelps to shoot at. Now, I figure if Phelps misses, the catcher—it was Ernie Lombardi—won't throw through but will let the pitcher cut it off and try to catch Brack napping at third.

I'm coaching at third and I move over to Brack. "Now this is going to be a hit-and-run," I tell him, "and you stay here. I don't want you to budge."

"Okay," he says.

The pitcher delivers, Manush goes, Phelps swings and dammit misses, and sure enough Lombardi doesn't go all the way with it but throws it to the pitcher. So I'm still in good shape because now I've got men on second and third and a hit puts me ahead. Except that the moment Lombardi fired the ball, off goes Brack. I couldn't believe it. I ran down the line after him; so help me, I was trying to tackle him. He slides in and of course Lombardi slaps it on him. Brack is kneeling there on all fours, shaking his head, and I'm so damned mad I run up and boot him right in the ass.

"What'd you do that for?" he asks.

"What'd I tell you?" I yelled.

"You told me to stay there."

"So how the hell did you get up here?"

"I don't know," he says.

He didn't know.

A few weeks or so before the close of the season in 1938, MacPhail called me in and told me there was going to be a change.

"I expected that," I said.

"Not surprised, eh?" he said.

"Can't say that I am," I said.

"Not really your fault," he said.

"You'd better be careful what you say," I told him, "or else I'll ask you why you're letting me out." We both laughed. Then he asked me if I had any suggestions as to who my successor ought to be.

"Yes," I said, "I think I do. You've got a guy right on the club now who's pretty smart, has got a lot of guts, and ought to be a damned good manager."

"Who's that?" he asked.

"Durocher," I said.

"Do you think so?"

"Yes, sir," I said. "I certainly do."

Shortly after that they signed Leo.

I'll tell you a funny tag to the whole thing. In the early twenties, when I was pitching for the Dodgers, Uncle Robbie sent me out to watch a game between Harvard and Princeton. He wanted me to look at a pitcher and if I liked him sign him up. Well, I went to the game, sized up the pitcher, and decided I didn't like him. But there was another fellow in the game, playing shortstop for Princeton. I liked him and brought him in and he stayed in the big leagues for fifteen years. It was Moe Berg. You didn't know that I brought Moe Berg to the Dodgers as a shortstop around 1923, did you? That's right.

Now, later on, in 1938, this other guy—this pitcher—is sitting on the board of directors of the bank that's controlling the Dodgers. God, you never know when they're going to turn up, do you? And he knew damned well I'd scouted him fifteen years before and put the kibosh on him. I can't believe that had anything to do with my getting canned in Brooklyn, but I couldn't help wondering if I didn't make a mistake back then in not signing the son of a bitch up.

3

EDDIE SAWYER

EDWIN MILBY SAWYER
Born: September 10, 1910, Westerly, Rhode Island
Managerial career: Philadelphia Phillies 1948–52, 1958–60

Eddie Sawyer served in the New York Yankee organization as player and later as player-manager. Moving to the Philadelphia Phillie organization, he worked his way to the top in 1948. In 1950 he piloted a young ball club to the National League pennant in an exciting race that had to be decided in extra innings on the last day of the season.

I signed with the Yankees as an outfielder in 1934 after having been scouted by Paul Krichell, who I think must have signed half the ballplayers the Yankees had in those days. I played throughout the organization for the next few years and hit the ball pretty well. In 1937 I was with Oakland in the Pacific Coast League, and I hurt my shoulder, which reduced my effectiveness as a player. At that point the Yankees decided that I ought to become a manager—at the age of twenty-eight.

The idea of managing appealed to me. I had always been interested in the game, in knowing it from the inside—from the strategical and tactical point of view. Also, I had done some coaching at Ithaca, where I'd graduated, so assuming authority on the field wasn't going to be a totally unfamiliar experience for me.

I could still play, even though my shoulder had never fully recovered from that injury. In those days in the Yankee organization, you had to play if you were managing. That way they could get two jobs done for the price of one. Typical Yankee efficiency. They weren't spendthrifts—let's put it that way. Those were the

days when Ed Barrow and George Weiss were running the
organization, and it was the most successful operation in baseball
from the top all the way on down, and nobody questioned their
way of doing things. In fact, there was one year when every team
in the organization, around eighteen of them, won pennants. That
gives you some idea of the type of ballplayers we had.

They started me managing at Amsterdam, New York, in the
Canadian-American League. This was in 1939. And I won the
pennant there in my first year. After Amsterdam they moved me
up to Norfolk, in the Piedmont League, and then to Binghamton,
in the Eastern League.

Well, it became my ambition to get to the big leagues as a
manager. That's a pretty special job—there were only sixteen of
them at that time. And the problem of competition in the Yankee
organization then was even more pronounced because of the
remarkable concentration of talent they had. During the years
when I was trying to get up there as an outfielder, they had at one
time or another fellows like Babe Ruth, Earle Combs, George
Selkirk, Joe DiMaggio, Charlie Keller, and Tommy Henrich. It
was the same thing with managers. At the top they had Joe
McCarthy, and then in the minors they had fellows like Bill
Meyer, Johnny Neun, and Bill Skiff. They were all ahead of me.
So when I was presented with a good opportunity outside of the
Yankee organization, I decided I had better take it.

In the winter of 1943 I was all set to join the Red Sox
organization. This was through my friendship with Herb Pennock, who was their farm director at the time. The winter
meetings were held in the New Yorker Hotel that year, and I went
down to New York to see Herb. When I got there, I found out that
he was no longer with the Red Sox; he'd become general manager
of the Phillies.

"Well, Herb," I asked, "how does that change things with us?"

"It doesn't change them a bit," he said. "The only difference is
you're going to leave the American League and go to the National."

So that's how I happened to join the Philadelphia Phillies
organization. I managed their Utica club for four years and then

Lou Gehrig, Joe DiMaggio, Bill Dickey in 1936

in 1948 took over the Toronto club in the International League, where the Phillies had established a working agreement.

One morning I got a call from Bob Carpenter, who owned the Phillies. He told me they were letting Ben Chapman out as manager and wanted to know if I was interested in the job.

"I guess I am," I said.

"Then it's yours," he said.

I had known that eventually I was going to get the job, though I didn't think it would come along that soon. Of course, it was something I'd been waiting for, for a long time. I had served a long apprenticeship managing in the minors—ten years. To me that was a great advantage. I had never played big league ball myself, but I didn't think that was a serious handicap. It's true that there's a certain tension in the major leagues that you don't find in the minors, but that didn't bother me because I had handled so many of these fellows when they were in the minors and knew them pretty well. At Utica, for instance, I'd had Richie Ashburn, Granny Hamner, Stan Lopata, and some of the others.

And, of course, there was the example of Joe McCarthy, who had never played a game in the major leagues either. I guess he had done all right as a manager in spite of it. Joe and I were good friends. He was headman on the Yankees when I was in their organization, and whenever I had the chance, I would sit up all night talking baseball with him. A lot of things I did as a manager were things I picked up from talking to Joe. For instance, he tried never to play a left-handed thrower in left field because of the angle the pegs came in on. The ball has a natural tendency to take off when a left-hander throws it, and when it bounces, it breaks away from the base, making it difficult to throw a man out, particularly at home.

McCarthy would talk about these things, and being a young, ambitious fellow, I sat down with him at every opportunity. We usually met at the winter meetings or at gatherings of the Yankee organization. The managers would get together, fellows like Neun, Meyer, and Skiff, and some of the scouts like Joe Devine, Krichell, and Bill Essick and talk baseball all night, letting the ideas flow. And many of those ideas were Joe McCarthy's.

He would talk about changing men around during infield practice—let the shortstop work out at second base and the second baseman work out at shortstop so they could get used to handling the ball to each other from the different positions and to learn just what kind of throw to make that the other fellow could most easily handle. He felt these kinds of exercises helped create teamwork, and those Yankee clubs always had great teamwork.

Joe used to have his catchers work out at shortstop so they would learn to handle low pitches. You want your catcher to handle low pitches from the ground up, dig them out, like a shortstop. He'd also have his outfielders work out at shortstop so they could learn how to pick up ground balls and how to charge them when necessary.

I put a lot of these ideas into practice when I was managing. There's an awful lot of behind-the-scenes work that goes into managing that the fans aren't aware of. It's like watching a man conduct an orchestra. All you see is him standing up there waving a baton. You don't see all those hours of rehearsal when he's working with the orchestra, trying to refine the music, and whatnot. But of course one of the charms of baseball is that the fans think they can manage better than the man in the dugout, and this is one of the things that has been drawing so many people to ball parks for so many years. Any good fan understands the fundamentals, but I wonder how many of them get the subtleties. When a fellow buys a ticket, he's not just a spectator but also a manager and an umpire too, and that's his privilege—it's part of the fun. And we all work hard to give him the best possible ball game to second-guess.

I was sort of a low-key manager. I was one of the boys, and yet I wasn't. I demanded respect, but at the same time I wanted a loose ball club; I wanted the boys to have fun and enjoy themselves. Curfews? Well, they're hard to enforce when you're playing so much night ball. What I did have was sort of a curfew in reverse. Every so often I used to have them work out in the mornings. Get them out of bed good and early and have them report to the ball park. This was a curfew, only I wasn't telling them what time to go to bed; I was telling them what time they would have to get up. If they knew they might be pulled out of bed early in the morning—there was never any advance notice—the chances were good they'd get to bed early at night because I ran them hard in those workouts. There was no fooling around.

I had another system I used now and then when I wanted to know who was staying out late. It was very simple. I gave the night elevator operator a brand new baseball and told him to get the players to autograph it for him. So as they came in at night, they'd sign the ball. The next day he'd show me the ball and tell

GEORGE BRACE PHOTO

Eddie Sawyer

me what time each man came in. So I'd go up to somebody and say, "You came in at two o'clock last night, didn't you?" "How do you know that?" he'd ask. Well, I knew because he'd signed in on that baseball.

But I never had any really serious problems with any of my players. Young players respond to a certain amount of discipline, if you handle it well. All you have to do is treat each one as an individual. You know, we did our traveling by train in those days, and there were certain advantages in that. For instance, it took twenty-three hours to go from St. Louis to Boston; you were together a lot and had those opportunities to talk to the players. Mostly we talked baseball, but if a man wanted to discuss some personal problems, then I made sure they knew I was available to them.

One summer nine of my players were expectant fathers. For many of them this was their first child. So they came to me, wanting to know how this was going to change their lives, how to handle the new responsibilities, what kind of insurance to get, whether to buy a house, and, if so, where—all of the normal concerns of any young father-to-be. To a lot of them I seemed the natural one to come to with their questions, and I was happy to respond as best I could. I was pleased that they had enough confidence in my judgment in these matters. At the time I thought that was part of managing a ball club, and I still think that it is.

I felt that you couldn't know enough about a ballplayer, about his personality, his background. I would always make an effort to meet the players' wives and parents; I wanted to know them. I think these things are important in the overall makeup of a ball club. I wanted to know just as much about them as they knew about themselves, and more if possible. Sometimes a man's off-the-field problems can have an effect on his performance on the field, and it can be helpful for you to have some understanding of them. You can't do this unless you make a study of it and spend a lot of time with your ballplayers and let them know you're sympathetic. I'll tell you, you can get a great understanding of human nature by managing a ball club, if you want to do it the way I did it.

So I've always felt that the most important thing in managing is
how you handle your men. I think your knowledge of the game
has to come second to that. How do you get along with twenty-
five different men under the pressures of a long season? Well,
usually fifteen of them are no problem. That's a pretty good rule
of thumb. The other ten give you the problems, and generally
they're the ones who aren't playing regularly. It's your job to keep
them interested, and you've got to keep them in shape for when
you need them.

Eddie Waitkus

You remember "The Whiz Kids"? That was my ball club. We had a lot of young ballplayers, many of whom had had the advantage of playing together in the minor leagues—don't underestimate the importance of that.

We finished the 1948 season in sixth place. In 1949 we finished third. I think that took some people by surprise, but it shouldn't have. Those were good young ballplayers we had, and I had begun to work them into the lineup. I put Hamner at shortstop and Willie Jones at third, and that strengthened the infield. Then we made a deal with the Cubs for Eddie Waitkus, and he became my first baseman. We had Andy Seminick and Lopata catching, and Ashburn, Del Ennis, and Dick Sisler in the outfield. And we had fine young pitchers in Robin Roberts, Curt Simmons, Bubba Church, Bob Miller, and a couple of older fellows, Russ Meyer and Jim Konstanty.

I've always felt that in a close race the manager who handles his pitching staff the best is going to win. Pitching is about 85 percent of the game. You might not have the best staff in the league, but if it's a good one and you handle it well, you're going to be a winner. You do this by pitching the right pitchers at the right time. You determine that by knowing your staff—their strengths, their weaknesses. You know just how much stamina a fellow has and so you count the number of pitches he makes in a game. I think I was the first one to bring in that idea of throwing so many pitches in a game. We counted them. If I knew that a fellow had thrown, say, 150 pitches, he might have to have an extra day's rest, whereas if he'd thrown only 80 or 90, I knew I could use him with a shorter amount of rest between starts.

Simmons had a great arm; he could really fire. When I took over the team, he was strictly a thrower. His problem was that he had received too much well-meaning advice. He had been overcoached more than any pitcher I ever saw. Everybody and his brother had tried to straighten him out because he appeared to be doing everything you're not supposed to do—he had that herky-jerky motion and he threw across his body, among other things. So he was getting all kinds of advice and instruction, and none of it seemed to be doing him any good. The only thing I ever did with Curt Simmons was call him aside and say, "Look, Mr. Pennock and the Phillies gave you a lot of money to sign a contract, right?"

"That's right," he said.

"You were with the Egypt, Pennsylvania, Legion team."

"That's right," he said.

"Now do me a favor," I said. "Would you go back and pitch just the way you did when you were on that Egypt, Pennsylvania, Legion team?"

He smiled and did just as I asked. It took him a while to shake off all that bad advice he'd gotten, and he finished the season with a 4–10 record. But he was happy; he was getting squared away. The next year, 1950, when we won the pennant, he had a great year. The only thing that ruined it was that he had to go into the service late in the season. Something a lot of people forget is that he had more wins when he went away than Roberts did. Curt was the number one pitcher on the staff. He had 17 wins and Roberts had 16. They were great buddies, and I got a little competition going between them to see who could win the most. It was a shame Curt had to go away; he'd been pitching in a marvelous groove. When he came back from the service in 1952, he was never quite the same again. He was a winning pitcher, but he was never again as overpowering as he had been in 1950.

I knew I had to get a strong bull pen because we were bringing young pitchers up to the big leagues pretty fast. We wanted them to throw as hard as they could for as long as they could, so we always had to have somebody ready to come in. That somebody was Jim Konstanty.

I brought Konstanty in from Toronto with me when I took over the Phillies. Probably the best-conditioned athlete I ever had play for me. He wanted to pitch every day. He'd pitched briefly in the major leagues before—for Cincinnati and the Boston Braves—but not very successfully. He had always been a starting pitcher, but when I had him at Toronto, I began using him in relief. I felt he had the ideal makeup for a relief pitcher. He was tough, and he had a great competitive spirit. I knew when I took over the Phillies that I wanted him as my relief pitcher.

Curt Simmons
"He could really fire."

He had outstanding years for me in 1949 and 1950. In '50 he was voted Most Valuable Player in the league—the first time that award ever went to a relief pitcher. He might have been a big surprise to the rest of the league, but he wasn't to me. They hadn't seen him develop as I had, and no one had ever used him the way I did.

Russ Meyer was a colorful guy. We got him from the Cubs after the '48 season. I always liked him because he had a great desire to pitch. He was what you call flaky, but, like Konstanty, he had a strong competitive spirit, something that I cherished in a pitcher. Another reason I wanted him was because his style of pitching was unlike anybody else's I had on the staff. I liked them all to be just a little bit different in their style of delivery and so forth. Russ had a good curveball, and he also threw one of the best screwballs in the league.

Meyer could be his own worst enemy at times. He never wanted to be taken out of a ball game. No good pitcher ever does, but Russ could take it particularly hard. I pulled him from a game one time in Cincinnati, and he came storming into the dugout and kicked a seat, where the batboy usually sat. Well, that seat had always been loose, but they had bolted it down the night before. So he figured to send it flying, but it didn't budge an inch. That night he had his leg in a cast. According to the X-rays he had a hairline fracture. It looked like he was through for a long time.

"I guess I'd better go home," he said. "I can't do you any good like this."

"Stick around until we finish the trip," I said.

A few days later he came to me and said, "You know, my leg feels all right."

"How can it feel all right if it's broken?" I asked.

"I don't know," he said.

He kept telling me he felt fine, so I finally sent him in to be examined. And it was the darndest thing, the kind of thing that could only happen to Russ Meyer. They found out that the hairline fracture they thought he had was really an old injury that had showed up on the X-rays. He didn't have anything more than a bruise. They took off the cast, and he pitched the next night and went on from there to have one of his finest seasons.

There was another story involving Meyer which some of the boys liked to tell. We were in New York, at the Commodore Hotel. Some of us were sitting around the lobby when Russ walked in with a pleased look on his face. It seems he'd bought a diamond ring from a fellow on the street. Paid something like three hundred dollars for it. A real bargain. He was showing it around to everybody. Bill Nicholson was his roommate and good friend, and it was Bill who finally put the question: "How do you know it's real?"

"Sure it's real," Russ said. "Look at it sparkle."

"You can't be sure," Nicholson said. "There's only one way to tell if it's a diamond or not—step on it."

"Go ahead," Russ said.

So Nick took the thing, put it down on the lobby floor, and stepped on it. The thing turned to dust—it was paste. Some New York sharpie had put one over on Russ.

Well, the funny thing about the story is that on our next trip into New York, Russ was walking down the street when he saw the guy who had sold him the ring. What are the odds on that happening in a city like New York? Anyway, Russ collared the guy and held onto him until a cop came by. When the cop wanted to know what was going on, Russ told him the story. The cop must have known the guy as an operator of some sort because he said to him, "How much money do you have on you?"

"Fifteen dollars," the guy said.

The cop looked at Russ and said, "What do you say?"

"All right," Russ said. "I'll take it."

So he took the fifteen dollars and closed the deal. Those were the kinds of things that happened to Russ Meyer. But I liked him. He always wanted that ball. He believed he could beat anybody, and he won a lot of big games for me.

Robin Roberts? One of the greatest pitchers of all time. If we'd had a little better ball club, with one or two more hitters, he probably could have won 400 games. He was a pleasure for any manager to have on his ball club. He was difficult to handle for only one reason—he wanted to pitch every day and thought he could. He completed many games with only 70 or 75 pitches, so there were times when I didn't think twice about letting him go out there with only two days' rest.

He would never throw at hitters. They knew this and would go up there and take a toehold, but he would still get them out. He did it with speed, control, and stamina. He seldom threw a ball above the belt, and most of the time he was right across the knees with it. And he had the ability to draw back and throw a little bit harder when he had to.

He had a very easy delivery. I call it symmetry of motion. It just flowed, pitch after pitch. He made it look easy. And do you know, a pitcher like that makes your whole ball club better out there. They knew Roberts was going to get the ball over the plate and make the batter hit it to somebody, so they were always ready. They never had a chance to get back on their heels, and as a result they made a lot of great plays in back of Robin. He was so good at

Robin Roberts
"One of the greatest pitch-
ers of all time."

his job that he made them better at theirs. That's about the way it was.

At the end of the season in 1949, just before we broke up to go home for the winter, I held a meeting and told everybody to come to camp in shape in the spring because we had a chance to win it. I honestly believed it. The Phillies hadn't won a pennant since 1915, and I felt we were about ready to break the drought. I had no illusions about it being easy though. The Braves, Dodgers, and Cardinals were all strong contending clubs, but I thought we could sneak in.

Well, we played good ball all year in 1950, and by the time September came around, we had built up a commanding lead.

But then things started happening to us. Simmons went into the service. And then Church and Miller suffered injuries. Church was pitching against the Reds and Ted Kluszewski hit him in the eye with a line drive. Ted hit through the box a lot, and this was a particularly vicious shot. The ball struck Church with such impact that it sucked his eyeball right out of the socket. He hit the ground with a thud and didn't move. We all thought he was dead. When I got out to the mound, I saw that his eyeball was hanging out over his cheek; it was one of the most gruesome things I've ever seen in my life. They took him to the hospital and put his eyeball back in the socket, and he never had any trouble with his eye—which is almost unbelievable, after the way he had looked lying there. But it did affect his pitching. Church was a tough kid and a fine competitor, but he couldn't help flinching a little bit after that when he pitched. That injury took something away from him, and he was never quite the same pitcher again.

Then we lost Bob Miller. He was going up the steps in Back Bay Station in Boston and slipped and pulled something in his back. That reduced his effectiveness significantly.

Simmons, Church, Miller—that was quite a large chunk of my pitching staff. We were thinning out and starting to lose ball games. With nine days left to go, we had a seven-game lead. That's when the trouble started. We lost two doubleheaders in a row to the Giants and all together lost eight out of 10 games, while the Dodgers were winning something like seven or eight in a row.

Surprisingly, there was very little depression on the team, and no panic. It was a young club, remember; I think the average age in our lineup was something like twenty-six. Nevertheless, the boys kept their heads. I think one thing that helped us was that most of them had played together in the minor leagues and knew each other and understood each other. And, of course, I had managed a lot of them in the minor leagues, so they knew me and I knew them. This helped immensely.

It finally came down to a two-game lead over Brooklyn with two games to play with the Dodgers at Ebbets Field to close out the season.

We lost the Saturday game. Erv Palica beat us, 7–3. That left us one game ahead with one still to play. As far as I was concerned, there was more pressure on the Dodgers than there was on us; we still had the lead. I was starting Roberts—for the fourth time in eight days—and they were starting Don Newcombe.

Was I afraid of hurting Roberts's arm with all that work? No. You see, I knew him. He could work with two days rest—not consistently, of course, but when he had to, he could. He had pitched four games in eight days, and given the number of pitches he threw in a game, it was the equivalent of two games. That made the difference. I knew exactly how many pitches he was throwing in each game. I could never have used Simmons that way even if he had been available; because he was a harder worker, he threw more pitches. With that easy delivery he had, Roberts seldom ever got tired. Konstanty was the same way. So those were the fellows I used that last week. I had to juggle the rest of the pitching staff around them, hoping to get three or four good innings out of a man. That's when a manager earns his money, under those circumstances. That's when your knowledge of your pitchers becomes crucial; you've got to know more about them than they know about themselves. And that's when your players have to have confidence in you.

That game went into the last half of the ninth inning a 1–1 tie. Newcombe was pitching beautifully and so was Roberts. In that last of the ninth, Cal Abrams led off for the Dodgers with a base on balls. Then Pee Wee Reese singled to left, and that put men on first and second with nobody out and Duke Snider up. You had to be thinking that Duke was going to bunt, at least give it one shot. But it was far from being a certainty because a good many times during the year he hadn't bunted in similar situations, particularly against Roberts. Snider liked to hit against Robin. Also, I was trying to think what Burt Shotton was thinking over there on the Dodger bench, and I surmised that Burt was thinking that Roberts might be getting tired and might make a mistake. So I was not sold on the idea that there would be a bunt.

And he didn't bunt. He swung away and hit a line shot into center field. Richie Ashburn came running in, took it on the first

or second bounce, and fired it home. He played that ball perfectly. Here you have to go back to something we talked about before.
I used to have him work out in the infield a lot, to get used to
picking up balls like that. He had to play that ball like a shortstop,
and he did—flawlessly. He didn't have the strongest arm in the
world, but he was playing shallow and was able to get off a good
throw.

Why was he playing so shallow in center field with Snider up?
Well, for one thing, Ashburn could play a shallow center field
because he had the ability to go back for a ball, particularly in
Ebbets Field, where the wall wasn't so far away. And another

Richie Ashburn

thing—and this comes from players knowing each other—he knew that Roberts wasn't going to let Snider hit a ball over his head in a situation like that.

So here comes Abrams around third with the winning run. What was I thinking at that moment? Well, I knew that in order to get him at the plate, everything was going to have to go right. Ashburn was going to have to charge the ball, pick it up cleanly, and get off a perfect peg home, and Stan Lopata was going to have to make the play there. Everything was going to have to go right, and things hadn't been going right for us lately. But Richie made the play, Lopata made the tag, and Abrams was out at home by a wide margin. But that still left men on second and third with only one out and three pretty good hitters coming up—Jackie Robinson, Carl Furillo, Gil Hodges.

I went out to the mound to talk to Roberts. I had no intention of taking him out; he was it for the day. In that situation you want to find out who your pitcher would most rather pitch to. They were all right-handed batters, so that wasn't a factor. We decided to walk Robinson and fill the bases. The decision was mutual, and it was a basic decision. First of all, you load the bases and it gives you a play anywhere. And I wasn't afraid of Roberts walking the winning run in because of his fine control. Also, Robinson was an extremely dangerous hitter; in that situation you were better off with him on first base than at the plate. So we put him on.

The next hitter was Furillo. Carl was a high-ball hitter, and Roberts made a mistake and got one up to him, but luckily it was popped up. When that happened I started to get the feeling that our luck might be changing. But we still had to get past Hodges. Roberts got him to hit a fly ball out to Ennis in right field—and not many people know this, but that ball was right in the sun, and it stayed in the sun. Del had to fight it all the way, and I don't know how he managed to catch it. But he did. I was glad to see that inning over with.

Then in the top of the tenth we got two men on and Dick Sisler hit a high line drive into the seats in left field, so we had a three-run lead. Roberts went out there in the bottom of the tenth, and you would have thought it was the first day of the season the way he fired that ball. He put them down 1–2–3, and the Phillies had their first pennant in thirty-five years.

Winning the pennant the way we did didn't give us much time to get ready for the World Series. We had two days off before we opened against the Yankees, and I wanted to give Roberts more rest. So I had to start Konstanty in the first game. He hadn't started a game all year, but that didn't concern me. Jim was an individualist with tremendous self-confidence and desire. I figured he might be the one to do it. I approached him the night before the Series opened and pulled him aside.

"You know the condition our staff is in," I said. "Well, I've got you down to start the first game."

"That's okay with me," he said. Nothing ever bothered him.

He came through beautifully, too, but we didn't hit for him and lost to Raschi, 1–0. That pretty much set the pattern for the rest of the Series—good pitching on both sides but not much hitting. We lost in four games, and the scores in three of them were 1–0, 2–1, 3–2. We were disappointed, naturally, but felt we hadn't disgraced ourselves. What the heck, the starters the Yankees threw at us were named Raschi, Reynolds, Lopat, and Ford.

The following year we finished fifth and then in the middle of the next year, 1952, I was fired. Why? I don't know. I haven't figured it out yet. I don't know what the rationale is for firing managers. It's true, we weren't winning, but it was only a year and a half after we'd won the pennant. I suppose part of that kind of move is to appease the fans. It's a point that's always made. You can fire the manager; you can't fire the players.

It happened just before the All-Star break. Bob Carpenter called me in after a game and told me he was going to make a change, that we weren't winning, and so forth. There wasn't anything I could say; his mind was made up. There was nothing personal about it. I had a fine relationship with Bob Carpenter and still do. As a matter of fact, he hired me back in 1958, after I'd been out of baseball for six years.

I took over the ball club from Mayo Smith in the middle of the season. They had gone downhill over the years and were pretty much a last-place club. We finished last again the next year, and it

UPI PHOTO

Dick Sisler scoring on his pennant-winning home run. Number 14 is
Del Ennis; number 1 is Richie Ashburn; number 4 is Eddie Waitkus.
Roy Campanella is the catcher, Larry Goetz the umpire.

didn't look too promising for the following year. So I did something that I guess was unprecedented. I had the ball club all through spring training, came north with them, managed on opening day, and then quit. That's right, after one game. I could see that things weren't going to get any better. I made one statement at the time: "I'm forty-nine years old and I'd love to live to be fifty."

JOSEPH VINCENT McCARTHY
CHICAGO N.L. 1926 - 1930
NEW YORK A.L. 1931 - 1946
BOSTON A.L. 1948 - 1950
OUTSTANDING MANAGER WHO NEVER PLAYED
IN MAJOR LEAGUES. THE MAJOR LEAGUE
TEAMS MANAGED BY HIM DURING 24 YEARS
NEVER FINISHED OUT OF FIRST DIVISION.
WON PENNANTS CHICAGO N.L. 1929,
NEW YORK A.L. 1932 - 6 - 7 - 8 - 9 - 41 - 2 - 3.
WON SEVEN WORLD'S CHAMPIONSHIPS WITH
NEW YORK YANKEES - FOUR OF THEM
CONSECUTIVELY 1936 - 7 - 8 - 9.

80

4

JOE McCARTHY

I never played ball in the big leagues. Not one game. Wasn't good enough, I guess. But I think I spent more time trying to get up there than almost anybody I know of. I was twenty years in the minor leagues, as a player and manager, before I made it. When I finally got into the big leagues, I thought, Well, I've got it made now. But once I got up there and had a look around, I realized my work had just begun. I was starting all over again. It was no bed of roses. But I was lucky. I had some great ballplayers who played for me. They're the ones who made it possible for me to be in the Hall of Fame today. I can't praise them enough.

I was born in Philadelphia in 1887 and grew up in Germantown, which was a suburb. I always loved baseball. Can't think of a time when I didn't.

Connie Mack was my idol when I was a kid. I used to wait outside the ball park just to look at him when he walked out. His Philadelphia Athletics were great around the turn of the century. They had Rube Waddell. Do you know his name? He was a great pitcher, one of the greatest. And they had fellows like Harry Davis, Lave Cross, Danny Murphy, Eddie Collins, Chief Bender, and Eddie Plank. It was a pleasure to go out and watch that team.

You know, when I went to Chicago to manage the Cubs in 1926, I took over a team that had finished last the year before. Well, some of my friends in Germantown gave me a dinner before I left for spring training, sort of to wish me luck. Connie was invited. When I got up to make my few remarks, I said I was glad that Mr. Mack was here with us tonight and that I hoped to have the pleasure sometime soon of meeting him in a World Series. Everybody laughed—they thought that was funny. But three

years later it really happened; we played the Athletics in the
Series in 1929. And, boy, what a lesson Connie taught me in that
Series! I've never forgotten it.

That was the Series when Connie started Howard Ehmke in the
first game. That was a big surprise. I'll say it was! Nobody
expected it. You see Ehmke hadn't done much pitching that year,
and Connie had Lefty Grove, George Earnshaw, and Rube
Walberg. Three ace pitchers. We figured on seeing one of those
fellows. So did the Athletic players themselves. When they saw
Ehmke go out to warm up, some of the A's said, "My God, are we
going to work *him*?" Connie never blinked an eye; he knew what
he was doing. You see, Ehmke had a delivery that was rough on
right-handed hitters, and we were loaded with them. We had
Rogers Hornsby, Kiki Cuyler, Hack Wilson, and Riggs Stephenson. Every one of those fellows hit over .340 that year.

But it proved out for Connie. Ehmke pitched a great game. He
beat us 3–1 and struck out 13, which at that time was a record for a
World Series game. Connie never did start Grove against us. He
held him back to be a relief pitcher. That's some relief pitcher,
Lefty Grove. He came in in the late innings of a few games, and
there wasn't a thing we could do with him. Was Lefty the fastest I
ever saw? Well, he wasn't the slowest. I saw plenty more of him
when I went over to the Yankees. Too much of him. There were
times when I preferred having a left-handed hitter in there
against him. Why? Well, the righties always thought they could
pull him. That was a mistake. Grove was too fast. The lefty batters
knew better—they never even tried.

That was also the Series where the A's took a game from us that
we should have won. We were leading them 8–0 going into the
last half of the seventh inning, and they came up with ten runs.
Hard to believe, isn't it? But it happened. I'll say it did. Actually,
they shouldn't have got more than three. Hack Wilson missed two
fly balls in the sun, and there was an easy chance in left field that
Stephenson should have caught. Everything went wrong at the
same time. The only piece of luck we had in that inning was with
a fellow named George Burns. Connie sent him up to pinch-hit,
and he came around twice in the inning, and we got him out each

Joe McCarthy, manager of the Chicago Cubs, 1929

Hack Wilson
"A wonderful little fellow."

time. Trouble was, we had to face eight other hitters between his
at bats.

Grover Cleveland Alexander was with the Cubs when I took
over in 1926. He was getting along in years then but still quite a
good pitcher. I had to get rid of him though. He didn't obey
orders. Wouldn't go along with me. A fellow asked me one time if
Alex followed the rules. "Sure he did," I said, "but they were
always Alex's rules." So I had to let him go. St. Louis took him
and he helped them win the pennant. That didn't bother me; he'd
been with the Cubs the year before, and they had still finished

last. If they finished last again, I'd rather it was without him. That's how I figured it. But he was a nice fellow. Alex was all right. Just couldn't keep to the rules, that's all.

We got Hornsby from Boston in 1929. Had to give up a lot for him—five players and a sock full of money. I didn't want to give up that much, but that's what they wanted. So we got Hornsby. He hit .380 for us, so I guess you might say he did his share. He was an outspoken man, but I never found any fault with him. He played to win and that's all I could ask for.

Hack Wilson was a wonderful little fellow. I had him in 1930 when he had that great year—56 home runs and 190 runs batted in. Do you know how we got him? We stole him from the Giants. That's right. They had sent him to the minors and then forgotten to recall him. A clerical mistake. So he was unprotected when the draft came around. The Cubs had finished in the cellar the year before, so we had first pick. We took Wilson for $5,000. McGraw hit the ceiling when he heard about it. I don't think he ever got over it. Wilson led the league in home runs four out of the next five years.

Hack was small, but he was powerful. Wasn't afraid of anybody. There was a guy on the Cincinnati club that liked to ride him. One day in Chicago Hack couldn't stand it any longer and charged right into the Cincinnati dugout and began to maul him. Hack was a tough kid—don't worry about that—and he knew how to punch. He did a job on this fellow before they broke it up.

That's the way it was with Hack. Good-natured as could be, but things seemed to happen to him. I guess people picked on him because he was small. They never did it twice, I can tell you.

I was let out in Chicago in 1930, and it wasn't too long before the Yankees came around. Was I surprised when they offered me the job? Well, I don't know how to answer that. Maybe I was; maybe I wasn't. I was in Philadelphia watching the World Series between the A's and the Cardinals. Paul Krichell, the Yankee scout, came up to me in the grandstand and told me Colonel Ruppert wanted to see me the next day in his office. That was the first inkling I had that the Yankees were interested. I'd had feelers from a couple of other clubs. I remember I called Judge Landis during the Series to talk to him about it. He was staying at the Bellevue Stratford Hotel. I told him I had a chance to go to two or three clubs and wanted his opinion.

"I want you to get the best job in baseball," he said.

"I can't," I said.

"Why not?" he asked.

"Because you've got it," I said.

He laughed and said, "Then get the next best."

I guess managing the Yankees was it.

Colonel Ruppert was a wonderful man to work for. He never bothered me. He let me run the team. He was a real fan and he loved to win. Naturally, everybody loves to win. I remember that after we beat the Giants in the 1937 World Series, I went to see him. He was sick in bed and hadn't been able to get out to the game. So as soon as it was over, I dressed and went right from the clubhouse in a taxi to his apartment on Fifth Avenue. When I came in, he had a big smile on his face—he'd heard the game on the radio. We shook hands and I said, "Colonel, you're the champion again."

"Fine, fine, 'McCarddy,' " he said. "Do it again next year."

Those were the only orders I ever got from him, after each World Series, "Do it again next year." And generally we did. You've got to follow orders, right?

I won my first pennant with the Yankees in 1932. We played my old team in the Series that year, the Cubs. Beat them four straight. It wasn't a very friendly World Series. There were some pretty rough bench jockeys on both sides. The Cubs were on Ruth an awful lot. Babe had a knack for stirring things up, you know. That's the Series where they say he called his home run. That's a good story, isn't it? A lot of people still believe today that he really did that. Did he? No. You see, the Cubs were riding him from the bench every time he came to the plate, and finally he pointed over at them. Then he hit the next pitch out. After he hit the ball, somebody said, "Did you see where he pointed?" Well, a lot of them did see his hand go up and they said "maybe he did point that way." That's how the story began. Tell you the truth, I didn't see him point anywhere at all, but I might have turned my head for a moment.

Babe went along with it. He was a great showman, you know. But later on he admitted that he never pointed to the bleachers. Gabby Hartnett said the same thing, and he was the catcher. Charlie Root, who was the pitcher, also said that. They said he pointed to the Cub dugout.

The first time I ever saw Babe Ruth was in 1914. I was playing second base for Buffalo, and he was pitching for Baltimore. This was in the International League. Years later, when we were both with the Yankees, somebody gave him an old clipping and he brought it around. It was a box score of a game he'd pitched and had beaten the Buffalo club.

"Look at that, Joe," he said. "You didn't get any hits off of me."

I looked at the box score and told him, "That's true, Babe, but look where I was hitting." I was hitting fourth. That was the only comeback I had. He'd been a first-rate pitcher, you know, with a very good fastball.

I had Earle Combs playing for me when I was managing Louisville. The Yankees wanted to buy him—that was around 1924. We told them we'd make the deal if they would throw in this kid they had at Hartford named Gehrig. Sure, we knew about him. But they wouldn't turn him loose. We made the deal anyway, and when Combs was leaving, he came over to shake hands and I said, "I'll catch up with you again one of these days." I was only kidding. But when I took over the Yankees in 1931, there he was in center field, and there was Lou on first base.

What a wonderful fellow that Gehrig was! Always hustled. Never gave a moment's trouble. Just went out every day and played his game and hit the ball. I'll say he hit the ball, and in all directions—right, left, center. No, I never asked him to bunt, not once in eight years. I don't think that would have been very good strategy.

Today it's hard to believe that streak he had—2,130 straight games. I remember one day in Detroit, right in the middle of it, he came up with a bad back and couldn't play.

"Come out to the park anyway," I told him, "and let's see what happens."

So he came out and I led him off, listed at shortstop. Bad back or no bad back, he saw a pitch he liked and hit a double. Then I took him out and put Crosetti in. But if you look in the record book, you'll see that Gehrig had one game at shortstop, and that's how it happened. That was around 1934, and it stopped his streak from being broken.

Five years later, though, again in Detroit, he finally had to come out. He had slowed up an awful lot. Nobody knew what was wrong, but the decline was painfully noticeable. He wasn't hitting the ball for any distance; when he did get the bat on it, it was usually just a single. You could see it. And he realized it too.

We had an off day, going from New York to Detroit, and I stopped off in Buffalo, where my home was. When I rejoined the team in Detroit the next day, Art Fletcher, my coach, came up to me and said, "Lou is looking for you. He wants to talk to you."

"Send him up to my room when you see him," I said.

A little later there was a knock on the door and Lou came in. I told him to have a seat. He was troubled, I could see that.

"Joe," he said, "how much longer do you think I should stay in this game? When do you think I should get out?"

"Right now, Lou," I said.

He didn't say anything right away, just sat there. Then he said, "Well, that's what I wanted to know."

"That's what I think," I said.

"That's the way I feel too," he said. "I'm not doing the ball club any good."

I told him that maybe some rest would help and then we'd see what was going to happen.

Then we went out to the ball park. Lou was the team captain, you know, and it was his job to take the batting order up to the umpire. Well, just before he did that, the public address announcer got on his microphone and announced that Lou Gehrig was breaking his string today, that he would not play. There was a big crowd in the stands, and when Lou took the batting order up, they all got to their feet and gave him the damnedest ovation I ever heard.

I knew there was something wrong with Lou, but I didn't know what it was. His reflexes were shot. I was afraid of his getting hit with a pitched ball. He wouldn't have been able to get out of the way, that's how bad it was. That was my chief concern, to get him out of there before he got hurt.

Two years later he died. We were in Detroit when we heard about it.

DiMaggio was like Gehrig in many ways. Good team man, great hustler, never gave the manager any headaches. It was a pleasure having a ballplayer like that. Joe had perfect judgment on a ball field, whether it was in the field or running the bases. He almost never made a mistake.

His hitting streak sure was exciting, wasn't it? Day after day, everybody waiting to see what he was going to do. Fifty-six games in a row. They finally stopped him in Cleveland one night. There was a tremendous crowd out to see the game, close to 70,000, I'll bet. They were there because of Joe. They wanted to see him make a hit. But the Indians shut him out. After the game I saw the president of the Cleveland ball club, and he was so happy and excited that his pitchers had stopped Joe. He was congratulating everybody in sight. But the next day, you know what happened, don't you? The park wasn't half-filled. He was glad they'd broken the streak, but the next day he was wondering where everybody was. That's what happens.

I think that Hack Wilson and Jimmie Foxx could hit a ball as far as anybody. I remember one game we played the Red Sox in Yankee Stadium. I had a fellow named Johnny Broaca pitching. In the top of the ninth the Red Sox have the tying run on first base, two men out, and Joe Cronin is up, with Foxx on deck. Broaca starts pitching to Cronin and he's not even coming close to the plate. I couldn't believe it—he's walking Cronin to get to Foxx. This was unbelievable. I yelled out to Dickey, "What the hell's

Lou Gehrig and Joe DiMaggio

going on?" But Bill just shrugged. There wasn't anything he
could do about it. And Broaca was pitching such a good ball
game I couldn't take him out.

So Foxx comes up, and now the tying run is on second. And
Jimmie laid into one. He hit it into deep center field. It was hit as
far as any ball I ever saw in Yankee Stadium that wasn't a home
run. DiMaggio went out there and caught it. It didn't miss by
much from going into the bleachers in dead center. But Joe got it
and the game was over.

We went into the clubhouse, and I went over to shake hands with Broaca.

"Johnny," I said, "that was quite a game you pitched. But will you tell me why you didn't pitch to Cronin?"

"I was afraid of Cronin," he said. "But I knew I could get Foxx."

"You did, eh?" I said. I looked around and DiMaggio still hadn't come in with the ball.

No, I didn't get thrown out of many ball games. I learned early on that you couldn't do your ball club much good if you weren't there. I generally got along okay with the umpires. I remember one time I pulled a good one on Bill McGowan. We were playing in Washington and Arndt Jorgens was catching—I used to put him in once in a while to give Dickey a rest. A runner slid into the plate and Jorgens tagged him and thought he had him, but McGowan called the man safe. Jorgens jumped up and pushed McGowan. Naturally McGowan ran him out of there.

So I went up there and said to McGowan, "Mac, what the hell did you put him out for?"

"You saw what he did, didn't you?" he said.

"Why, he just gave you a little push like that," I said, and I demonstrated it by giving him a push.

"Isn't that enough?" he asked.

"You mean to tell me," I said, "if a fellow gives you a little push like that"—and I demonstrated it again—"you're going to run him out of the game?"

By this time the crowd was yelling like crazy. They didn't know what we were talking about. All they knew was that I was standing there pushing McGowan, and he wasn't doing anything about it. But then he got wise to it and said, "Goddammit, don't do that again."

"Okay, Bill," I said and winked at him and walked away. For the rest of the game, the fans were on him something awful for not having thrown me out. McGowan never let me forget that. Years later he'd say to me, "You put one over on me that time, didn't you?"

A lot of people have asked me through the years, "Joe, what does it take to be a manager?"

"Just about three things," I say. "A good memory, patience, and being able to recognize ability." You've got to be able to recognize ability; that's so damned important. And not only recognize it, but know what to do with it.

Joe Gordon came up as a shortstop. He'd played a year in the Coast League at short, and that's what he was when he came to Newark. But I wanted him to play second base because Lazzeri was on the way out then. So I worked with Gordon one spring down at St. Petersburg and helped make a second baseman out of him because that's what we needed. He played one year at second with Newark and then came up to the Yankees in 1938 and was one of the best.

You make these changes now and then. Red Rolfe was originally a shortstop, too, but he didn't have the real good arm for making that long throw. I told him I was going to play him at third base.

"It's one of the easiest jobs in the infield," I told him. "You average about three chances a game. And don't worry about those hot smashes. That's a big joke. You've got a glove and you can stop them."

"Okay," he said.

He broke in at third up at Fenway Park. The first ball hit down to him took a bad bounce and hit him in the eye and blackened it. He came into the dugout holding his eye and said, "Joe, you gave me some bad information." But he became a good third baseman.

So you see how these teams were put together. It wasn't as easy as it looked. They were all good ballplayers, but you had to work with them to put them where they could be most helpful to the ball club.

When Charlie Keller came up, he wasn't a pull hitter. He'd never had to be, you see, because he had been playing in the International League, where they had a lot of small ball parks, and he was hitting home runs to left field. But he couldn't do that in Yankee Stadium. His first year up he hit only 11 home runs. So the next year I said to him, "Why do you think they built such a short right field in this ball park?"

"For Ruth," he said.

"That's right," I said. "So why aren't you taking advantage of it? You're a left-handed power hitter."

I told him I wanted him to pull everything he got his bat on. It wasn't easy for him because he wasn't used to it. In batting practice I told the pitchers to throw every ball inside to him so he could pull the hell out of it. Charlie didn't know that. That's how we got him used to doing it. So you see, there are a lot of things managers never talk about, that people think just happen. But things don't just happen. I don't want to sound like I'm bragging. I'm just explaining the way things work.

When I took over the Red Sox in 1948, people used to say to me, "Well, Joe, now that you've got Ted Williams, who do you think is better—DiMaggio or Williams?"

"I'll tell you," I'd say. "When I was managing the Yankees, I was crazy about DiMaggio. Now I'm crazy about Williams."

How the hell are you going to answer a question like that? Some people thought I might not get along with Williams. I don't know where they got that idea from. What the hell, I'd had Hornsby and Ruth and Gehrig and DiMaggio. Williams was no problem. He was in the ball game every today. He played. He hustled. Followed orders. He followed orders perfectly. Of course I only gave him one order—hit. No insubordination there. He hit.

We ended up in a tie for first place with the Indians that year. First time there ever was a play-off in the American League. It was a one-game play-off. I started Denny Galehouse against them, and I still hear from the second-guessers about that because he wasn't one of my first-line pitchers. The truth was I didn't have anybody else. Remember, we were in a close race all the way, and my starters were all used up from getting us into the play-off. And Galehouse had pitched a great game for me against the Indians the last time we were in Cleveland. I was hoping he

Ted Williams

would do it again. But he didn't, and we lost. What the hell, I could have started Parnell or Kinder or one of the others, but then I would have been second-guessed for starting a tired pitcher. No matter what you do, you get second-guessed.

I quit in 1950. I'd gotten tired, and I wasn't feeling well. I guess it begins to catch up to you. I began to feel I wasn't a good manager anymore. So I quit.

I still follow the game today. I read the box scores, but I don't know the names of half those players. It's a whole new generation in there now. Sometimes I look back and I find it hard to believe it's all so long ago.

But people still remember. I get mail from all over the country—from California, Texas, Ohio, and all over. Wanting autographs. And a lot of them from kids. You'd be surprised. One kid, he wrote and said he's nine years old and has been a fan of mine all his life. Can you imagine that? All his life.

5

WALTER ALSTON

WALTER EMMONS ALSTON
Born: December 1, 1911, Venice, Ohio
Managerial career: Brooklyn–Los Angeles Dodgers, 1954–76

Walter Alston has achieved a record for longevity that is remarkable among big league managers. Only Connie Mack and John McGraw managed longer for a single ball club. Handling Dodger teams in Brooklyn and in Los Angeles, Alston has won seven pennants and four World Championships.

No, it hasn't been dull. There's been a little bit of everything. I wouldn't trade it for any other job I know of. It hasn't always been easy—there's a lot of grief and aggravation you have to put up with—but at the same time it's been gratifying and exciting. I think you have to enjoy it and be prepared to take what comes, the ups and the downs; otherwise you'd better not be in managing.

I guess I always wanted to be a ballplayer, going back as far as I can remember. My dad was a pretty good athlete himself. We lived on a farm, and as soon as I was big enough to swing a bat, once in a while he'd get me out there to play catch or pitch to me up against the barn door.

I went to school at Miami University in Oxford, Ohio, a few miles from where I was born. I played ball there and hit pretty well. The day after I graduated, Frank Rickey, Branch's brother, came driving down the back roads to where I lived and offered me a contract to play in the Cardinal farm system. I can still remember it. My dad and I were working at trying to build a house for ourselves when Rickey drove up. We talked some and then he asked me if I wanted to sign a contract.

"For how much?" I asked.

"One twenty-five a month," he said.

I don't know why I was even asking about the money. I was so anxious to play ball I would have signed for half that amount!

In 1936, my second year in pro ball, I played at Huntington, West Virginia, and led the league in home runs. The Cardinals brought me up at the end of the season. I was a first baseman, and at that time they had Johnny Mize and Rip Collins, who were two pretty good first basemen. Frankie Frisch was the manager, and they had Dizzy Dean, Pepper Martin, Leo Durocher, and Joe Medwick. That was the Gas House Gang.

Medwick was kind of hard on the rookies. I could throw pretty well, and they had me pitching some batting practice just about every day. When I was finished throwing, I'd go over and work out at third base because they had two first basemen. One day Medwick hit a line drive down there, and I dove after it and caught it. When he was through hitting, he came trotting out toward left field and when he went past me said, "What are you trying to do there, show me up?" That was a hell of a thing to say, wasn't it? How is some rookie going to show up a guy like Medwick?

I didn't get to know any of them very well. A rookie was next to nothing in those days—you were lucky to get a swing in, in batting practice. But Pepper Martin was nice to me, and I got friendly with Jess Haines. I think Haines liked me because we were both from Ohio.

I sat around on the bench until the last day of the season. We were playing the Cubs. Collins had been used earlier, and then Mize got thrown out of the ball game for arguing with the umpire. All of a sudden I was in the game, playing the last few innings. I came up to bat against Lon Warneke, hit one foul pretty hard, and then struck out. I didn't know it then, but that was going to be my one and only time at bat in the major leagues.

I heard later on that in 1940 Branch Rickey had decided I

Walter Alston
Star of the Darrtown High School
baseball team

would never make it to the big leagues as a player. Would I have quit in 1940 if I had known of Rickey's assessment? No, I don't think so. I liked playing too much. I loved what I was doing. Of course, I wasn't making all that much money, but I did have a teaching certificate and I taught school in the off-season. Between baseball and teaching I managed to get enough beans and potatoes.

In 1944 I was playing for Rochester. I hurt my back in a game and soon after that the Cardinals gave me my release. I guess they felt I was through as a player. I came back home to Ohio feeling pretty down. That was the low point for me in my baseball career. Of course, I had the school job, but I knew I was going to miss baseball. I liked it and hated to give it up, and it sure did look like I was giving it up—or more precisely, I should say baseball was giving me up. If anybody had come along at that time and told me that I was going to be spending the next thirty-plus years in baseball, more than twenty of them managing the Dodgers, I would have told him to go have his head examined.

I was back about a week when I found out Branch Rickey had been trying to reach me by telephone. Well, we didn't have a telephone in those days. He finally called the grocery store here in town and the grocer came on up to get me. I went over to the store and spoke to Mr. Rickey, and he offered me a job in the Dodger organization—he was running the Dodgers now—at Trenton, New Jersey. That's how I got started with the Dodgers.

I was playing-manager at Trenton in 1944 and '45 and then took over the club in Nashua, New Hampshire, in 1946. That was the first year for black players in organized ball. Jackie Robinson was at Montreal, and on my club I had Campanella and New-combe. I tried not to worry too much about the situation, even though it was something new. There was some abuse, but mostly it came from other clubs and other managers. I caught a lot of it when I was out coaching on the line. As far as my getting along with Campanella and Newcombe, I had no problems. They were top-notch ballplayers, and each was a hell of a good man. They got along fine with the rest of the team. I guess I got particularly close to Campy. He just loved to play ball. He was like a little kid about it, that same sort of enthusiasm, and he never lost it, even when he became a big league star.

As I said, the abuse came from the other clubs. There was one guy, a manager, who used to ride me from the bench, asking me if I'm sleeping with Campanella. One day I met him outside the clubhouse between games of a doubleheader and I stopped him.

"Listen," I said, "you've been wondering if I sleep with Campanella. Well, the answer is no. The Dodgers go first class; we all get to sleep in separate rooms. But if you gave me my choice of sleeping with Campanella or with you, I'd sure as hell take Campanella. Okay?"

I guess it was okay because he didn't say anything more about it.

After Nashua I managed for the Dodgers at Pueblo, St. Paul, and Montreal.

Roy Campanella, left
"He just loved to play ball."

The Dodgers won pennants under Charlie Dressen in '52 and '53. Charlie had been working under one-year contracts, and after the '53 season he asked for a three-year contract. He seemed pretty stubborn about it, but it never entered my mind that he would eventually turn down what he was offered. Hell, he'd just won two pennants and had a great ball club in Brooklyn. I couldn't believe he'd back out of there. But he did, and the Dodgers began looking for a new manager.

I didn't apply for the job. I'd been in the organization a long time. I figured they knew me and knew my record, and if they wanted me, they would let me know.

I can remember the day—November 23, 1953. The rabbit, pheasant, and quail season had opened in Ohio, and I was up the road here about four or five miles hunting. I got back early in the afternoon, and there was a message for me to call Buzzie Bavasi, the Dodgers' general manager. I called him back, and all he would tell me was that he wanted me to come to Brooklyn right away. He didn't say I was getting the job, but I kind of had a feeling that was what it was about. I didn't see any other reason for them bringing me out to Brooklyn in the middle of November. In addition, Buzzie told me to come in under an alias. I guess he didn't want the newspapermen sniffing out the story, somebody hearing that Walter Alston was suddenly in town. He wanted to break it at a press conference the next day. So I bought a ticket under the name of Matt Burns.

The next day "Matt Burns" became Walter Alston again, and Walter Alston became manager of the Brooklyn Dodgers.

I realized I was stepping into an unusual situation. I wasn't getting the job because the previous manager had failed. In fact the contrary was true—Charlie had just won two pennants. But the thing that made it a little easier for me was that there were seventeen guys on that club who had been with me in the minors at one time or another—guys like Campanella, Newcombe, Carl Erskine, Clem Labine, and a lot of others. So I was not a total stranger to them, nor were they all going to be strangers to me.

Another thing that made it easier for me was that I got an awful lot of help and cooperation from Pee Wee Reese, Gil Hodges, and

Campanella. They were three great guys. They could have made it tough for me. After all, here's a guy coming out of the minor leagues who had never really played in the majors—coming in to manage what was virtually an All-Star team and telling those guys what to do. Remember, we also had guys like Duke Snider, Carl Furillo, Billy Cox, and Jackie Robinson. That was a hell of a team. You could turn them loose on the field without a manager, and they'd win their share of games. So they could have made it difficult for me, but they didn't, and I'll always give Pee Wee and Gil and Roy a lot of the credit.

The pressure was there, no question. The club had been winning, and I knew it was sort of expected of me to win. Nobody demanded it; there was no ultimatum from upstairs. But I knew what everybody was thinking.

I felt the pressure, sure. I'm not going to lie to anybody about that. But I don't think I felt it as much as people thought I did. I've always felt that if I did the best I could, I wasn't going to worry about something I couldn't help. I do the best I can and the hell with the rest of it.

I can remember when I was managing in the Dodger system and we'd be at Vero Beach in the spring, twenty-four minor league managers and about fifty scouts. Every time the word went out that Mr. Rickey was coming to town, goddamn, they'd all start to bust their asses, doing this, doing that. I'd think, well, hell, I can't do any more than I've been doing. I didn't give a damn whether he was there or not. I didn't mean any disrespect, of course. I liked and respected Mr. Rickey. We got along fine. I simply felt I'd been giving it everything I had and couldn't do any more just because he was coming. If I waited for him to show up before I put out, then I had no business being there in the first place.

I felt the same way when I took over the Dodgers: Do the best I could with the players I had, and if it wasn't good enough, let the club get somebody else.

I guess I had a problem or two with Robinson when we first went to spring training. I think he was kind of testing me out a little bit. We'd be out doing calisthenics, and he'd stop on the side to talk to a writer or someone. This went on for two or three days,

"That was a hell of a team." Five members of the 1954 Brooklyn Dodgers. Left to right: *Duke Snider, Gil Hodges, Jackie Robinson, Pee Wee Reese, Roy Campanella*

and I talked to him about it. I think he just wanted to see what I'd take and what I wouldn't. I had to let him know that I would treat him fairly, no more and no less than any other ballplayer. Who he was or how good he was never entered my mind. It smoothed out all right with Jackie, and I think the longer we worked together, the better we got along.

Well, we didn't win it in 1954—we finished second to the Giants. But if 1954 was a disappointment to some people, 1955 was not. We came back and won the pennant by 13 games. And there, as usual, were the Yankees, waiting for us. Remember, up to that time the Dodgers had never won a World Series, and most of the time it was the Yankees who had beaten them. In fact, the Yankees had beaten the Dodgers in five World Series since 1941. And damn if it didn't look like it was going to be the same old story in '55. We lost the first two games at Yankee Stadium. But then we turned it around by beating them three straight at Ebbets Field. We lost the sixth game at the Stadium and that tied it at three games apiece.

I started Johnny Podres in that seventh game, and he did a hell of a job. We were ahead 1–0 in the sixth inning, and I did a little maneuvering there that was going to turn out just right for us. Let's see if I can remember just how it worked out. Reese led off with a single. Snider sacrificed, there was an error in the Yankee infield, and we had men on first and second. Then Campanella sacrificed them to second and third. Furillo walked. Hodges hit a sacrifice fly and that made it 2–0. Then I did a little brainstorming. I sent George Shuba up to hit for Don Zimmer, who was playing second base. I was hoping to pick up another run, but I was also figuring that I would set myself a better defensive alignment for the late innings. Shuba made out, and after the inning was over, I moved Gilliam from left field to second base and put Sandy Amoros in left.

That move paid off in the bottom of the inning. The Yankees got men on first and second with nobody out and Berra was up. With Yogi up, Amoros naturally shaded over toward center. Well, Berra sliced one down the left-field line, where he seldom hit them. It was kind of high, but still Amoros had a long, long way to go. At the last second he reached out with his gloved hand and caught the ball. The thing I admired about Amoros making that catch is that he never shied away from the fence; he went awfully close to it to get the ball. Could Gilliam have gotten it? You have to wonder. Gilliam wore his glove on his left hand, remember; he would have had to reach across his body to get the ball. Amoros, wearing the glove on his right hand, reaching way out, just did get it.

I don't think anybody in the ball park believed he had a chance for it, including the Yankee base runners, because there was a relay back to the infield that doubled the man off of first. That broke

the back of it. The score never changed and we won it, 2–0. It was
a particularly sweet win for Brooklyn and a particularly sweet one
for me. You never forget a World Series victory, and especially the
first one.

The most important part of managing? Be your own self. To me
that's probably the most important part of it, more so than the
strategy part. If you know yourself, you'll know your players—
how to handle them, how to keep them happy, how to get a
hundred percent out of them, which ones to pat on the back,
which ones to give a kick in the ass now and then. I occasionally
raise hell at meetings if I think it's for the good of the whole club,
but mostly I take a guy into the office and talk to him. The
winning of the ball game and the good of the team comes first.
You've got to keep that uppermost in your mind. Individual
grievances and pet peeves have got to go by the wayside.

Generally, you don't have to worry about the guys who are
playing every day. It's the guys who are sitting on the bench that
are the ones that get needles in their pants. I can understand
it—they wouldn't be worth a damn if they were content to sit
there. They've got to be on edge. I think anybody who's a good
athlete and a good competitor has got to be a little high-strung;
it's part of what makes them what they are. You've got to
understand it. Of course, with that first club in Brooklyn, where,
as I said, you virtually had an All-Star at every position, the guys
on the bench didn't have a hell of a lot to moan about. But in the
past few years I've had guys on the bench who were just about as
good as the guys playing. That can be a tough situation.

I don't get too many comments from my players about strategy.
They're content to let you do the worrying. Sometimes a pitcher
will come in and ask you why you took him out. All you can do is
tell him. Of course, when you've got a relief pitcher like Mike
Marshall ready to come in, that's explanation enough. I must say
I've been blessed with outstanding relievers during my years
with the Dodgers, going all the way back to Brooklyn. We had
Clem Labine and Don Bessent there, then later on Larry Sherry,
Ron Perranoski, Phil Regan, Jim Brewer, and Marshall.

I always think of Jim Gilliam when I think of a good team man.
To me he was always underrated. He never made the headlines
that often, but I would rather see Gilliam up at bat with a man on
second base and nobody out than anybody I know of because he
would do the job for the team. I think we're getting fewer and
fewer of that kind in the league. I think more and more of the
younger players are individualistic—concerned with their own
records—and whether the team wins or loses is not quite as
important as it used to be. I guess a lot of that is a reflection of the
times. Most young people who are playing ball today have come
up through prosperity. It hasn't been such a tough life for them. A
lot of them got big money to sign and didn't have to spend five or
six years in the minors riding the buses the way players used to.
So it's changed, and the best you can do is roll with the punches.

I don't care how long a guy's hair is or how wide his mustache.
That's his business. I know when I was a young man, I never
liked anybody telling me certain things, so I let a fellow pretty

Jim Gilliam
"I always think of Jim Gilliam
when I think of a good team
man."

much have his way—as long as he's giving me a hundred percent out on that field.

I think that probably the fewer rules you have, the better off you are. I would rather do what I could to motivate players to stay in condition and take care of themselves than have to force them. Anyway, I don't think you can force them. So I let them use their own judgment, unless of course somebody gets way out of line.

Naturally there are times when things get a little rough and you can't help getting hot. One time we were in Pittsburgh—I guess this was around '63—and we'd lost a few games in which we didn't play too well. I think everybody was feeling a bit edgy. We got on the bus to go to the airport. The Pirates were leaving the same night, and we saw their bus go around us. It was a sleek Greyhound, air-conditioned. Our bus wasn't air-conditioned, and it wasn't too sleek either. It was a warm night and some of the guys in the back started bitching and moaning about the bus.

Lee Scott, our traveling secretary, finally got mad, and he turned around and said, "Win a couple of games and then you can complain."

I asked the driver to pull over to the side and stop. Then I got up.

"If anybody wants to complain about the bus," I said, "he can come directly to me."

Scottie started to say something, but I told him to keep quiet, that I'd handle it from here.

"First of all," I told him, "from now on I want you to get a goddamn bus that's no better and no worse than anybody else's."

Then I told the players I'd had all the bitching I intended to listen to. I said we could talk about it now and get it all straightened out, and if anybody wanted to talk individually, I'd be happy to step outside with him. There I was, challenging twenty-five guys to step outside. I was so mad I was about ready, too. But everybody seemed satisfied and we went on.

I think the AstroTurf has changed the playing of the game in certain respects. There's more of a premium on speed now, especially in the outfield. You want speedy outfielders who are able to cut the ball off before it gets through the gap. And I think the sacrifice bunt is a little harder to execute on AstroTurf than it is on grass. Also the bunt defense has improved; they've got all kinds of trick plays now, charging from both sides and so forth. You used to try and bunt down the line towards first and third, but with these guys charging in from the corners today, we kind of feel now that if you bunt the ball straightaway and deaden it halfway to the pitcher's box, you've got just about as good a chance as any. Of course, it's much harder to deaden the ball on AstroTurf than it is on grass. I think a lot of managers feel that the AstroTurf is to the advantage of the hitters, and I think they turn them loose a little more than they used to.

Right now in the National League it's split about half and half between the teams that have the artificial surface and those that don't. So you have to keep adjusting back and forth, and what you do is before the game have your guys take a few extra ground balls to get them accustomed to what they're playing on.

Naturally your ball club is always changing, and that's going to determine how you play your game. For a long time there, when we had Wills and Koufax and Drysdale and that team, we didn't score many runs, but we did have a couple of guys who could run like hell. So you had to rely on a base on balls, a bunt hit, a stolen base, a ground ball, or a sacrifice fly to get your run or two and then hope that your good pitching would hold them.

We moved out to Los Angeles after the '57 season, and our first year out there we dropped to seventh place. There were a number of reasons for that. First of all we lost Campanella—he had that accident that winter. He was the one guy who I think would have popped them over that short left field we had out there in the Coliseum, where we played the first few years. Another thing was, when Drysdale went there, he decided he was going to pitch everybody outside because of the wall. But his best pitch was a fastball that he threw in on a right-handed hitter. He'd break half a dozen bats a game with that pitch. But when we first got out there, he didn't want to throw it. So it took him a while to adjust. Nothing went right for us, and we finished seventh.

But then the next year, '59, we turned it right around and, with pretty much the same club, won the pennant. We finished the regular season in a tie with Milwaukee and then beat them in a play-off.

One of the key players for us that year was Maury Wills, who joined the club in mid-season. You know, outside of his legs he was not born with the greatest natural abilities. He had a pretty good arm, but he had to learn to play shortstop. He had to learn to field a ground ball. He became an excellent bunter and, with the help of Bobby Bragan, a switch-hitter. He was a man of tremendous determination and ambition—always working hard, trying to improve.

In 1962 he stole 104 bases. That was the record, of course, until Lou Brock broke it a few years ago. Was there pressure on me as

Maury Wills stealing third in a 1962 game against the New York Mets. The third baseman is Felix Mantilla.

the manager because he was going for a record? No, I wouldn't say so. I had a stop sign for him. There were certain situations when I didn't want him to run. For instance, with a man on third I would sometimes nail him to the bag because I was afraid if he stole second, they might walk the next man to set up a double-play situation that I wanted to avoid. But a lot of the time Maury was on his own. I trusted his judgment. His going for a record never bothered me. Hell, look at it this way. He stole 104 bases and was thrown out only 13 times. He wasn't just setting a record. He was helping us win ball games.

What helped Wills that year I think was that he had the perfect man hitting behind him—Gilliam. Gilliam could handle the bat. He could take a lot of pitches. He wasn't concerned about having two strikes on him. But there was one advantage for him. When Wills was running, it pulled one of those infielders out of position and gave Gilliam some daylight to hit the ball through. But I know he took a lot of pitches, letting Wills go. I'll tell you something else about Gilliam. He could adapt up at the plate as well as any hitter I ever saw. I had him in the minor leagues and several times this situation occurred: Man on first, I give the hit-and-run sign, the guy on first doesn't go, and Gilliam doesn't swing. After it happened a couple of times, I started to give them both hell for missing the sign.

"Well," Gilliam said, "he didn't go. I can see if he's going."

"You can follow the ball and the runner at the same time?" I asked.

"Sure," he said.

Well, it had happened a couple of times, so I had to believe him. He was able to handle those situations, he was that quick up at the plate. So the same sort of thing happened frequently with him when Wills was on first. He'd see Maury break, and if he could afford to take the pitch, he would. That's what I mean about Gilliam being a team man. He could have hit more that year, but he knew the base-stealing was helping the team win games, and he wanted to give Maury as much room as he could. That's my kind of ballplayer—Jim Gilliam.

In 1954 we signed a wild, hard-throwing left-hander to a bonus contract. His name was Sandy Koufax. The scouts had brought him in, and I saw him working out on the sidelines at Ebbets Field that summer. I liked what I saw. He had an outstanding fastball and a pretty good breaking ball.

The next time I saw him was in spring training the following year. He was in a little warm-up area behind the barracks playing catch with somebody. They were about sixty feet apart, and I would say that about half of his return throws were going over the other guy's head. I looked at that and said to myself, "What the hell have we got here?" We had to keep him with the big club because in those years there was a rule stipulating that if you signed for a bonus, you had to stay with the club the next year.

It was years before Sandy could master control of the ball. But we always felt that he had good enough stuff and that if he ever

Sandy Koufax in 1955

got control, he was going to be a winning pitcher. We stayed with him, trying to pitch him as much as we could. We were in pennant races those years, and I just couldn't give him as much work as I would have liked to. I think that bonus rule hurt him. If he could have gone out to the minor leagues and pitched regularly, he would have come along a lot sooner. But I think you've got to give Sandy a lot of credit, along with Joe Becker, our pitching coach, for all the patience and hard work that they put in.

All at once Sandy got control. And I don't mean control in the sense of just throwing the ball over the plate. He could throw the fastball where he wanted to—to spots. When you have that kind of stuff and that kind of control, well, they just stopped hitting him. And it all happened in one year. Whether it was a matter of rhythm or whatever, I don't know, but there it was.

He was the greatest pitcher I ever had, although I would say that Drysdale was a pretty close second. Sandy had the fastball and the curve, while Drysdale never had the really good breaking ball. But they both were outstanding. Having two pitchers like that on a ball club can make you a mighty smart manager.

In '65 we played the Twins in the Series and went down to the seventh game. That day I had to make what was probably the toughest decision I ever had to make as a manager. Very often things work themselves out—you know what you want to do or circumstances tell you what you have to do. Now, there I was with one more game to play, and I had Koufax with two days' rest and Drysdale with three. With two pitchers like that, of almost equal ability, ninety-nine times out of a hundred I would have said give me the man with the most rest. But I'll do the best I can to explain to you why I didn't.

First of all, Drysdale hadn't gone too well against the Twins in the games he pitched. I didn't think he was quite as sharp as he had been. That's one reason. Number two, I felt the Twins were a little bit more susceptible to left-handed pitching than they were to right-handed. Number three was the fact that I had Perranoski in the bull pen, a strong left-handed reliever. If I start a left-hander, Koufax, and then have to go to Drysdale and they do much switching right and left, I come in with Perranoski. So it's

Don Drysdale pitching to Bill Mazeroski

left, right, left, which works out to my advantage. Another thing was that I felt better about Drysdale coming out of the bull pen in a jam than I did Koufax. His control was better in those situations than Sandy's. Koufax was sometimes wild to the first batter he pitched to. And it took him a longer time to warm up. If I'm going to rely on him in the bull pen, I've just about got to have him throwing the whole damn game.

So that was my reasoning, for whatever it was worth, and I decided to start Koufax. Before the game I talked to him alone, then I talked to Drysdale alone, and then I talked to them both together. I told Drysdale my thoughts and he was great about it. After all, he was an ace pitcher, fully rested, being passed over in the seventh game of a World Series.

"Skipper," he said, "whatever you decide is fine with me."

It turned out to be fine with everybody. Koufax shut them out on three hits, 2–0.

You know, I think I was as proud of the team in '74 as I was of any I've ever managed. We started putting that team together in '73. Ordinarily if you bring in one or two young ballplayers and expect them to help you become a pennant contender, you're darn lucky if they do. In '73 we kind of stuck our necks out and decided this was going to be our club. We went with them. I'm talking about Ronnie Cey, in his rookie year; Bill Russell, who we were trying to make into a shortstop; Davey Lopes, also in his rookie year; Steve Garvey, who we were making into a first baseman; Bill Buckner, a young outfielder; Joe Ferguson and Steve Yeager, two young catchers; and a few pitchers. We started the season in '73 with those guys, hoping they'd take us somewhere. We ended up winning 95 games and I was damned proud of them, just as proud as I was the next year, when we won the pennant.

I've got to give a lot of the credit to the organization—the front office, the scouts, everybody. They've always given me a lot of fine young players to work with.

I guess Frank Howard was just about as big and strong a man as has ever been in this game. We used to have some fun with him on occasion. We brought him up at about the same time we did Tommy Davis and Ron Fairly and a kid named Don Miles. They'd all received pretty good bonuses, and we decided to have a look at them at the end of the year. This was around '58. I put Miles in a game in Chicago, and he crashed into that brick wall and banged himself up. Then in the same game Fairly hit a foul tip off of his toe, and he was out for a few days. Now it was big Frank's turn. We went to Philadelphia. Second time up he hit a line drive into left field, and as he was rounding first, he tripped over the bag and fell and hurt his leg. So he was out for a while.

After that some of the veterans like Hodges and Reese, who were a couple of pretty good agitators, went into the dressing room and said, "Hey, Skip, they're not putting the stuff into these young fellows like they used to, are they?" They saw Howard on the rubbing table getting worked on—he stuck out over both ends, he was so big—and they brought him a pillow and a glass of water and asked him if there was anything else they could do for him. They enjoyed getting on him because he was sort of easygoing. This went on for four or five days.

Then I got Frank off to a side.

"Hey, Frank," I said, "goddamn, you don't have to take that from them. They're getting a little too rough, don't you think?"

"Oh, no," he said. "It's okay."

"No it isn't," I said. "I think they're going too far. I tell you what you do. Why don't you just take that Pee Wee up and shake him a little bit? Gently, of course."

"Pee Wee's a nice guy," he said.

"You listen to me," I said. "They're just going to drive you nuts if you don't quiet them down a little bit."

Then I went over and sat down beside Reese.

"Hey," I said, "I'd sure like to try some more of those kids out. Why don't you get on that Howard and agitate him a little bit and see if I can't get him back into the lineup?"

That suited Pee Wee just fine. I sat back and folded my arms while he got up and went to the other end of the bench and started needling Frank. Next thing I see is Frank standing up, his back to me, and he's got Reese up off the floor shaking him up and down, and old Pee Wee's arms and legs are flapping and his eyes are shining as big as half-dollars.

Later on Reese came up to me cussing. "Hey, Skipper," he said, "what's going on?"

"Just having a little fun," I told him.

"Fun?" he said. "I think you're trying to get me killed."

The one-year contracts? People always ask me about them. Well, up to this moment I've signed twenty-three of them, so I don't see where there's anything to complain about. I was tickled to death to get the first one and glad to get each and every one after that. You can call it stubbornness or pride or whatever, but I know I wouldn't want to be there if they didn't want me. I don't care about a two-year contract. The Dodgers have been fair with me all down the line. We've had some thin years, and maybe in another organization I would have been fired. But I wasn't fired. And we won some pennants. So I'm not concerned about a one-year contract. Why should I complain about that after the ball club has stuck with me through the thin years?

Walter Alston in 1964

6

PAUL RICHARDS

PAUL RAPIER RICHARDS
Born: November 21, 1908, Waxahachie, Texas
Managerial career: Chicago White Sox, 1951–54; Baltimore
   Orioles, 1955–61; Chicago White Sox, 1976.

After a playing career that included service with the
Brooklyn Dodgers, New York Giants, Philadelphia Athletics,
and the Detroit Tigers, Paul Richards turned to managing
and soon developed a reputation as one of baseball's keenest
and most respected minds. After being out of uniform for
fifteen years, Richards returned to the field as manager of the
Chicago White Sox for the 1976 season.

As far back as I can remember, the only thing I ever wanted to
do was play baseball. My father was a schoolteacher, so I was
taught pretty early on to read, and my favorite reading was the
box scores and accounts of ball games that came down with the
Dallas newspapers.

I started out as a third baseman and pitcher in high school.
Strangely enough, I was an ambidextrous pitcher and actually did
some ambidextrous pitching in professional ball at Macon, Georgia, and Muskogee, Oklahoma. At Macon, in 1930, our club had a
few of its catchers get hurt, and there was a call for volunteers to
go behind the plate. I volunteered and all of a sudden I'm a
catcher, and I stayed a catcher for the rest of my career.

I played on a high school team that won 65 consecutive games.
Naturally that attracted some attention. So a bird-dog scout from
Dallas came down to Waxahachie to see us play. He went back
and called the Brooklyn Dodgers and spoke to Wilbert Robinson,

who was managing them at that time. Uncle Robbie sent his old ace pitcher Nap Rucker to Texas to look the team over, and Nap signed me to a Brooklyn contract.

He was a great fellow, Nap was. One of those homespun country gentlemen, a good storyteller and a very interesting character. He'd had the experience of breaking into the old South Atlantic League with a fellow named Tyrus Raymond Cobb. They were roommates, and he told many stories about Cobb's early days—how Ty fought and scratched and scrambled to be first, whether it was going to bed first or taking a bath first or getting to breakfast first. Whatever it was, Cobb had an obsession about being first, even way back then at the very beginning.

Incidentally, the Detroit Tigers trained right here in Waxahachie around 1917, in a park that was then called Jungle Park and is now called, excuse me for saying so, Richards Park. John McGraw's Giants were training not too far away in Marlin Springs, and they came up here for an exhibition game. Naturally I went out to see the game. Well, in the very first inning Cobb dropped an easy fly ball that was right in his hands. I've never forgotten that. The greatest player in the world drops a ball. It's odd the things you remember, isn't it? If he had gone four for four, I would probably have forgotten it a long time ago because he was supposed to do that. But I can still see that easy fly ball dropping out of his hands to the grass.

Years later, when I was managing in the big leagues, Cobb would call me whenever we were in the same town together and he would come over to talk. The interesting thing that I noticed about him was that he was always hesitant about answering questions, but he would ask you questions by the hour—about various players, about techniques, about how they were doing this or that today. He wanted to know everything that was going on in baseball, but he didn't want to tell you anything.

He was a fascinating character. They say that playing against him was always an experience. The drive he had to excel was incredible, and sometimes frightening. You know, you just don't become a Ty Cobb when you put your spikes on. There's got to be

Nap Rucker in 1914

something more to it, something born in you along with the
natural ability. There was a force in Cobb that demanded he excel
no matter the cost, and there was a cost—he was very unpopular
with his teammates as well as with the opposition. And it didn't
seem to bother him in the least. Certainly he didn't court
popularity.

Did I ever see another ballplayer with that kind of inner drive?
Well, yes. I'd say that Ted Williams had it as a hitter. The
intensity of his concentration and determination at the plate was
awesome. And I'd say that in some respects, without the ultimate
ability of a Cobb, certain players that I knew had it, like George
Kell, Nelson Fox, Minnie Minoso, and Brooks Robinson.

Ty Cobb
"The drive he had to excel was incredible, and
sometimes frightening."

Did I always want to manage eventually? Well, even as a youngster of ten or twelve years old I had my own teams. We used to hitchhike to various little towns around the county to play. Later on, in pro ball, I always observed the moves the managers made and occasionally talked to them later about their strategy and tried to analyze their thinking.

Donie Bush, whom I played for at Minneapolis, was very influential in my career. He was a strict manager, even with the former big leaguers who came down, fellows like Jess Petty and Rube Benton and Carmen Hill. I liked that. I liked the way he handled men. And he was a student of the game, always bringing things to your attention, no matter how minute. One thing I learned from him, and always remembered and drilled into my players when I was a manager, was that no player should ever be doubled on a line drive with nobody out. And we actually went seven years in Baltimore when I was managing without ever having a player doubled with the bases full and nobody out. Sometimes you see a man doubled off on a line drive and later on somebody will say, "He couldn't help it." Well, that's wrong. He could help it. He could have stayed on the bag, for one thing, although I'm not advocating that. But you can teach a fellow not to break until he *knows* that ball is in the outfield or on the ground.

Another thing Bush insisted on was, with runners on first and third and one out, the man on first should never be tagged when a ground ball is hit to the second baseman, which can prevent that run from scoring. Yet it happens quite often, and they say, "Well, he went a little too far." That's exactly right. He went a little too far. The second baseman charged the ball, tagged him, and threw on to first for the double play. The run doesn't count. But if he can make the second baseman throw the ball to first and *then* run him down, that man on third is going to score. How do you do it? It's very simple—just don't run when the ball is hit to the second baseman. Now, that is a fundamental. The fundamentals start and end with the simplest things you can think of, and I actually get embarrassed talking about them because they are so simple. But these fundamentals are not observed in the major leagues the way they should be. How many times have you seen a man on first go to third on a base hit and the batter wind up on second because the outfielder threw the ball to third? The next batter hits a ground ball which should be a double play, but it isn't.

You would think they'd learn these things in the minor leagues. Well, let me tell you something about the minor leagues. You can bring a boy up and tell him something, and he'll say he never heard of it. The chances are he was told about it but probably didn't pay any attention. There's the old story about hitting a mule over the head with a two-by-four to get its attention. Well, you can't hit your ballplayer over the head, but you've got to get his attention and stamp the lessons into him. How many times have you heard a third-base coach say he told that guy to tag up on line drives to the outfield? "I told him twenty times." Okay. But maybe he should have told that guy *fifty* times because twenty wasn't enough—because the guy still broke when the ball was hit and then wasn't able to get back and tag up and score when it was caught.

But those things aren't the player's fault. They're the manager's fault. He's responsible for everything that happens on that field, good or bad. If he's got good players and trains them well, it's to his credit. And let's say the player does something out of the ordinary that's good, something that the manager hasn't taught him. Well, in my contention, the manager gets credit for it because he has trained his player to expect these situations, to be instinctively alert for them, and to take advantage of them. On the other hand, if the player misses third base while he's scoring the winning run, that's the manager's fault. He should teach his players to touch those bases. Everything that happens on the field during the course of the game is either something good for the manager or something bad. What the fan is seeing is the end product of what the manager has done before the game.

And I've often wondered how much of this game of baseball the fan actually sees and perceives. The competition between the pitcher and the hitter, for instance, can be quite interesting for the perceptive fan. He can see the outfielders and the infielders move a step or so, which tells them the pitcher is going to try and pitch a

Paul Richards

certain way to the hitter, and sometimes he'll see the hitter adjust himself a little to try and meet the challenge. It's all quite subtle and interesting, if you know what to look for and how to watch it. I've always contended that baseball is made up of very few big and dramatic moments, but rather it's a beautifully put together pattern of countless little subtleties that finally add up to the big moment, and you have to be well versed in the game to fully appreciate them.

I'll say this. It is much, much easier to teach winning baseball on a winning team than it is on a losing team because a little failure in the third inning on a losing team doesn't make a whole lot of difference if you're getting beat 10–2. But if you get beat 2–1 in eleven innings, that failure in the third inning beat you. So the winning team gets into the clubhouse and they say, "Wait a minute. We'd have won that game if it hadn't been for that one little thing." So those things go together. You can teach the game better if you're winning than if you're losing because those little mistakes are all the more glaring and obvious. It means the losing manager has got a tougher job, and he's got to stay with it longer.

One thing you can't do—that's fool your players. A ballplayer knows when he's wrong, and he doesn't mind being told about it. And this business of being tough, don't try it unless you know you're right, and not a hundred percent but a hundred and ten percent because once you start down that road, there's no turning around.

All players are not alike. That's another very simple thing to know and to understand, and you had better know it and understand it. You've got twenty-five different players and each one calls for different handling, and you'd better give them that handling. You see, when you take over a ball club, you have to prove to the ballplayer that you know what you're doing and that what you're doing is best for the ball club. Now, the player may not like it, but deep down he will respect it. You may be sitting him down against left-handed pitching, for instance, and he's going to gripe about it, but he knows that this is right. You've got to prove to them that your moves are the right ones for the ball club. You've got to get their respect. You don't necessarily have to have them like you. Managers who try to get too close to their ballplayers are making a mistake because invariably you'll get too close to two or three and leave the others out in the cold, and they're not going to like that.

Is it easy for a club to lose confidence in a manager? It sure is. Very easy. If it's obvious that he's playing up to the sportswriters or he's playing up to the general manager and not giving full attention to what's going on on the field, sure he's going to lose his players' respect. And you'd be surprised how many managers will do that in order to keep the newspapers from criticizing them. Sometimes they'll use strategy that goes against their better judgment, just to appease the newspapermen, rather than do what they know they should do and stick with it.

The newspapermen have their job to do, of course, and it's up to you to get along with them. You have to be a pretty good diplomat and sell yourself to them in a manner that does not in any way reflect adversely on your ballplayers. The writers come right on into the clubhouse after a game, and there are a few who try to get somebody to say something controversial. They work at it. The manager has to be very careful. If you've got a player who messed up your ball game for you, your first reaction many times is to say, "Well, if so-and-so hadn't booted that ball, we'd have won it." Or the writer may say to you, "What do you think of so-and-so making that error?" My answer to that sort of question was always this: "Well, I remember last week when he made a great play and saved the game. That's what I prefer to remember."

It gets back to what I've always felt is absolutely essential for being a good manager. It's wrapped up in one word, one thing you must by all means be sure that you're capable of understanding, and that is restraint. He must restrain himself when things are tough, when things are not going well. Restraint under duress is absolutely necessary. And, boy, I can tell you, sometimes that's not easy—sometimes the more restraint you're trying to exercise, the more duress you put yourself under.

You know, the problem of disciplining a player has changed considerably since the time I came up to the big leagues. Back then, you could do almost anything you wanted to a ballplayer.

Not anymore. Today they've got player representatives and they've got Marvin Miller. Today it is absolutely necessary for the manager to be one hundred percent right in a dispute with a ballplayer. He can no longer be arbitrary or unduly severe in dealing with a player. He knows that his decisions might well be contested by a labor relations law and all other facets of that particular union. You get back to the manager not having so much to exert discipline as to exact respect from the players so that they will keep themselves in condition and be ready to play. If you can't get them to respect you, you're in trouble.

I came up to the Dodgers in 1926, stayed on the bench for a couple of months, and then was shipped out. Wilbert Robinson was the manager, and they had Dazzy Vance, Zach Wheat, Rabbit Maranville, and Burleigh Grimes, among others—and, by the way, they're all in the Hall of Fame today. Wilbert Robinson was more or less a manager who took the older players and put them on the field and just let them play. He didn't do a whole lot of managing or instructing. In fact, I don't think any team in baseball did less instructing than the Dodgers in those days.

I came back to Brooklyn again, briefly, in 1932. Hack Wilson was on the club at the time, a little past his peak but a great personality. We had Van Lingle Mungo, who had a world of stuff but was saddled with a mediocre team; and Lefty O'Doul, who was one of the brightest, most observing ballplayers that I was ever around and a very fine hitter.

The Giants bought me in 1933, and I joined them under Bill Terry. Terry was probably the finest defensive manager that I knew in baseball. He concentrated almost entirely on defense. His theory was not to let the other club score and they'd beat themselves. Naturally most ball games are lost rather than won. Terry took it far beyond anybody I ever knew—his entire approach to every game was defense. He didn't hit-and-run. He didn't go for the stolen base or any fancy offensive plays at all. He just figured to score three or four runs. And he had the good pitching staff to win—Carl Hubbell, Hal Schumacher, Roy Parmelee, Fred Fitzsimmons—and a good bull pen.

Bill Terry

Could a fellow like Terry have managed differently with a different type of team? I don't think so, and I think perhaps he proved it later on, that without the great pitching staff and without the good defense his managing fell apart. I don't think he was able to adjust to another type of managing. His whole concept was defense, and when he didn't have it, he couldn't manage. But when he did have his kind of club on the field, he was very skillful in leading it.

Terry was not a personality manager. He had no feelings for the ballplayers, no particular friends except those who courted him. He had a couple of players who made a point of doing that, and he wasn't aware of the fact that that was what they were doing. That sort of thing was to the detriment of the other players, and they criticized it severely.

Terry was a marvelous ballplayer. A lot of people don't know this, but he was the fastest man going down to first base in the National League. He was a superb fielder. And he hit .400. Terry had only one weakness. When he was at bat and the pitcher was winding up, Terry had a tendency to drop his bat slightly while he timed the pitcher's motion and then brought it back up again. When the pitcher was holding a man on and working out of a stretch, Terry did the same thing, only this time he had a tendency to drop the bat too fast and then couldn't get it back. You know, he got the reputation for not driving in runs. Well, if the bases were full, he could drive in runs because the pitcher was winding up. That was Terry's only weakness.

Did I ever mention it to him? No. He was hard to talk to. I stayed as far away from him as I could, frankly. I can give you an example. Roy Parmelee was one of our good pitchers on the Giants. I had him down in the bull pen one day. He had a sailing slider-fastball kind of pitch which was effective. I asked him if he could sort of let it out a different way, with his big finger instead of his forefinger. He tried it and it sank like a spitball. I told Terry about it and asked him to watch it and see what he thought of it.

"Leave him alone," he said. "He's doing fine."

So I forgot about it. But I'll always feel that Roy Parmelee could have been one of the real great pitchers if he could have used that pitch—if somebody had demanded he use it. I always felt that under no circumstances do you rule out a certain pitch for a pitcher until you know it's not effective. The Tigers, when Cobb was managing, got rid of Hubbell because he had a screwball. They just didn't think much of that particular pitch in those days.

I don't think that experience with Terry was lost on me. When I was managing, I wanted a player to feel free to come to me with what he felt were constructive suggestions. It's true that I wanted to keep them at arm's length, but no further. The door was always open, as far as baseball was concerned, but "Please don't ask me to have dinner with you or a drink with you or go visit your family."

I don't mean you should be cold and unrelated to a ballplayer. If he's got a serious problem and he comes to you for advice, sure, help him, do whatever you can. But it depends entirely on circumstances. I'll tell you something that I've stated many times, and I'll repeat it: I learned more as a player what not to do than what to do. You learn more through the mistakes of the managers you play for than you learn through their good points.

Another thing I tried to hold firm was that the players not bring their kids when they come to the ball park. Some managers say it's going to be one big family—that the kids are welcome, the wives are welcome, and so on. Well, I'll tell you, the worst thing you can have is one of the players' kids in the clubhouse. He gets in somebody's way, maybe a guy who's mad about something, and pretty soon you've got trouble on your hands, trouble that's absolutely unnecessary.

I caught Hubbell in quite a few games. Who called the game when he was pitching? Well, I did, but I will have to say that he did not have to accept any sign that I gave. But after I'd caught him a couple of games—and I think he'd verify this—he seldom, if ever, shook me off.

Catchers and pitchers are another category entirely. When I was managing, I tried to teach our catchers, and especially young fellows catching older pitchers, that you don't try to be too smart. You try to figure your pitcher out and determine what he would like to throw, early in the game especially. If you're giving him the pitch that he likes to throw early, then along about the eighth and ninth innings, when he's tired and undecided about what he wants to throw, he'll go along with you. You've convinced him you've been right all day, why aren't you right now? That gives him confidence. But you almost never insist on asking a pitcher to throw a certain pitch because in most cases if you do that, he will not give it the good effort. So I learned that if a pitcher was strongly in favor of a certain pitch at a certain time, I'd rather he give me his pitch good than my pitch bad. Essentially it's a combination of things wherein the catcher has to gain the complete confidence of the pitcher for the time when the tough situations arise late in the game.

Of course, it doesn't always pan out. You know, there are certain personalities about baseball people. There are some players who remember only the games they win. There are other players who only remember the games they lose. Dizzy Dean never remembered a game he lost. Hubbell seldom remembers a game he won. Well, as a catcher, I go back through the years, and I remember the bad calls I made rather than the good ones. I remember Joe Cronin pinch-hitting against us one time when I was catching for Detroit. We threw him five consecutive fastballs and ran the count to three and two. I figured now's the time for the curve. So I called for it and the pitcher busted off as good a curve as you could throw, and Cronin hit it in the seats. I've never been able to understand that. Was he guessing? How could he be guessing after five fastballs? To this day it worries me.

I saw Pie Traynor when I was in the National League. He had a bad arm then, but he could get the ball away quickly and that compensated for his errant throws. He had a marvelous ability to dive for balls. That was what impressed me about him. I really think, though, that Brooks Robinson is his superior as a fielder. Brooks is the greatest defensive third baseman that ever lived. There's no doubt about it as far as I'm concerned. Of course, I can't go back to the guy the old-timers say was the greatest, Jimmy Collins. But I saw Ken Keltner, George Kell, Traynor, and Billy Cox, and I'd have to say that Brooks just made plays that nobody else makes, or ever made, as far as I saw.

Would I call Brooks a natural? No, I wouldn't. In fact, we had two scouts bring in bad reports on him. We only signed him after our third scout went down and saw something in him. He had a little trouble with his hitting when he first came up, but his defensive ability was so good that the pitchers didn't care whether he ever got a hit or not. They wanted him in there.

The best throwing arm I ever saw on a catcher probably belonged to Gabby Hartnett. And he was accurate. He was just a great throwing catcher. Better than Johnny Bench? Yes. The fans used to come out early to watch infield practice just to watch Hartnett throw the ball around. That's quite a tribute to a fellow's throwing arm, wouldn't you say? He didn't go through

Ernie Lombardi
"One of the nicest people I ever
met in my life."

infield practice as a matter of routine. He made a theatrical performance out of it because he knew the fans liked to see him pop
that ball to second base and to third base, and you could hear it
all over the park.

Another one of my favorites behind the plate was Ernie
Lombardi. One of the nicest people I ever met in my life. He
came to the Brooklyn club one spring when I was there—a big,
powerful kid from California. He reported with a little cap on and
a satchel about the size of one a doctor would carry. The
ballplayers put together some money to buy him a hat. Everybody
liked him. The first game he caught he was catching Dazzy Vance.
Somebody swung at a ball and Lombardi ducked and the ball hit
him on top of the head and bounced all the way back to the
bench. A blow like that would have knocked out an ordinary man,

but Lombardi just crouched down and gave another sign, just as if nothing had happened. I've seen him catch hard-throwing pitchers with his bare hand and just toss the ball back to them. Carl Hubbell once said that Lombardi was the one hitter he didn't want to pitch to. The only way you could get him out was pitch him low outside, and if you didn't throw it perfectly, he was liable to hit it back through the box and kill you. Ernie was a great hitter, and if he would have had just normal speed afoot, there's no telling what he would have hit.

In 1935 I was traded to the Philadelphia Athletics. Had a chance to play for Connie Mack. To tell you the truth, I wasn't terribly impressed with the way he managed. I'm sure he was a very learned baseball man, but he didn't seem to be stretching himself that year. We had a team that included Jimmie Foxx, Eric McNair, Wally Moses, Bob Johnson, Pinky Higgins, and Doc Cramer, which is a pretty good team. But nothing was done with them. Nobody seemed to pay much attention, and we finished last.

I wasn't in the American League all that long at that time, but I did have an opportunity to see some of the great players they had there then. Charlie Gehringer was one of the best. Nobody in the league knew how to pitch to him. Most of the time he'd spot you a strike, for some reason or other. But then at the most inopportune or unexpected time he would not do that, and he'd hurt you. When it came down to driving in the tying or winning run in the ninth inning, Gehringer is the man that you wanted at the plate, above all others in my opinion.

In the field he was just as great. He made the double play beautifully and covered tremendous ground. He was, along with Bobby Doerr, one of those second basemen who could run toward the base and pick up a ball backhanded and flip it out of his glove to the shortstop. He started many a double play doing that that he might not otherwise have made. It's not an easy play to make; there are some second basemen who won't even try it.

Lefty Grove was throwing a fork ball when I batted against him. He was no longer real fast. I never hit at him in his heyday, but I did see him pitch. He was terrifically fast. You know, a left-hander's ball has a tendency to tail a little bit, but Grove threw it so hard it didn't tail—it didn't have time. It was on top of you before you knew it. Lefty had the type of fastball they tell me Satchel Paige had. You thought it was waist-high when you swung at it, but it was actually letter-high. The ball was four or five inches higher than you thought it was, which made the hitters think it was jumping, but it wasn't jumping. It came so fast it created an illusion.

Bill Dickey and Mickey Cochrane? I'd have to pick Dickey. He didn't have the fire that Cochrane did. Cochrane had a lot of flair, and he was a great catcher and a good hitter. But he didn't have the arm Dickey had, and he didn't have the power Dickey had. So I would take Dickey over all the catchers I've known. He's number one. And I'll tell you something else—that Berra's not too far behind. I remember one time a New York sports-writer came into our clubhouse moaning about Berra not hitting—Yogi was around .270 or so at the time.

"I'll tell you what," I said to him. "You go back to the hotel tonight and check back through your scorebook and see what Berra's hitting when the seventh inning starts."

He showed up the next day with a sheepish look on his face and said, "Well, I give up. From the seventh inning on he's hitting .430."

That's right, from the seventh inning on. And in close games that's when they change the marbles, right there. Berra was a game winner, and he was a better thrower than people gave him credit for being. And you know, in spite of what some of the Yankee pitchers said, he was a little smarter than they gave him credit for. He knew what was going on.

When you get to talking about hitters, there's no doubt that Ted Williams has to be the best left-handed hitter I ever observed. No doubt about it at all. Up at the plate he had the concentration and determination of a Cobb and it blanked out everything except what he was up there trying to do. I remember one day we were playing them a doubleheader in Detroit. This was the year they won the pennant, 1946. In the first game Williams hit a couple of home runs and a double, and the times we got him out, he nailed the right fielder to the fence with line drives.

Freddie Hutchinson is going to pitch the second game of this doubleheader. I don't think there was ever a tougher competitor on the mound than Hutchinson, or one who got angrier while he was at it. I'd caught the first game that day and gone out for a pinch hitter late in the game. I went into the clubhouse and Freddie's on the table getting rubbed down. He's telling the trainer that he doesn't care what Williams was doing out there or how great a hitter he was, he just wasn't going to hit Freddie that

George Kell

way. Freddie was going to knock Ted down the first time up. The game hasn't started yet, but Hutch is already steamed up.

The second game starts and he goes out to pitch. Williams comes up the first time and Fred throws one close, which didn't faze Ted. Second pitch he really knocked him down. Ted gets up and steps back in, snapping that bat back and forth. Never blinked an eye. Then Hutch threw the next one in. I can see it to this day. You know, along around Thanksgiving I read in the paper where some writer asked Ted what was the longest home run he'd ever hit in his life. Ted said that there had been one Sunday in Detroit when he caught the wind going out in the second game of a doubleheader and Freddie Hutchinson gave him a fastball which went for a pretty good ride.

Hutch didn't last very long in that game. Just an inning or two. I had to go into the clubhouse and there he is, good and mad. He's throwing chairs and equipment and whatnot. I got over near the door and said, "Hutch, boy you really scared that Williams." I closed that door just as a chair came crashing against it.

So that was Ted Williams. No use throwing at him. First of all, you're not going to hit him. And second of all, you're not going to bother him. Best thing to do with him was to let him do what he was going to do anyway and then concentrate on getting the next man out.

In 1936 I went back to the minors, with Atlanta. I managed at Atlanta for five years, then later on, after the war, managed Buffalo for three years and Seattle for one, before taking over the White Sox in 1951.

I was always willing to try out a new idea. One year, when I was at Buffalo, Sam Jethroe was tearing the league apart with his base running. In 1949 he stole 89 bases. You just couldn't stop him. We were playing Montreal one day and a situation came up that we had talked about. It was the eighth inning, we were leading by a run, there were two out, and the Montreal pitcher was at bat. Jethroe was on deck. If we get the pitcher out, we have Jethroe leading off the ninth. Well, if he leads off in the ninth and gets on base, he's going to steal second and very possibly third.

We had it figured out that anytime he led off an inning and got on first, his chances of scoring were ninety percent. We had statistics on it.

So, if we walk the pitcher intentionally and let Jethroe hit with the pitcher on first base and two out, the only way that Jethroe's going to hurt us in that particular situation is with a triple. If he gets a hit, the chances are the pitcher is only going to second, and even though Jethroe is on base, he can't hurt us with his speed because he's got the pitcher in front of him. So we tried it, and it worked.

Branch Rickey, running the Dodgers at that time, who owned Jethroe, happened to be in the ball park and he carried that story back with him to the All-Star Game, and it upped the price on Jethroe from $25,000 to $75,000. Mr. Rickey actually told me that himself.

That maneuver drew some attention to me, and so did another one. This one involved putting a pitcher at third base, bringing in a relief pitcher to work to one man, and then taking him out and putting the first pitcher back on the mound. That got a lot of publicity because it happened in a big league game. And you'd be surprised at the baseball people who didn't know you could do that.

What happened was, I had Harry Dorish pitching against the Red Sox in the top of the ninth. Ted Williams was leading off, and I wanted a left-hander to pitch to him. So I moved Dorish over to third base and brought Billy Pierce in. Pierce got Williams out and I took him out of the game and put Dorish back in to pitch to the right-handed hitters. Was I worried about Dorish having to handle a difficult play at third? Well, no. I'd never seen Williams hit a ball to the third baseman.

Billy Pierce was quite a pitcher. You know, I first ran into him when I was playing with Detroit in 1945 and he was working out with them. In fact, he got into a few games that year. He was just a kid. His father owned a drugstore about a block from where I was living. I'd go in now and then to buy something, and there was this kid clerking behind the counter. I never paid any attention to him. Then out at the ball park we had this little left-hander who

I'd warm up occasionally. One day he walked up to me on the field and said, "You know, you won't even speak to me when you come into our drugstore."

"What are you talking about?" I asked.

"That's my father's drugstore," he said. "You were in there last night."

I took a good hard look at him and, sure enough, he was the clerk.

You know, the Tigers made a mistake with him. They traded him before anybody knew what a fine pitcher he was going to be. Sent him over to the White Sox, which was fine for me because when I took over that club in 1951, there he was. I worked a little with him on his windup to help his delivery and convinced him that he had to throw a slider and an occasional change of pace, and that was all he needed.

Billy had a nice sense of humor. He's pitching against the Yankees one day and they're hitting him pretty well, but Jim Busby out in center field is catching everything they hit. I went out to ask Billy how he felt and he said, "Don't ask me how I feel, ask Busby how he feels."

I went back out in the eighth inning and asked him again. I know he's got to be tired by this time.

"I'm all right," he said. "I'll stay out here and lose it."

"No you won't either," I said. "We'll let somebody else lose this one." He was a real cute kid. I was fond of him.

Another one of my favorites with the White Sox was Nelson Fox. I think a fellow like Nelson Fox is a tremendous compliment to baseball, as well as a great asset. Here's a fellow who didn't possess overwhelming physical ability but still went out and made himself into a fine ballplayer.

I've never seen anybody who wanted to play more than Fox did. In spring training you had to run him off the field to get him to rest, and I mean just literally run him off. During the season Frank Lane, who was the general manager, would get on me from time to time to give Fox a rest. I didn't want to, but finally I said all right. So I took him out of the lineup one day in Detroit. The game starts, I'm sitting up there at the end of the bench, and here

Nelson Fox
"One of my favorites."

comes Fox. He sits down next to me and starts yelling at the pitcher, yelling and yelling, giving him hell, calling him everything. He goes on for nine innings like that, loud as he could. Doing it on purpose, you see, just to give me a headache.

Finally I turned to him. "Foxie," I said, "let me tell you something right now. This is the last time you're ever going to sit on this bench with me. I don't care if Lane or anybody else says you need a rest, you're not going to get it. Just remember that."

Well, that satisfied him. He didn't want a rest. He never wanted

Minnie Minoso

a rest. And I sure didn't want him sitting next to me for nine innings screaming his head off.

Minnie Minoso was another favorite of mine. To my way of thinking he was undoubtedly the most colorful player of his era. I once heard another ballplayer say that with Minoso on the club, if you don't hustle, you really look bad. He had an effect on the whole team. I asked Billy Pierce one day who he thought would lead the team in stolen bases, Busby or Minoso.

"Busby," he said.

"Why?" I asked.

"Because Minoso doesn't stop at first," he said.

That was the way he played ball, all the time. He was one of the great people in baseball—one of the finest, most lovable men.

In 1955 I was offered the job at Baltimore and I accepted it. What we were faced with there was a complete rebuilding job, practically from scratch. I got myself a lot of scouts, and we signed a lot of ballplayers, a lot of them. What we were doing was using the old Branch Rickey formula, which was "There's got to be some quality in quantity." And that proved to be right. We went out on a limb several times with players. We took a little chance on a guy like Brooks Robinson. Milt Pappas had a bad knee, but we took him. We had a scout out in California who picked up Chuck Estrada and Jerry Walker and Wes Stock. Then we added Steve Barber and Jack Fisher. All good young pitchers. They called it the Kiddie Korps. In addition we had Jim Gentile, Ronnie Hansen, Marv Breeding, and Brooks.

It was a fine young team, and it came right along. In 1960 we made a run at the Yankees. We played them a four-game series in New York in September, when it was all up for grabs, and they wiped us out. That was always the problem, during all my years of managing—the Yankees. They always seemed to have a little more—more power, more pitching. They outmanned you; they outgunned you. Well, I guess I'm not the first manager who's sung that song.

Handling pitchers? Well, I guess I had my own approach, my own system. You know that a certain pitcher must have four days' rest or five days' rest. Once in a while you run into a guy that can pitch with three days' rest, but with night baseball that runs into problems. You don't recover from night pitching as you do from day pitching. Night pitching stiffens you up more. You have to know how to use your staff to maximum efficiency. So many times you have a star pitcher who wants to pitch with three days' rest regardless of anything. Well, that upsets your whole pitching staff. It means one guy might have to take six days' rest, another five, and so on. If somebody needs the extra throwing, let him get it on the sidelines. I don't care what pitcher it is, he's got to have more stuff with four days' rest than he has with three. I'm a firm believer in that. He'll have more stuff, harder stuff. He may not have as sharp control, but let me tell you—hitters worry about stuff more than they do about control.

Some managers will work their top pitchers with three days' rest. All right. They'll win 20 games for you, but they'll also lose

14 or 15. You're not getting maximum efficiency from them. Also, you're wearing them out and at the same time not developing a pitching staff.

You've got to come back to the fundamentals. I can't say that often enough. My drilling of my players did not stop when spring training ended. It continued on throughout the season. You cannot assume a player has been taught a particular fundamental and then when he messes up in a ball game, blame him for it. You have to *know* that he's been instructed along those particular lines. Game conditions, the score, the inning, everything is a factor. John McGraw used to have an automatic fine, and I had one also, if his coaches didn't know how the wind was blowing. If my coaches couldn't tell me when I walked into the clubhouse if the wind was blowing to right field or left field, they were fined. The coaches have to know so they can tell the players.

I don't care how experienced a player is, you've got to keep after him. There are an awful lot of small details that add up to the winning of a ball game, and it's up to the man in charge to see that his players are always drilled in and constantly alert to those things. So if anybody tells you a manager has no effect on a ball club, he's telling you that he doesn't know baseball.

Paul Richards in 1960

7

OSSIE BLUEGE

OSWALD LOUIS BLUEGE
Born: October 24, 1900, Chicago, Illinois
Managerial career: Washington Senators, 1943–47

Ossie Bluege spent his entire big league career with the
Washington Senators as player, coach, and, in 1943 through
1947, as manager. In 1945 Bluege took a team that had
finished last the year before and brought it to near victory,
missing the pennant by a narrow margin.

I used to watch McGraw when I was a kid. He'd bring his Giants
to Chicago to play the Cubs—that was a great rivalry in those
days. I was lucky growing up in a town that had two big league
clubs. I saw my first big league game when I was ten years old.
That would be 1910. So I saw all those fellows—Tinker, Evers,
Chance, Three-Finger Brown, Honus Wagner, Ed Walsh, Smoky
Joe Wood, Nap Lajoie, Shoeless Joe Jackson. Then there were
some that I saw that I had the opportunity to play on the same
field with later on, like Ty Cobb, Tris Speaker, Babe Ruth, Eddie
Collins, and Walter Johnson.

I loved to play baseball, always enjoyed it, but who the devil
ever thought about becoming a big leaguer? I was never very big,
but I had a lot of nervous energy and was always keyed up out
there.

I was going to school at night, taking accounting courses, and
holding down a job during the day with International Harvester.
Through a fellow named Jack Doyle, an ex-major-leaguer, I
started playing some pretty fast semipro ball around Chicago. I
was getting fifteen dollars a game—not bad money in those days.

As I was leaving the ball park one day, I was stopped by a fellow named Bill Jackson.

"Listen," he said, "I'm the manager of the Peoria Tractors in the Three-I League. I watched you play today, and I've got a contract for two hundred a month for you."

This was in 1920. I was still a minor, so he told me to take the contract home, have my father sign it, and then join the Peoria ball club in Rock Island. I was flattered—I didn't know I was that good. So I took the contract home and showed it to my father. He didn't know too much about baseball. He was a strict old German gentleman who believed in hard work and in going to church on Sundays and holding the Bible up in your hands where everybody could see it. He wasn't too impressed with that contract.

"You want to give up all your accounting training, all your schooling?" he asked.

"Dad," I said, "they make five and six thousand dollars a year playing major league ball."

He couldn't believe that. "They pay men that much money to chase that ball around?"

"That's right," I said. I told him I didn't have to give up my accounting, that I could always go back to it.

So we talked and talked, and finally I told him that if I didn't make the big leagues in three years' time, I'd come back and push the pencil. That satisfied him, and he signed the contract.

The next day I caught the night train to Rock Island and got there at four in the morning. I checked into the hotel, slept a few hours, and at 7:30 was up and ready to go. That was my normal routine—get up early and go to work. I hung around the lobby until nine o'clock, and nobody had showed up. What is this? I asked myself. So I rang Jackson's room and told him I was there.

"What the hell are you calling me up at this hour of the morning for?" he asked.

"It's time to go to work, isn't it?" I asked.

"For who?" he asked.

That's when I began to get the idea that this was going to be a different life.

I was there for just a little while when Bill Jackson said to me,

Three-Finger Brown in 1910

"Kid, next year you're going to be sold to a major league ball club." Boy, when he told me that, the wheels started turning in my head. You know how it is when you're a kid. You've got all that ambition, and it doesn't take too much to get your imagination warmed up. But he knew what he was talking about because next year, sure enough, Joe Engel of the Washington club came by and bought my contract for $3,500.

I split the '22 season between Washington and Minneapolis and in '23 became the Senators' regular third baseman. Donie Bush was the manager in '23. Then Bucky Harris took over in 1924 as playing manager. He was the one who put me in the line-up to stay. You see, I'd hit only .245 my first year, and they felt the team needed some more punch in the lineup. So they brought a few guys in and tried them out at third while I sat on the bench. I didn't say anything—didn't make any fuss. But I could see that things were happening around third base that shouldn't be happening, and we were losing ball games. Then early in May we lost a couple of games because of some shenanigans around third base. I'll never forget this. I was in the shower after the second game, cleaning up. Bucky walked by, and I could tell by his face he was annoyed. Suddenly he looked at me and said, "You're playing third base tomorrow and from here on in, come hell or high water."

From that day on we went. We started clicking. We won the pennant and the World Series.

I can remember John McGraw and Bucky Harris having a managerial battle of wits before the seventh game of the 1924 World Series. Looking back on it now, it was really something. Here is the young Harris, in his first year as a manager, trying to outsmart the Giants' great John McGraw.

You see, McGraw was platooning at first base. He was starting George Kelly against the left-handers and Bill Terry against the righties. Terry was murdering us, and we wanted him out of there. So Griffith and Bucky did a little scheming. There was a lot of rivalry there, between Griffith and McGraw. You have to go way back on this. Griff was the first manager to represent the American League in New York. He managed the Yankees in 1903, when they were known as the Highlanders. McGraw didn't like that; old John J. thought New York was his private kingdom. There was an enmity there for years and years.

So Bucky started Curly Ogden, a right-hander, and McGraw put Terry in the lineup. Ogden pitched to two batters and then we

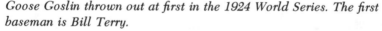

Goose Goslin thrown out at first in the 1924 World Series. The first baseman is Bill Terry.

brought in George Mogridge, a lefty and a good one. We were leading them 1–0 in the sixth inning and, sure enough, McGraw hit for Terry. Then Bucky turned around and brought in Fred Marberry, a right-hander. Bill Terry told me later that they were telling McGraw right from the start not to pay attention to what we were doing, not to platoon, otherwise they'd get caught short. But McGraw didn't listen.

We were tied at the end of nine innings, 3–3, and we brought Walter Johnson in at that point. The shades of night were falling now, and Walter was throwing bullets. The Giants had roughed Walter up twice in the Series, but they weren't hitting him now.

Then we got lucky in the bottom of the twelfth. Muddy Ruel hit a double and then Earl McNeely hit one down to Freddie Lindstrom at third that hit a pebble and bounced over Freddie's head just as he was getting set to make the play. That was it, brother. Muddy came in with the winning run, Walter was a winner, and we all were winners. That was the greatest thrill of my life, winning that Series—the only one the Washington Senators ever won.

It was a good ball club. Do you remember Joe Judge? He was our first baseman, and I'll tell you, he was a better first baseman than Sisler ever was. This is not to take anything away from Sisler, but Joe was a genius around that bag. And we had Roger Peckinpaugh, Muddy Ruel, and Sam Rice. Sam was a heck of a ballplayer. He's in the Hall of Fame today. You want to hear something? Sam ended up with 2,987 hits. That's right, just 13 short of 3,000. Why didn't he go on and get those last 13? I don't know; I guess he wasn't interested. Ballplayers didn't pay as much attention to their records in those days as they do today. Today they wouldn't let a man retire under those circumstances. They'd make a big promotion out of his getting those last few hits.

We weren't a power team. We hit only 22 home runs that year. That's right—22 home runs for the entire season. And Goose Goslin got 12 of them by himself. Goose was a great hitter. You couldn't throw the fastball by him. They would try. They would set him up for it with other stuff and then try to slip it by, and he would always zing it. He was a character, too. I remember one time he was going stinko. There was a guy up in the grandstands, one of those louts with the foghorn voices, and he was on Goose something terrible. "Goose," he's yelling, "where were *you* last night?" Things like that. Boy, that Goslin, he was coming in every inning getting redder and redder in the face.

Finally the old man, Griffith, who was sitting right behind our dugout, sent a note down to Bucky. The note said, "Take Goslin out of there. Let him take care of that guy." So Bucky took him out, and Goose went back to the clubhouse, changed into his street clothes, and went up into the stands and took that guy by the collar and gave him a good shaking.

To me the two greatest thrills in joining the Washington ball club were playing in the nation's capital and playing on the same team with Walter Johnson. Walter was like a little god as far as I was concerned. Playing behind him was a pleasure. If you booted a ball, he'd come over and say, "That's all right. You'll get the next one."

When I saw him, he'd already been pitching for about fifteen years, and he was still as fast as anyone in the league. He used to like to pitch batting practice, so I had the chance to bat against him quite a bit. He used to sort of flip that thing up there sidearm, almost underhand, and you'd think that ball was going to come right at you, and you'd back off and swipe at it, but it was right over the plate. That ball would rise; it would swoosh and rise. Try and hit it. And when Walter got in a tough spot in a game, he could reach back for that little extra. Very few pitchers can do that. Walter always seemed to have a little in reserve. But he was something to watch when he was in trouble out there. First he would put his glove down on the mound. Then he would open his belt and pull it in a notch. Then he would pick up a little dirt and let it ooze through his fingers. When he did that, brother, look out—the current was on. He had turned the switch.

After Bucky left as manager for the first time, in 1928, Griff hired Walter. Walter was not a good manager. You know what his chief weakness was? He didn't know how to handle his pitchers. That may sound strange, but the truth was, Walter didn't know

*Frankie Frisch and
Bucky Harris during
the 1924 World Series*

very much about pitching. All he knew was that you reached back and fired—that was the way he had done it for twenty years, and nobody ever did it better. And that's what he expected his pitchers to do. Bucky, who was a second baseman, knew more about pitching than Walter did.

I think Griff knew about Walter's weaknesses, but he hired him anyway. The old man was something of a sentimentalist. He liked to hire his own boys to manage. He put Clyde Milan in there, then Bucky, then Walter, then Joe Cronin, then Bucky again, then me, then Joe Kuhel.

Ty Cobb? Sure, I saw plenty of him. Old Tyrus Raymond. I don't think the fires ever went out in him, not till the day he died. I remember one game late in the season in 1928. We were playing the Athletics in Philadelphia. They were fighting the Yankees for

the pennant that year. As a matter of fact, they lost out by only a
game or two. That was the year Connie Mack had Cobb, Speaker,
and Eddie Collins on the team, all of them right at the end of the
line. Collins was a player-coach, but Cobb and Speaker got into
quite a few games. In this one game it was the bottom of the
ninth, one out, Collins is on third, we're leading them by a run,
and Mack sends Cobb up to pinch-hit. Tyrus Raymond himself.

Naturally the infield was pulled in, especially with that Cobb
up there. Well, he hit one down to Harris at second on two big
bounces. Collins breaks for the plate and Harris throws the ball
home, to Muddy Ruel. I come in from third, and we've got
Collins in a rundown. Now, here was a play we'd worked on in
spring training. Instead of throwing that ball back and forth,
which gives the batter time to get to second, Harris wanted us to
run the base runner back and then at the last split second throw
the ball. That way, there's a minimum amount of ball handling,
and you can keep the batter from taking that extra base. Well, we
worked it to perfection. Muddy got the ball, Collins put on the
brakes, Muddy ran him back, I came in, Muddy gave me the ball,
and I put it on Collins. Then I turned around and there's Cobb
racing to second. I fired the ball to Harris, and he put the tag on
Cobb. Boom—double play and the game is over. Tyrus Raymond
couldn't believe it. He figured Collins would have jockeyed
around long enough for him to get to second. He just stood there
with his hands on his hips and yelled, "*How* long has that guy
been playing ball?"

Cobb was a smart ballplayer. Shrewd. Don't you think he
wasn't. But so was Griffith. Do you know what the old man used
to do when he was managing and they were playing the Tigers?
He would have one of his ballplayers get on Cobb. Ty had a low
boiling point, you know. Finally it would get to the point where
Cobb couldn't take it any longer, and he would go after the guy.
There would be a fight, and they'd both be thrown out of the
game. That's how Griff dealt with Tyrus Raymond.

Cobb was always thinking out there, always doing something
to irritate you. If he stepped out of the batter's box to get some dirt
on his hands, he always bent over with his backside to the

pitcher. He always had contempt for the opposition, nothing but contempt, and he wanted you to know it.

I can give you another illustration of the way Cobb played ball. I was just a rookie. Ty's on first base and Harry Heilmann hits a line drive single to right field. Well, Cobb seldom stopped at second. He just kept on going and you had to throw him out, that's all there was to it. On this particular play Sam Rice picked up the ball in right field and fired it in to me, and now I've got the ball at third base just as Cobb is rounding second. And he doesn't care; he's coming. I'm thinking to myself, this is going to be interesting! Instead of waiting at the base, I took a few steps out to meet him, in a little bit of a crouch, waiting to tag him. Well, this is no exaggeration now. He didn't slide. He just took off and came at me in midair, spikes first, about four or five feet off the ground, so help me just like a rocket. He hit me in the upper part of my arm, just grazing the flesh but tearing open the sleeve. I made the play. I tagged him out, but I was so mad I was going to konk him with the ball while he was lying on the ground. But Billy Evans, the umpire, pulled me away. Then he threw Cobb out of the game for making such a vicious slide.

The next day I was standing around the batting cage waiting my turn to hit when up walks Mr. Tyrus Raymond. Just as sweet as apple pie. He's apologizing.

"Son," he said, "I hope I didn't hurt you."

"I'm all right," I said.

"Good," he said. Then the look in his eyes changed just a little, his face got mean, and he said, "But remember—never come up the line for me."

But that wasn't what had got him mad. I'll tell you what got him mad—he knew he was going to be out. That was like waving a red flag in a bull's face. When he knew you had him, it seemed to make him a little crazy, like a cornered animal. That's when he was most dangerous.

As an infielder, I always tried to take everything into consideration, anticipating every possibility—if the ball was hit to me and at what speed; who is the runner on first and if he runs like a deer or a donkey; who was covering the bag in case I had to throw there, the second baseman or the shortstop? And it's all got to be automatic because you don't have time to think out there. If you've got to stop and think out there, you'd better quit.

I used to try and drill these lessons into my players when I was managing. You see, I was known as a pretty good fielder in my day and I prided myself in that. To my mind, fielding is the artistry of the game. You watch a third baseman coming in to scoop up a ball bare-handed and throw a man out on a bunt, or you watch the double play being made or the outfielder making the fine running catch. This is all very beautiful when it's being executed well. And the fans appreciate it too; don't think they don't. A great play in the field always gets a standing ovation, whether it's for the home team or against.

I couldn't emphasize some of these things enough to my players. I used to tell them that we were not all gifted alike, that some of us had quicker reflexes and better hands than others, but at the same time I would let them know how they could become better ballplayers simply through observation and anticipation. Sit on the bench when the other team is taking batting practice, study those hitters, and never mind going into the clubhouse and sitting around because in batting practice the opposing hitter will show you where his strength is. And watch him when he bunts one because he's going to tell you something then too—whether he squares off to bunt or just drops the bat on the ball. If you can pick up those little tip-offs, then you're going to be able to get a split-second jump on him, and that often can make all the difference.

Another thing I would tell my infielders was not to watch the pitcher during the game. Too many of them used to watch the pitcher wind up and throw. Forget that, I'd tell them. You study that hitter, you keep your eye on *him* because if you're keen enough, you can almost instinctively know what he's going to do. When I was playing third base, I never took my eyes off the hitter, and in time I got to where I could almost sense when he was going to knock one down my way. You don't believe that, do you? Well, it's true. And that's why I was able to go to my right as well

Ossie Bluege

as my left. I know this sounds egotistical, but anybody who saw me play ball will tell you I could do those things. And it was the product of hard work and observation, that's all. You can get a lot more out of your God-given abilities if you keep your eyes open.

I mentioned that seventh game of the 1924 World Series against the Giants. Okay, we're in extra innings now. Here again I'm talking about observation. The Giants came in from the field, and I was looking over at their dugout. There's McGraw talking to Freddie Lindstrom, who was going to lead off. Lindstrom had pretty good foot, he could run. I said to myself, Oh-oh, something's up. Extra inning ball game, the man is leading off, you know they want to try something. So I got even with the bag and watched his bat. I was *anticipating,* you see. Sure enough, he dropped it down. And it was a perfect bunt, rolling up the third-base line. But I was moving in the moment he moved that bat. I got that ball and fired it to Joe Judge at first base, never straightening up, and nailed Lindstrom.

After we'd won that game, and the Series with it, McGraw came into our clubhouse to congratulate Harris. And before he left, he came over to me and shook my hand and said, "Son, you're the best ever." Well, coming from John McGraw, who was an old third baseman himself and sparing with his praise, it just made my chest swell out and I never forgot it. I don't want to sound like I'm popping off; I made plenty of errors too. But when John McGraw makes a statement like that to you, you can't help but be proud of it.

Right after the season closed in 1942, I went to Chicago to visit my family. One day I got a phone call from Griff.

"When are you coming home?" he asked. Home was Washington.

"I'm not sure," I said.

"Well, why don't you get in your wagon now and get back here?" he said. "I want to talk to you."

I knew right then and there what it was all about. Bucky had been released as manager shortly before, you see. It was the second time for Bucky. So I drove back and when I got to Washington, I went out to Griff's house. He took me into his study, and we sat down.

"Well," he said, "I had to release Bucky." And when he said it, tears came into his eyes. That's how he felt about Harris. You don't always want to let a manager go; sometimes you just have to. Then he said, "Do you want the job?"

To tell the truth, I never had any ambitions to be a manager. I never thought I was cut out for it. I had been working as a coach under Bucky, and after having been in the big leagues for more than twenty years as a player and a coach, I knew all the problems one had to deal with. You had to be a teacher and an instructor and a psychologist, and some players take it kindly and some don't. I always felt, Why go through it? But of course it's easy to settle all that in your mind when nobody has made you an offer. I guess that's human nature—you say you're not interested in something, until somebody offers it to you.

I knew it would be a real challenge. I felt confident that I knew the game well enough. Of course, I knew I'd be managing players who had been my teammates, which is sometimes rough. But you don't like to say no, do you? Not many men are asked to manage a big league club, and when you're asked, it's very hard to refuse.

So I said yes, and we shook hands on it. He said he couldn't pay me a lot of money, but that was of no concern to me. I was never a materialistic man. I knew he would be as fair as he could be, and that was good enough.

Then we assessed the ball club, the strengths and weaknesses. We had some good ballplayers, like Mickey Vernon, Jerry Priddy, George Case, Stan Spence, and Jake Early, and a few good pitchers like Early Wynn, Dutch Leonard, and Mickey Haefner. We went over the rosters of the other ball clubs to see who might be available. The war years were upon us then. A lot of fellows had been drafted or were about to be, and good ballplayers were hard to come by. Bob Johnson of the Athletics had retired, but we induced him to come back and play for us. He gave us some power and was a pretty good outfielder. We needed a third baseman, and we got Harlond Clift from the Browns, still a solid ballplayer even though he'd seen his best days. In those war years you had to do a lot of cutting and pasting to make a ball club.

We finished second in 1943, which was the highest a Washington club had been since 1933. In 1944 it turned completely around and we finished last. You see, in those years, with ballplayers going into service, your whole team could change overnight. But then the next year, in 1945, we turned it right around again and almost won the pennant. We finished second to the Tigers by a game and a half. I think that was the most peculiar end of a pennant race there ever was. We finished the schedule a week ahead of everybody else because Griff had agreed to give the Washington Redskins the use of the field. At the time the agreement was made, nobody expected us to be in the race. What the heck, we'd been dead last the year before. So it was very peculiar that last week. We were fighting for the pennant, only we weren't fighting—we were sitting around to see what the Tigers were going to do.

We wound up our season with a doubleheader against the Philadelphia Athletics, and I'll never forget that. Of course we knew that every game was going to be precious to us. I had Dutch Leonard going for me in that first game, and we were ahead by a run or two in the late innings. Buddy Lewis had come back from military service in the middle of the year and was in right field. Late in the game somebody hit a ball into short right field. Buddy came in for it and caught the ball and in almost the same motion started to flip it to George Myatt, the second baseman, who had come running out. Well, when he started to flip the ball, Buddy dropped it. Eddie Rommel was the umpire, and he ruled that Buddy hadn't had possession of the ball long enough for the batter to be out, which was plain nonsense.

Now, I had seen that Rommel hadn't been watching it all that closely. So I went charging out there.

"Eddie," I said, "I was watching you, and you weren't anywhere near the play."

He knew he was wrong. I could tell by his reactions. I kept chewing him up until finally he said, "That's enough out of you. You want to stay in this game, you'd better clear out of here."

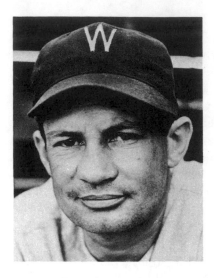

Buddy Myer

That made me even madder.

"You want to throw me out for arguing something that you know you're dead wrong about?" I said. Oh, I really started to give it to him then. "You want to throw me out?" I said. "Then go ahead." I don't think I was ever hotter on a ball field.

Well, he did throw me out. His bum call cost us the ball game. Anyway, I went back to the clubhouse and the clubhouse man said to me, "Os, Tommy Connolly is in the ball park. He's sitting right behind the dugout." Tommy Connolly was the American League's chief of umpires. When I heard he was there, I got dressed and went out to look for him. I was still burning. When I got upstairs to the box seats, he wasn't there. He had scooted.

I sat there and watched us lose that game, and after it was over, I headed for the umpire's room. That's sanctum sanctorum you know; nobody's allowed in there. I knocked on the door and Tommy Connolly opened it.

"May I come in, Tommy?" I asked. "I'd like to talk to you."

"Come on in," he said.

Rommel and the other umpires were there, and Rommel's face was flushed. Tommy must have just got finished eating him out.

"Tommy," I said, "I'm not going to discuss that play. You know how I feel about that. All I'm asking is that you grant me permission to sit on the bench and direct the ball club in the second game."

You see, in those days the rule was if you're thrown out of the first game of a doubleheader, you're out for the whole day. Well, we were fighting for a pennant, and I wanted to be in there, especially after having been thrown out for disputing a call like that.

He looked at me and grunted and in his Irish brogue said, "No, I can't do that. Those are the rules."

"Tommy," I said, "this is something special. You can waive that rule at this stage of the game. This is the last day we've got to play. I'm sure the league would back you up on it."

"Can't do it," he said. He was an old-timer from the old school. Strict.

That was it. I went back and sat behind our dugout for the second game. And I had to be careful. I was dying to give some signs and instructions during the game, but if my coaches had been caught looking at me or if I had started doing some wigwagging, it would have been a violation. So I had to sit there like a wooden Indian the whole game, which we won anyway. But if we had won that first game, it might have been a different story at the end because we lost by just a game and a half. The Tigers won on the last day of the season when Hank Greenberg hit a grand-slam home run in the ninth inning against the Browns.

And that was the only game I was ever thrown out of as a manager.

I never argued with the umpires very much. They seldom change their decisions, as you know. But you do have to go out there from time to time to put in your two cents worth. There are reasons for it. Sometimes you try to lay the groundwork for the next close call that comes up. If you handle it nicely, you might get that call. If you run out there like you're going to fight a pack of wolves, you're only going to get them mad at you, and that's not going to help your cause any. What you try to do is convey to them that they *may* have missed it. After all, they're not infallible, and they know that. If he was out of position to call that particular play, you go out there and let him know that you know it.

Another thing is, if one of your players is arguing, you've got to go out there and back him up, even if you think he's wrong. In those cases you might run out there and get in a little wink at the umpire while you're hollering at him, just to let him know that you know what the story is. He knows you've got to come out there and wave your arms. The fans enjoy it, your ballplayer is satisfied, and there's no harm done. Another reason you're out there is to prevent your player from getting thrown out of the game. You'll see the first thing a manager does when he goes out is to get between his ballplayer and the umpire.

I can tell about one experience I had with Bobo Newsom. I don't have to tell you what a character he was. He was like a big kid, playful and easy going. But at the same time he could drive you nuts out there. I knew him well enough after so many years. I could tell when he was getting tired on the mound—he'd start yapping at the umpires. In fact, that's a good rule of thumb to use with certain pitchers. Different pitchers show it differently when they're getting tired, and with a lot of them it's barking at the umpire. Particularly if it's a close ball game. That's when you know they're losing it, because every pitch is becoming labor to them and they want every close call. This was Bobo.

One day we're in a one-run ball game, and everything is going along fine. All of a sudden around the seventh inning Bobo starts giving the plate umpire a going-over on every other pitch. It was big Cal Hubbard, one of the best. Bobo is walking down off the mound, yelling, and walking back. He got out of the inning all right, and between innings Hubbard called me out.

"Os," he says, "you'd better get somebody ready because that guy isn't going to be around much longer. The next time he comes walking down to give me his opinions, I'm going to run him out. I'm telling you as a friend."

Sure enough, the next inning Bobo starts up with him again. Now, I knew he was getting tired, but he was still getting them out, and I wanted to keep him in there as long as I could because a tired Bobo was still better than what I had fresh in the bull pen at the moment. So I went charging out there. He's storming around on the mound.

"For Pete's sake," I said, "calm down and pitch." He gave me some lip and I lost my patience and said, "Listen, you big fathead, do you know where that last pitch was? It was high. So what are you yelling about?"

"You think that pitch was high?" he said. Now he's mad at me.

"That's right," I said.

"Nuts," he said.

"Nuts to you," I said.

So there's the manager standing out on the mound in a close ball game arguing with his pitcher. All I was trying to do was keep the big lout in there. I managed to do that, and he struggled through to win it. But that's the kind of guy he was. He could

GEORGE BRACE PHOTO

Bobo Newsom
"I don't have to tell
you what a charac-
ter he was."

drive you crazy. But he was harmless and lovable and a good pitcher. He was always being traded back and forth. I think he was with the Washington ball club four or five different times. Griff kept getting rid of him and kept bringing him back.

But when he was out there, he had the heart of a lion. I can tell you that right out of experience. This happened on opening day in 1936. We were playing the Yankees. Ben Chapman laid down a bunt, and I came in for it. I had to hurry because Ben could run. It was one of those do-or-die plays, when you line first base up in your mind and come up throwing, which I did—and there's that big hulk of a Bobo standing there. The ball hit him right in the jaw. He came staggering over to me and said, "What'd you do that for?"

"Why didn't you duck?" I said.

"I don't know," he said.

You know something, he had a broken jaw—they wired it up later—but that son of a gun wouldn't come out of there. He stayed in and finished the game and won it. That was Bobo.

You know, I went out and pitched batting practice practically every day of my managerial life. That's right. And I would hit fungoes too. Joe McCarthy used to say to me, "Ossie, that's against all rules of the union." I pitched batting practice because I loved it, but the reason I had to hit the fungoes was because I didn't have anybody else to pick up the bat. I wanted Clyde Milan, my coach, to keep his eye on things during the workout. We didn't have all the specialists around that you have today. The manager had to get out there and work.

One of the great things about baseball is it's an unpredictable business. You never know when something interesting or exciting is going to happen, and that's why you can't wait to get out to the ball park every day, no matter how many years you've been at it. I can give you an example. We had a tryout camp at Sanford, Florida, one spring. I think it was '37. Joe Engel was running it. Naturally a lot of kids showed up for it. One day in walks this big, robust kid wearing dungarees and a work shirt. He was only

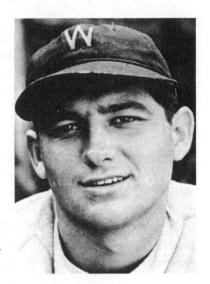

Early Wynn
"He was only seventeen, but he
looked like he could take care of
himself."

seventeen, but he looked like he could take care of himself. He walked up to Joe Engel and said, "I want to play ball."

Joe looked him over and said, "What are you?"

"I'm a pitcher," the kid said. "And I can hit, too."

"You can, eh?" Joe said.

"That's right," the kid said. He didn't lack for confidence.

So they gave him a uniform and let him work out, and on the strength of what they saw, they signed him to a contract. That's how the Washington ball club got Early Wynn. Just walked in and announced himself. A few years later he was in the big leagues, on his way to the Hall of Fame. But I'll tell you something, he didn't become a real good pitcher until we traded him to Cleveland. When he pitched for me in the early forties, he had a good fastball, but that was it. When he went to Cleveland, Mel Harder got hold of him and taught him how to throw the good curveball and change-up, and that's when Early became a great pitcher.

Signs can be a troublesome thing, although they shouldn't be, particularly with big leaguers. But you know, on opening day, after spring training, you call a meeting and go over the signs with your ball club. This is the bunt. This is the take, the steal, the hit-and-run, and so on. Everybody got them? They nod their heads. Okay. But the minute you turn around, they start putting their heads together and whispering to each other, "What's the bunt sign? What's the take?" I saw it as a player and I saw it later on as a manager.

Of course, you're going to have problems with individual players. Sometimes the fans see a man thrown out stealing second and they want to know why a guy was stealing in that particular situation. Well, the truth is he wasn't stealing—the batter missed a hit-and-run sign and the runner was shot down. That's when a manager gets gray. No, I never fined a player, for that or anything else. I never believed in taking a man's money. I always tried to reason with them. Sit down and have a talk. And sometimes that can make you even grayer. I'll tell you what I mean.

I had a fellow named George Binks playing for me during the war. Bingo Binks. He was a good ballplayer. One day he's on first base and Rick Ferrell is up. Rick was slow afoot and was an easy double-play man, so very often he would hit-and-run. I let him call it anytime he wanted to because I trusted his judgment. Well, he put it on, but Binks didn't go. Now, this wasn't the first time that had happened. Rick was pretty frustrated. He pulled me aside after the game and said, "Os, that Binks just can't get a sign."

"Okay," I said. "I'll talk to him."

The next day I called Binks into my office.

"George," I said, "do you know all the signs?"

"Sure," he said.

"What are they?"

He went through them and he had them right.

"Good," I said. "Now, do you know the hit-and-run signs of the players that are hitting in back of you?"

"Sure," he said.

"What's Rick Ferrell's sign?"

He told me.

"Okay," I said. "Now we're getting to the question. You were on first base yesterday and Rick gave you the hit-and-run sign."

"That's right," he said.

"Well, you didn't go. Why didn't you run when the ball was pitched?"

He looked at me very seriously and said, "I was afraid he was going to miss it."

That was the answer. And so the manager gets gray. And grayer.

8

BOB SHAWKEY

JAMES ROBERT SHAWKEY
Born: December 4, 1890, Brookville, Pennsylvania
Managerial career: New York Yankees, 1930

For years one of the American League's finest pitchers, Bob Shawkey was the Yankee manager between the Miller Huggins and Joe McCarthy reigns. He later served as baseball coach at Dartmouth.

Miller Huggins had died suddenly, you see. It happened late in September, just before the season ended, in 1929. There were just a few games left, and Art Fletcher and I were running the club. We'd been coaching under Hug.

One day during a game Colonel Ruppert, who owned the Yankees, and Ed Barrow, who was the general manager, sent somebody into the dugout to tell me to come meet them under the stands. When I walked up to them, Barrow said, "Bob, how would you like to have the job?"

I wasn't particularly surprised to be asked. I'd been with the Yankees a long time and had always got along well with everybody.

"I think I'd like to give it a try," I said.

So that's the way it came about. That's the way I was hired to manage the Yankees in 1930.

An awful lot of prestige came along with that job. Seemed like everybody in New York knew you. Wherever you went, you got the royal treatment—in restaurants, stores, all over. It sure was a long way from the farm where I'd grown up. That was in Sigel, Pennsylvania.

I played ball as a kid—sandlot ball. But we didn't know anything about the big leagues. We were just a little country town and didn't hear too much about what was going on outside.

I made up my mind pretty early that I wasn't going to stay there. As soon as I was old enough, I went up to the lumber woods and got a job cutting and hauling logs. Then when I was eighteen, I went down to Oil City and took a job with the Pennsylvania Railroad. I'd been playing ball here and there whenever I could and in 1911 signed up with Harrisburg in the Tri-State League. Two years later Connie Mack bought me for the Athletics.

The 1913 Philadelphia Athletics. I'll say that was a good ball club. That was when they had the $100,000 infield—Stuffy McInnis, Eddie Collins, Jack Barry, and Home Run Baker. Connie had quite a good pitching staff, too. He had Chief Bender, Bullet Joe Bush, Eddie Plank, and Jack Coombs. Coombs had a bad arm then, but he'd been a 30-game winner a few years before.

You don't hear too much about Eddie Plank today, but take my word, he was one of the greatest left-handers that ever pitched. He had a good curveball and fastball, and he knew where he was throwing that ball. And I can't praise Chief Bender enough. He was a veteran and a great star, and I was just a kid, but he took time to work with me on improving my delivery. I was throwing too much with my arm, and he showed me how to get my body into it more and how to be better balanced on my follow-through so I could field a bunt. The Chief had a great curveball, but I'd say his greatest success came on the change-up he threw off his fastball. They'd swing at his motion, and that ball would come floating up there. It was beautiful to watch.

I'd say that those A's were one of the two greatest ball clubs I ever saw. The 1927 Yankees was the other, of course, and I was privileged to play with both of them.

Connie broke up the team in 1915, and I was one of the players to go. I went over to the Yankees in the middle of the season. The Yankees had a terrible team then. Wild Bill Donovan was the manager. He was a nice fellow, a regular guy. If a bunch of us were standing around the lobby and decided to go to a picture

Three of Connie Mack's stalwarts
First baseman Harry Davis and pitchers Jack Coombs and Eddie
Plank, circa 1911

show, he'd get up and go along. Now Connie would never do that. Connie was altogether different. You never saw him after the game. The only time you ever saw him outside of the ball park was on the train or in the dining room. He never mixed with the players, but at the same time he always had tremendous morale on his clubs. He knew how to handle men. He was very shrewd, and gentle, and always talked to you like a father. The boys worshipped him.

The Yankees didn't begin to shape up until a few years later when they got Ruth and some of those other fellows. You see, the man who owned the Red Sox, Harry Frazee, was a theatrical producer, and he was losing a lot of money in his ventures. So in order to raise some cash to pay his debts, he had to sell off his good ballplayers. He and Ruppert were close friends, and over the next few years the Red Sox sold the Yankees Ruth, Herb Pennock, Joe Bush, Sad Sam Jones, Waite Hoyt, and Carl Mays.

You know, I was there when Carl Mays hit the Cleveland

shortstop, Ray Chapman, in the head with a pitched ball. Chapman died soon after—only big leaguer ever to die after being hit. He had changed his batting style that year; he was leaning over the plate more. That didn't make any difference to Mays, of course—he'd knock a man down anytime if he thought it would do some good. Was he throwing at Chapman that day? I wouldn't like to say. I don't know. It never seemed to bother him afterward though. Nothing bothered him. He wasn't too popular with the boys. Down south in the spring the next year none of the regular players would mix with him. He corralled some of the younger players and told them "If you got to knock somebody down to win a ball game, do it. It's your bread and butter." He says this after killing a man! That's the type he was.

He was a stinker. One winter I worked for an insurance company in Philadelphia, and I insured his automobile. He went out and hired a guy to steal it in order to collect on the insurance. He promised the guy a certain amount of money to do it and then never paid him. That's how I happened to find out about it—the fellow called me up and told me what Mays had done. Of course, we didn't pay Mays anything. Then he went to Cincinnati and did the same thing with somebody else. That's the way he was. A stinker.

The league was full of great ballplayers in those years. You can name them: Cobb, Speaker, Joe Jackson, Nap Lajoie, Eddie Collins, Sam Crawford.

Lajoie was something to watch out there. He was a big man, and for his size the most graceful man I ever saw. Up at the plate he was murder. He wouldn't swing at the ball unless it was a strike, wouldn't budge that bat.

How did you pitch to fellows like that? Well, you had to figure out which was the best way they hit you, and then go accordingly. There was no one set way to pitch to them. Connie had that all down in black and white. He knew how every hitter did against his pitcher. He had it written down on a scorecard which he kept on the bench with him. Cobb, for instance, might hit me in one direction and Bender in another. Connie knew all that. He'd have a meeting before each ball game to tell his pitchers

Carl Mays

where to put the ball and his fielders where to play each hitter. He was very scientific and in a lot of ways ahead of his time, with all his charts and records.

The only hitter I could compare with Ted Williams is Joe Jackson. They were built the same way, tall and rangy. I don't think Joe had a weakness up at the plate; you just had to pitch to him and hope for luck. He was very hard to fool because he could watch that ball until it was right on top of him. He must have had exceptional eyesight, same as Williams.

There are three of them it's awfully hard to judge between: Williams, Jackson, and Cobb. I'd say that Cobb was the greatest all-around player I ever saw, and the smartest. He studied everything. He'd get to know how you were trying to pitch him, and he'd shift his feet accordingly. If he knew you were watching his feet, he'd wait until the very last second before he did it. And

if you did manage to fool him with a pitch, then he was quick
enough up there to bunt at you and beat it out.

You've got to include George Sisler when you're talking about
the cream of the crop. There's a fellow who hit .400 a few times,
but then he ran into a bad situation. George developed sinus
trouble, and it bothered his eyes a great deal. He had to lay off for
a year. When he came back, we soon learned something. And this
shows you how mean it was in those days. When he was up at the
plate, he could watch you for only so long, and then he'd have to
look down to get his eyes focused again. So we'd keep him
waiting up there until he'd have to look down, and then pitch. He
was never the same hitter again after that.

Huggins took over the Yankees in 1918. I was in the navy that
year, so I didn't get to know him until the next year.

Bob Shawkey in 1914

Huggins was a very fine person and a good baseball man. He knew the game and he knew how to get the most out of his ballplayers. Most of the boys liked him very much. He was a quiet man by nature. He tended to keep things to himself—very seldom exploded about anything. I think in certain ways he patterned himself after Connie Mack, who was the greatest manager I ever played for. Neither man would ever criticize you in front of the other players. If you made a mistake, Connie would call you up to his office the next day and have a little talk. Hug was the same way.

Hug's style of managing was completely different from John McGraw's. I played against McGraw's Giants in the 1913–14 World Series when I was with the Athletics and then later again when I was with the Yankees, in 1921–23. You could hear McGraw all over the ball park, cussin' his players out. And then after the game, if he'd lost, you could hear him through the clubhouse wall—yelling and cursing, laying them out cold. But he was a very successful manager, and so was Hug, each in his own way.

Of course, Hug could be tough when he had to be. He had an awful lot of patience, but there was a limit. Guess who was the fellow who finally went beyond the limit? That's right, Babe Ruth. Babe never slacked off on the field; he always gave you a hundred percent there. But away from the field he broke every rule in the book and probably a few others that weren't in the book. On the road he never stayed in the hotels. He'd go right from the ball park to some girl's apartment. Babe loved the girls. I've always said that if there were seven wonders in the world, then he was the eighth because I don't know how he could carry on the way he did and still be the great ballplayer that he was. He was amazing. You've heard Ping Bodie's comment, haven't you? Ping was Babe's roommate on the road, and one day somebody asked him who he roomed with and Ping answered "Babe Ruth's suitcase."

Anyway, it finally got to the point where Hug felt he had to do something about it. We were in St. Louis when it happened. The ball club was out on the field loosening up, and I was in the

Miller Huggins and Babe Ruth

clubhouse with Hug. Just the two of us. I was about to go out on the field and he said, "Wait a minute." He was sitting on the bench with his eye on the door. I sat down next to him. We talked for a while, not about anything in particular, and all the time Hug kept watching that door.

Then the door opened and in walked Babe, in his street clothes. I was surprised to see him. I thought for sure he was out on the field with the rest of the boys. He took off his jacket and hung it up in his locker. But then Hug said, "Babe, you don't have to dress today. You're fined and suspended. The secretary has your fare back to New York."

Babe took his jacket out of the locker, put it on, and started to leave. Then he turned around and called Huggins every name under the sun. Hug got up and walked over to him—he was about half Babe's size—and said, "Babe, some day you're going to thank

me for what I'm doing now. You're never going to play another
ball game for the New York Yankees until you straighten yourself
out."

Babe stormed on up to Chicago to see Judge Landis, but he
didn't get any satisfaction there. Then he went back to New York
to see Colonel Ruppert, but Ruppert backed Huggins all the way.
The fine was a whopper—$5,000.

When the team got back home, there was Babe hanging around,
wanting to play. Hug kept him out for about ten days.

I don't know if a manager could fine a man that much money
today, what with the Players Association and agents and lawyers.
It's different today. But of course you don't have a Babe Ruth
today. He was special, any way you look at him. You can't believe
the publicity and attention that man got and how little impression it made on him. He'd hardly ever look at his mail. He would
dump stacks of it into his locker and now and then ask me or one
of the other fellows to look at it for him to see if there was
anything interesting. I'd go through it and find lots of opportunities for him to make money, by endorsing cigarettes or bubble
gum and things like that. I'd show them to him and he'd say
"Okay, okay," and then forget about it. But on the other hand,
he'd almost never turn away somebody who wanted a handout,
and he'd never say no to a kid asking for his signature. He would
stand in the middle of a crowd of kids and sign for every one of
them.

I pitched to him a few times, you know, when he was still with
the Red Sox. I recall one game when Hug brought me in, in the
top of the ninth to pitch to Babe. We were leading them by a run
and they had the bases loaded with two out. I struck him out. We
had a big crowd that day, and I never saw so many straw hats fly
onto a ball field in my life. They don't do that anymore today, do
they—throw their hats out in appreciation?

I didn't have any problems with Ruth when I was managing.
We got along just fine. I had no trouble whatsoever with anybody
on the team, the only exception being Waite Hoyt. Waite liked to
hang around with theatrical people in the different cities, and it
got to a point where I felt he was staying out late too often and not

Bullet Joe Bush
in 1916

taking care of himself. I spoke to him about it, and he said okay, he'd watch that. I always told my pitchers a day ahead when they were starting so they'd be ready. One day in Boston I told Waite he'd be starting tomorrow. Well, he stayed out pretty late that night. The next day he didn't last more than three or four innings. Next game I started him was in Philadelphia, and the same thing happened.

When we got back home, Ruppert said to me, "What about Hoyt?"

"He's pitched his last game as a Yankee, as far as I'm concerned," I said. "I'd like to make a deal for him."

"Good," he said.

So we traded him to Detroit.

Now, I didn't have to go out of the hotel to know what was

going on at night. Heck, we had a man watching them—the ones we knew we had to watch. Usually it was the hotel detective that reported to us. He would tell us who was coming in after curfew, and that's how we knew. The ball club paid these fellows a few bucks for their trouble. It was that way with just about every club.

One year we had a detective traveling with us. He was going along as a friend of some of the boys, which he was, but at the same time he was reporting to Ruppert and Barrow about who was doing what and when. They brought him back again the year I was managing. He went on a couple of road trips with us. It was Ruppert's idea—in fact, that's how he found out about Hoyt. Ruppert could be very fussy about things. He took a lot of pride in his ball club and wanted to be sure the boys were taking care of themselves.

You see, in those years we took those long road trips by train. Sixteen, eighteen hours—trips like that. It wasn't like it is today, those short plane rides from here to there. On the train there was a lot of mingling among the players, and this detective fellow was right along with us. He got to know them pretty well, so he always knew what was going on.

When we'd get a report on a man, I'd call him in and talk to him. I'd say "Listen, you were in such and such a place at such and such a time. Now you'd better watch your step or I'll lay a fine on you." There wasn't much they could say about it because they knew it was true. Some of them were downright confounded by how much we knew. They never suspected that their good friend was a detective working for the ball club. It came out a few years later, but by that time he was long gone and had the good sense not to come around anymore.

The year I was managing I had just two coaches—Art Fletcher and Charlie O'Leary. Some teams didn't have even that many. They'd put a player on to coach at first. Today, for heaven's sakes, they've got a pitching coach who sits on the bench with the manager, a bull pen coach, and two men out on the lines, and some of them even carry a batting instructor. That's quite a change. You've got a lot of specialists around today. You very seldom see a manager on the coaching lines anymore.

We didn't make as many pitching changes in those days as they do today. A pitcher was expected to go nine innings; he was taught to pace himself, to hold back a little extra for when he got in a spot. You see, we didn't carry more than seven or eight pitchers in those days. If you look at the records, you'll see there were many more complete games then than there are today. I could usually tell when a man was beginning to lose his stuff—he would get wild. That's the way Connie always figured it. I heard him say it once, "When your arm gets tired you start to get wild."

The year I had the ball club, we were rebuilding. We had some new faces, especially in the infield. Connie had put together another great team in Philadelphia, with Foxx, Grove, Simmons, Cochrane and those fellows, and we had to make some changes if we were going to keep up with them. That caused a little problem for Gehrig. He was so used to all those good boys throwing strikes to first base that he'd got into the habit of taking his foot off of the bag too quickly. Because he knew the ball was going to be there, you see. Well, with some of the new boys the pegs weren't always so good, and he was getting off the bag to catch them and then not getting back on.

"Lou," I told him one time, "someday you're going to cost us a close ball game doing that. You'd better keep that foot on the bag as long as you can."

"These boys don't throw that ball as accurate as some of the other ones did," he said.

"I know that," I said. "But that doesn't make any difference. You've got to keep that foot on the bag because one of these days they're going to call it against you."

Well, one day in Chicago we lost a 1–0 ball game because of that. When we got into the clubhouse, all I said to him was "There's that game I told you about, Lou." He sat down on the bench and cried like a baby. He was that type. Very sensitive boy. Later on, after he'd had his dinner, he came up to my room and apologized, promised it would never happen again. And it didn't. He stuck to it after that.

As I said, we were rebuilding that year, trying to make what good trades we could. One day Ed Barrow came to me and said, "We can get one of three pitchers from the Red Sox—Ed Morris, Danny MacFayden, or Red Ruffing. I think we ought to take Morris or MacFayden."

MacFayden was a good pitcher, but he had never impressed me all that much, and I knew that Morris was a loner, a straight whisky drinker who went to the bar after his ball game and sat there and drank.

"Get Ruffing," I said.

"Why?" he asked.

"Because when he pitches against us, we can't do anything with him until after the fifth or sixth inning, and I think I can help him." He was pitching all with his arm, you see, and his arm would get tired, he'd lose some of his stuff, and we could get to him. I explained that to Barrow. He was not too sure about it but went along with me. So we got Ruffing, and I worked with him for about ten days to get him to throw more with his body—the same way Chief Bender had worked with me when I was a rookie with the Athletics. Ruffing became a winner after that, one of the biggest winners the Yankees ever had. All it took was a very slight changeover.

But in the end they gave me a dirty deal. Just before our last road trip I had a meeting with Ruppert and Barrow. They told me that the team had drawn more people than it had done in quite a while and that they were very happy with the way things were, even if we did come in third. They told me that I was going to be there next year. I wanted to sign the contract right then and there, but Ruppert said, "No, let's wait until the season is over. That's the way I always did it with Hug."

One day after the season had closed, I went up to the office to talk over some business. I was heading for Barrow's office when the door opened and Joe McCarthy came walking out. I took one look and turned around and got out of there. I knew what had happened.

Bob Shawkey, New York Yankees manager, in 1930

9

AL LOPEZ

Alfonso Raymond Lopez
Born: August 20, 1908, Tampa, Florida
Managerial career: Cleveland Indians, 1951–56; Chicago
    White Sox, 1957–65, 1968–69

In fifteen full years as a manager, Al Lopez's ball clubs
were never out of the first division, and only three times were
they lower than second place. Lopez's 1954 Cleveland Indians set an American League record with 111 wins. Lopez
holds the major league record for lifetime games for a
catcher—1,918. He was elected to the Baseball Hall of Fame
in 1977.

In 1925 a team of big leaguers came barnstorming through
Tampa right after the World Series, planning on playing each
other or playing against a local pick-up team. When they got to
Tampa, they thought it might be a good idea to get one of the local
kids to play with them, to attract some customers. I was only
seventeen years old at the time and had caught just one season in
the Florida State League, so you can imagine how scared and
excited and delighted I was to play with big leaguers.

"Great," I said. "Who's pitching?"

"Walter Johnson," they said.

"Walter Johnson!" I asked. This was a little more than I
expected.

"Do you think you can catch him?"

"I don't know," I said. "But I'll try."

So they advertised it: Walter Johnson pitching, Al Lopez
catching. I thought that was pretty funny, me being an equal

Al Lopez

drawing card with Walter Johnson. But they figured it would attract a lot of people from over in Ybor City, where I lived.

Johnson was very nice. Just before we went out to warm up, he came over to me and said, "Look, I'm not going to really let out. I'm going to bear down on just two fellows—Ike Boone and Jack Fournier. They hit me pretty good, so I'm going to bear down on them. You be ready when they come up."

He bore down on them all right. He pitched just five innings that day, so he faced those guys twice each and he struck them out twice each. Johnson must have been around thirty-eight years old then, but still a great pitcher. He could still fire it when he wanted to. And you know, he was easy to catch. You could follow his ball, and he was always around the plate. After it was over, he told somebody, "That boy did real well back there. Handled himself fine." You can bet that made me feel good.

The Dodgers bought my contract and brought me up from Macon, Georgia, at the end of the year in '28. I sat around on the bench the last few weeks, not doing anything until the last weekend of the season. We were playing the Pirates and all of a sudden Wilbert Robinson put me in to catch. I found out later the reason I caught was because Burleigh Grimes was pitching against us that day and none of the other catchers liked to hit against him. Burleigh was kind of mean.

I caught that day and went 0 for 4. The next day we had a doubleheader and Robbie let me catch both ends. This is when the Pirates had Pie Traynor and Glenn Wright on the left side of their infield. Well, I was strictly a pull hitter and I hit some good hard shots to the left side. I'd take off for first figuring I had myself a hit, but each time to my astonishment I saw that peg zinging into the first baseman's glove. I knew, I just *knew,* that at Macon those would have been hits. It was practically impossible to hit a ball past Traynor or Wright. I was 0 for 8 in that doubleheader and went home that fall wondering what a fellow had to do to get a base hit in the big leagues.

Wilbert Robinson—we all called him Uncle Robbie—was a fine man, very easygoing. It really hurt his feelings if one of his

*Dolf Luque and Dazzy Vance,
Brooklyn Dodgers pitchers, in
1930*

players disliked him. He tried to have everybody's goodwill. I think that's the reason he traded away Grimes; he and Burleigh didn't see eye to eye all the time. Dazzy Vance was one of his pets. Robbie liked big strong pitchers who could throw hard, and Vance was just that. Dazzy also had one of the finest curveballs I ever saw.

Dolf Luque was there too. He was a real old-timer when I joined the club. To me he was a real pitcher; by that I mean he was a craftsman out there. He could spot that ball anywhere he wanted. He was strictly overhand, with a curve that broke straight down—they called it a drop. He could pitch to left-handed hitters better than he could to righties by throwing them that curve. Catching him was a real education. I learned an awful lot about pitching to hitters from catching Luque.

Babe Herman was another one of Robbie's favorites. Babe was a great hitter, one of the best I ever saw. I roomed with him a couple of years, and the funny thing is I had good years with the bat then. Maybe it rubbed off. You know, he had the reputation for being clumsy in the field, but the truth is he became a good outfielder. He was a fine ballplayer for the Dodgers. One year he hit .393—and didn't lead the league. That was 1930, which was probably the biggest hitting year the league ever had. I believe the National League as a whole averaged over .300 in 1930. It was a good ball to hit that year, very lively.

They changed the ball after 1930. I think McGraw complained about it, and McGraw had a lot to say about things then. When he said something, they listened. The Giants were the powerhouse of the National League, and probably of baseball, when it came to influencing things.

I can remember one game very distinctly. The Giants had a pitcher by the name of Roy Parmelee, a wild, hard-throwing right-hander. He was pitching against us this day in the Polo Grounds, the bases were loaded, and Glenn Wright was up—he was with the Dodgers now. Parmelee threw him a fastball; his fastball had a natural sliderlike break to it. Glenn started to swing, saw the pitch breaking away, and kind of half threw his bat at the ball, almost one-handed. He got out in front of it and hit it down the left-field line. Remember the Polo Grounds, how short it was down the lines? Well, Glenn hit it just hard enough for the ball to drop in for a grand-slam home run. We could see McGraw throw up his hands in the dugout, and, we heard later, he said, "What kind of baseball is this?" I think he made up his mind right then and there that the ball was too lively and that something had to be done. The way I understand it, that was the beginning of softening the ball up a bit.

McGraw was tough as nails on the field. He wouldn't tolerate mistakes, whereas Robbie would. You could get away with mistakes with Robbie. But McGraw made a fine impression on me as a manager. I didn't know the man personally, but when you played against his team, you knew you were playing against one of the best. They weren't going to make too many mistakes. There was something about them that made you know they were in good shape to play baseball, especially in the spring. I heard that he really drove them in the spring because he wanted to get off to a good start. Another thing, when they threw the ball around during infield practice, they really fired it; that's the way he wanted them to do it. When you watched that Giant team on the field, you could always feel McGraw's hand everywhere. He was all business on a ball field, and so were they. There was never any clowning on that club, not even around the batting cage. With every other team the guys would get around the batting cage and there would be a lot of kidding, but not with the Giants.

What you saw with the Giants was discipline. That was the way McGraw worked. In those days a ball game started at three o'clock in the afternoon. Well, McGraw insisted his players be in the clubhouse by ten o'clock in the morning, and if they weren't there on time, they'd be in trouble. No, there's no way a manager could run his team like that today—there'd be a revolution.

But with all his strictness, McGraw had the respect of his players. You can get away with all the strict discipline if your players respect you. And I think that's the main thing in managing. That's all I ever wanted when I was managing. It's not too difficult to earn their respect. All you have to do is treat them the way you wanted to be treated when you were a player. I understood that a man was going to make a mistake, and as long as he didn't do it over and over again, I'd go along with him. You don't want to be rough on players who are trying their best.

Bill Veeck once said that if I had a weakness as a manager, it was that I was too decent. Well, I never took that as a negative comment. In fact, it was nice to hear that said. I'd like to think I'm a decent guy. Nothing wrong with that, is there?

A ball club can reflect the manager's personality. McGraw was businesslike and efficient, and so were his ball clubs. Uncle Robbie was easygoing, and so were his clubs. Of course, they weren't the "Daffy Dodgers" any longer when I got there, but some of those guys could still be pretty tricky. One day I had an argument with Bill Klem over a close play. We had a good go at it, and that was that. The next day there was a picture in the paper of

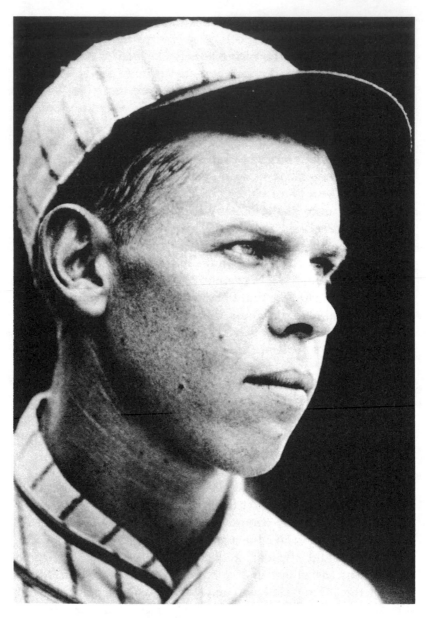

Babe Herman
"One year he hit .393—and didn't lead the league."

that play, and it showed Klem was wrong. One of the guys—I think it was Mungo—cut the picture out, taped it over home plate, and then covered it with dirt. I didn't know anything about it.

Just before the first pitch was thrown, Klem went around to clean off the plate. I was crouched there watching him. He bent down and started whisking his little brush back and forth. He uncovered a corner of the picture, turned his head, and gave me a dirty look. Then he went on brushing, his hand moving slower and slower, his face getting redder and redder. Little by little he cleared off the whole picture. I tried not to laugh because I could see how sore he was. He thought I had done it and, boy, was he burned up! "You dumb busher," he said. "I didn't do it, Bill," I said. But I don't think he even heard me because he just kept chewing me out.

Klem, by the way, was a great umpire. The best I ever saw.

You know, when you're managing a ball club, you're constantly being interviewed. The writers are always around looking for a story. Well, you've got to be darned careful not to say anything that's going to offend anybody. Remember that crack Bill Terry made when he was managing the Giants: "Is Brooklyn still in the league?" Well, that was just a flip remark made on the spur of the moment in spring training. But I think he probably was sorry later on that he ever said it.

You see, we came down to the last two games of the season playing the Giants at the Polo Grounds. This was 1934. The Giants were tied for first place with the Cardinals. We were going nowhere. We were down in sixth place, I think. Now, that remark of Terry's had never bothered the Dodger players any, but it seemed to have rankled the fans. They took it up and made a big thing of it. I think there must have been more Dodger fans than Giant fans in the Polo Grounds at those two games. They were running up and down the aisles waving banners and yelling and really cheering us on.

We were up for those games. Van Lingle Mungo beat them the first game, and the next day we came from behind to beat them again. That knocked the Giants right out of the pennant. You can imagine what went on there. You should have heard those fans. It couldn't have been any wilder out there if we had won the pennant ourselves, but I guess knocking the Giants out of it was just as sweet to the Dodger fans. You can't believe how bitter that Dodger-Giant rivalry used to be. You don't have anything these days to compare to it.

Stengel was managing the Dodgers at that time. He told me something afterwards about that last day. After we'd beaten the Giants, he was going to go to their clubhouse and tell Terry how sorry he was that they'd lost out. But then he thought better of it, figuring that Terry was probably feeling pretty lousy about things. The Giants had led most of the season, you see. So Stengel went on home. Then at the winter meetings he met Terry. "You know, Bill," he said, "I was going to come in after that last game and pay my respects." Stengel said Terry was still burning from what had happened, and Bill scowled at him and said, "Well, it's

Bill Klem in 1946
"'You dumb busher,' he said."

a goddamn good thing you didn't. You would have been thrown out on your ass."

I don't know if Terry's wisecrack had anything to do with the way we played those last two games, but when everything was over, it made him look bad. I'll tell you, I learned my own lesson soon after I joined the Dodgers. A writer came to me one day and asked me which pitchers I liked to hit against. "Listen," I said, "they're all tough." That's what you're supposed to say, right? But I wanted to be a nice guy and give him some kind of answer, so I went on and added, "But I've had pretty good luck with Bill Walker." Bill Walker was a left-hander with the Giants, and a good one. Anyway, that's what I said. But it came out in the paper that I said Walker was easy for me to hit. You can imagine what he thought when he read that. I had a devil of a time with him after that. He really bore down against me, pushed me back, knocked me down. I didn't blame him. All he knew was what he'd read in the paper. But I'd never said what was attributed to me.

I used to warn my players not to antagonize anybody unnecessarily, especially the cellar clubs. Don't wake them up. Be nice to them, joke with them, get them relaxed—and then go out and beat their brains out. In a nice way.

Durocher seemed to want to do the opposite. He'd stir you up. I remember one time when I was with the Pirates and Durocher was managing the Dodgers, he got into an argument with Vince DiMaggio. Leo yelled something over from the Dodgers' dugout, and it got Vince angry. Vince had a short fuse anyway. Next time up, he popped out, and that made him angrier. They spent the rest of the game yelling back and forth at each other.

In the ninth inning we're one run behind. This was in 1941, and the Dodgers are fighting for the pennant. Every game means something to them. Anyway, DiMaggio comes up in the ninth with one out and doubles off of Hugh Casey. Somebody hits a ground ball to second and Vince moves over to third. That made two out and I'm the hitter. Now, Casey had a way of going down to the ground in his windup and then coming up. Just as he goes down for his windup, DiMaggio makes a tear for the plate, as if he's going to steal home. He came so far down the line I actually thought for a moment he was coming all the way, but then he stopped. He must have distracted Casey because Hugh hesitated for just a fraction in his motion—I thought he did anyway so I jumped out of the batter's box and yelled "Balk!" Then the umpire, big George Magerkurth, ripped off his mask and yelled "Balk!" He saw it the same way I did. So DiMaggio is waved in and scores the tying run.

Well, you should have seen that commotion. Leo led a charge of Dodgers out to Magerkurth, and they went at it. Finally Leo got kicked out and play resumed. I'm still up at the plate and Casey is out there boiling. The first pitch is right at my head. Second pitch, same thing. I'm ducking, and so is Magerkurth. Finally Mage says to me, "Hey, Lopez. Is he throwing at you or is he throwing at me?"

"I don't know," I said, "and let's not try and find out—he's mad enough as it is."

"The hell with this," Mage says. "I want to know." And out he goes to talk to Casey. Well, when that happens, here comes Leo again—he must've been hiding in the runway behind the dugout—along with Charlie Dressen, Fred Fitzsimmons, and some others. They go at it again. Magerkurth finally clears them off, throwing Leo out again.

So I step in again and look at Casey. He's got murder in his eyes. He throws two more at me. The fourth ball almost took my head off. I go down to first base. The next hitter is a fellow named Alf Anderson. Alf isn't too much with the stick, but don't you think he hits the first pitch just fair down the right-field line? I start running as hard as I can, while Dixie Walker is chasing the ball down in right field. The ball hugs the line all the way, and I score from first base—and that's the ball game.

The moment I crossed the plate, Leo comes running back onto the field and follows Magerkurth all the way to the umpires' dressing room, jawing away at him. I understand he tried to break down the door there, which is not such a good idea since those doors are heavy and the fines for trying to break them down are even heavier.

But what hurt the Dodgers most was Leo getting on Vince DiMaggio. He should have left Vince alone. Instead he got him so worked up that Vince provoked Casey into balking, which got Casey so provoked he couldn't pitch to me. It ended up costing them the ball game. So when you hear somebody say "Let sleeping dogs lie," you'd better believe there's a lot of good sense to it.

Stengel was a great guy and a fine manager. He loved to teach. He would get a young fellow and sit with him by the hour and talk to him about baseball. I think he tried to pattern himself after McGraw in many ways. Of course, he was a different personality from McGraw, though he could cat you out on the bench if he had to. The difference between them was that a little while later he'd be kidding with you, which I don't think McGraw would ever have done.

My path and Casey's kept crossing in baseball. I was traded three times during my career and two of those times by Casey. In

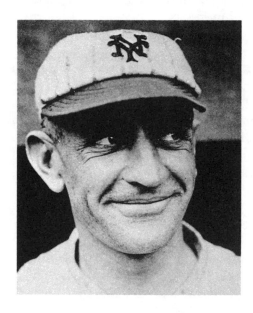

Casey Stengel
"I think he tried to pattern himself after McGraw in many ways."

the winter of 1935 I came up to New York on some business. I was having drinks in my room at the St. George Hotel with some friends when Casey came by. This was about three o'clock in the afternoon. Casey was such an interesting talker that the next thing we knew it was about nine o'clock, and we hadn't had our dinner yet. I suggested we go out and get something to eat. I invited Casey to come along, and he said he'd join us on one condition— that we let him pick up the check. We argued back and forth, but he was insistent. So we went across the street to a restaurant, ate dinner, listened to him talk some more, and then went back upstairs to my room. At two o'clock in the morning we were still talking. Finally my friends left, and Casey sat around to have one more drink. He became quiet for a few minutes, and I could see he had something on his mind.

"Dammit, Al," he said all of a sudden, "I'm going to have to make a trade. It's either you or Mungo, and I'd like to keep Mungo because he's younger and because he brings people into the park."

I could see it was bothering him. I guess it had been on his mind the whole time, and he had been sitting all afternoon and all night figuring out how to tell me.

"Casey," I said, "don't feel bad. If you think you can make a good deal, go ahead and make it."

"Okay," he said. "But if I trade you, it's going to be to a good club, a contender."

Soon after I got back to Tampa, I heard about the trade. Casey's intentions about sending me to a contender were well meant, I'm sure, but he ended up trading me to Boston, who the year before had set a league record by losing 115 games. Then a few years later he comes over to manage Boston and trades me to Pittsburgh.

I was a teammate of Al Simmons' at Boston in 1939. Here was one of the greatest right-handed hitters who ever lived, but on the decline now. Something happened that year that I'll never forget. The Braves had acquired Eddie Miller from the Yankees to play shortstop. For the Braves, who didn't have much money, it was a pretty big deal. They laid out some cash and gave up about four or five ballplayers for Eddie. And he was worth it, too. He was a good ballplayer.

One day there was a fly ball hit into short left, and Miller and Simmons went for it. It was one of those situations where you just want to close your eyes because you can see the collision coming, and there's not a thing you can do about it. They ran into each other with a smack and went tumbling to the grass.

Everybody went running out there to see how Miller was. He was the bright young ballplayer, the one they had the investment in. Hardly anybody paid any attention to Simmons. Well, Miller was all right, but Simmons had a hairline fracture above his ankle, and was out for quite a while. One day he came into the clubhouse and sat down next to me. He had a wistful little smile.

"You know something, Al?" he said. "Ten years ago, when I was playing for Mr. Mack, if that collision had happened, they would have sent a goddamned kid shortstop nine hundred miles from Philadelphia for running into me."

I'll never forget him saying that.

In 1946, after the Pirates let Frankie Frisch go, a Pittsburgh newspaper took a poll to see who the fans wanted to manage the club. It turned out that I was their choice. But the new owners, Frank McKinney and his associates, wanted Billy Herman. That was fine with me. I thought Billy was a great guy and would be a good manager. But at the same time it left me in kind of an uncomfortable position. I knew that sooner or later we'd have a few bad games and the fans would start yelling "We want Lopez." I didn't want that to happen, so I went to the front office, explained how I felt, and asked to be traded. They sent me to Cleveland. I played there in '47, which was my last active year in the big leagues. I was thirty-nine years old then.

After the season in '47 Bill Veeck, who owned the Indians, and Lou Boudreau got into some kind of a hassle. I forget what it was about, but there was a story in the paper saying that Boudreau might not be back to manage in '48. At the same time I was in New York for the World Series and was also shopping around for

*Al Lopez obliging some young fans
at the Polo Grounds in 1934*

a job as a coach or a minor league manager. I got a call from
Veeck. We were both at the New Yorker hotel, and he wanted to
see me. So I went up to his room.

"You get a job yet?" he asked me.

I told him that I had a few feelers out and that things looked
promising.

"Look," he said, "don't do anything until I get back. I'm going
to Chicago to talk to Boudreau. If things don't pan out, you might
have the job."

"Bill," I said, "I don't want the job. I was there one year as a
player, and I don't want people thinking I was after the job, that I
might have been undermining Boudreau."

I told him I'd prefer going out somewhere to manage, to get that
experience, and then if later on he still wanted me, I'd be glad to
work for him. So he went to Chicago and straightened things out
with Boudreau, and I wound up in Indianapolis, where I managed for three years. Eventually I did get up to manage the
Indians, but it wasn't until 1951.

That's when I began chasing the New York Yankees. I spent year after year chasing them. I finished second to the Yankees nine times. I did manage to beat them out a couple of times, in 1954 with Cleveland and again in 1959 with the White Sox. Those were the only years between 1949 and 1964 that the Yankees didn't win the pennant. In '52 we finished two games out of first place. The frustrating thing about that was we won something like 18 of our last 21 games, and the Yankees did the same thing. We just couldn't gain an inch on them.

A manager has to adapt his style to what material he's got. There's no other way to do it. In 1954 with Cleveland I didn't have too much speed on the club—we only stole around 30 bases—but we did have guys who could hit the ball out of the park, like Vic Wertz, Al Rosen, and Larry Doby. So our game was to hold the other side with our good pitching and wait for somebody to sock one out.

Now, my other pennant winner, the White Sox, was set up differently. Outside of Sherman Lollar we didn't have any really serious long-ball threats. It was a Punch and Judy team, with fellows like Luis Aparicio, Nellie Fox, Jim Landis, and Billy Goodman. But you see a guy like Aparicio, how well he can run the bases, and you turn him loose. Just give him the go sign. His percentage of steals was over 90 percent that year, so it's hardly a profound tactical move to put a fellow like that on his own.

Letting Aparicio try to steal meant we didn't have to hit-and-run with Nellie Fox, who was behind him in the lineup. The hit-and-run is more of a defensive play than an offensive one, you see. You use it to keep out of the double play. And you have to hit at whatever the pitcher throws, his pitch rather than yours. So why should you have to handicap Nellie Fox, who's a .300 hitter, by hitting-and-running with him when you can get Aparicio to steal second base? You don't have to be much of a genius to dope that out.

I never believed in having one particular pattern for my pitchers to follow. The old wisdom used to be pitch high inside and low outside. Today I think they concentrate mostly on

John McGraw

pitching low. They claim it's harder to hit the low ball for distance, but I don't think so. If you're a low-ball hitter, you're going to hit it. And suppose your best stuff is high? If you're a high-ball pitcher with a riding fastball, I think you should pitch high, no matter who's up there. It's your strength against his.

When I managed Cleveland, I thought I had the best-balanced pitching staff ever in baseball, with Bob Lemon, Early Wynn, Mike Garcia, Bob Feller, and Art Houtteman for starters, plus Don Mossi and Ray Narleski in the bull pen. Well, when we held a meeting to go over the hitters, you found out there was no one way to pitch a man because everybody was a different type of pitcher. Wynn was a high-ball pitcher. Lemon threw a sinker and kept it low. Garcia was just overpowering, and he tried to pitch the right-handed hitters tight all the time because his ball bore into them. Houtteman pitched a little bit like Lemon. Feller no longer had the great speed, so he'd throw them curves and sliders in tight. They were entirely different pitchers, so I left them on their own.

I played for many managers and of course you learn a little from each one. I think I learned more about pitching from Bill McKechnie than from anybody else. He liked to keep his pitchers in rotation, no matter what. I tried to do that when I managed. Of course you plan ahead and set them up. I always wanted to have Lemon, Wynn, and Garcia ready for the Yankees because that was the club you had to beat if you were going to go anywhere. And Stengel was sure to shoot Raschi, Reynolds, Lopat, and Ford at us.

In 1954, when I was managing Cleveland, we finally caught the Yankees. It wasn't easy because they won 103 games. But we won 111, which is still the American League record. Then we went into the Series against the Giants and didn't win a game. We just got cold, that's all, and the Giants played great ball. They made the plays. Remember that ball Vic Wertz hit with the bases loaded at the Polo Grounds that Mays made the great catch on? Heck, that would have been a home run just about anyplace else. And nobody gives their third baseman, Henry Thompson, much credit, but he made some of the greatest plays I ever saw. And Dusty Rhodes got those big pinch hits.

They say anything can happen in a short series. Well, I knew that. I just never thought it was going to be *that* short.

10

DICK WILLIAMS

RICHARD HIRSCHFIELD WILLIAMS
Born: May 7, 1928, St. Louis, Missouri
Managerial career: Boston Red Sox, 1967–69; Oakland Athletics, 1971–73; California Angels, 1974–76; Montreal Expos, 1977–

Dick Williams had a thirteen-year big league career, primarily as a versatile utility man, with the Brooklyn Dodgers, Baltimore Orioles, Cleveland Indians, Kansas City Athletics, and Boston Red Sox. In 1967 he took a Red Sox team that had finished ninth the year before and led them to a pennant. Later, Williams went on to manage the Oakland Athletics to World Championships in 1972 and 1973.

You lay all your groundwork in the spring, and then you keep on it—on how you want them to play. I'm talking about the basic fundamentals. If a guy hangs a curve or a guy fumbles a ground ball, you can't do anything about it. Those are physical mistakes, and you don't get on a man for them because you know he's making an effort. They're going to happen, and they're going to happen again. But mental mistakes I can't tolerate. A man has to know what he's got to do on the field at all times, and it's got to be automatic. Missing a cutoff man looks like a physical action; to me it's a mental mistake. It shouldn't happen. I can't tolerate a guy missing signs. I won't tolerate it. And I tell these guys that. There's no excuse for missing a sign.

I enjoy managing. It's true the manager is very vulnerable. It's the most insecure position in the organization. But it's something I love to do. I love the challenge. I can tell you just when I began thinking about managing—in 1952, right after I dove for a fly ball in St. Louis and separated my shoulder. I was with the Brooklyn Dodgers then. I did a lot of bench-sitting from that point on and found myself doing some long-range thinking. Even though I wasn't playing, I tried to stay on top of every situation that came up because I knew I wanted to stay in baseball.

I had come up in an outstanding organization with outstanding tutors. Branch Rickey was running the Dodgers during the years I was there, and he always tried to surround himself with men of the highest caliber. I think this is borne out by the fact that so many men who were touched by Rickey in one way or another and became managers made it to the major leagues. I'm thinking of fellows like Eddie Stanky, Walter Alston, Leo Durocher, Bobby Bragan, Gene Mauch, Gil Hodges, and Danny Ozark. They all had their indoctrination through the Rickey system.

I've been asked from time to time who had an influence on my baseball career. I would have to say there are three men who influenced me more than any others—Charlie Dressen, for whom I played in Brooklyn; Bobby Bragan; and Paul Richards, for whom I played in Baltimore. I didn't agree with a lot of Paul's theories, especially on pitching, but his fundamentals were absolutely sound. He based his whole game on defense. I heartily agree with that. Sure, I'd love to have a lot of power hitters, but I do think if you have a sound pitching staff and a strong defense, you're going to be able to scrounge two or three runs in the course of a ball game. And that should be good enough to win, much of the time.

Charlie Dressen was another one who placed tremendous emphasis on pitching and defense. Even when he had all that sock in the lineup with the Dodgers in the early fifties, a lot of his thinking was centered on pitching and defense. In fact, he was his own pitching coach. Bobby Bragan shared a lot of those same ideas.

So, coming under the influence of these men, I base an awful lot of my thinking on strong pitching and good execution by my defense. Then you take what offense you have and utilize it. If you've got speed in the lineup, then you have to hit-and-run, run-and-hit, steal, take the extra base.

Coach Charlie Dressen and five members of Brooklyn's 1941 pitching staff
Left to right: *Whitlow Wyatt, Curt Davis, Freddie Fitzsimmons, Hugh Casey, Kirby Higbe*

Since I was never a pitcher myself, I'm in favor of a strong pitching coach. He's got to spend a lot of time with his men, which the manager can't do, and gain their confidence. As far as I'm concerned, he's the manager of the pitchers and I'm the chairman of the board. I make the final decisions, based on his advice.

I wound up my playing career with the Red Sox in 1964. They asked me to go to Seattle as a player-coach. I wasn't sure I wanted to do that, but they told me that if they moved the ball club to another city, I would have the opportunity to manage. There had been some talk about the Red Sox getting another Triple-A affiliation. Before I gave them my answer, I put in a call to Paul Richards to ask his advice. He told me to take it. It was good advice because, sure enough, that winter they moved the Seattle club to Toronto and I became manager. I managed there in '65 and '66 and we won the Governor's Cup both years.

Just before the season ended in '66, the Red Sox let Billy Herman go as manager. I set my sights on the job. I wanted it. I went to Boston for three days of organizational meetings after the season, wondering what was going to happen. After three days nobody had said anything to me, and I was getting set to fly home. I was having dinner with some of the front office people, and after dinner somebody said to me, "Dick O'Connell wants us to ride back with him." O'Connell was the general manager. I hop in the car and he reaches over and says, "I'd like to shake hands with the new manager of the Red Sox." I was really elated. And you know what happened the next year, in '67.

In 1966 they'd finished ninth in a ten-team league. Well, I wanted a better ball club than that. My first job was to get them believing that they could play together as a unit. Then I had to get them to believe they were a hell of a lot better than a ninth-place ball club.

So when we went to spring training, we started out right from scratch as far as fundamentals were concerned. This is what Paul Richards and Bobby Bragan would do. They began by taking the whole ball club up to the on-deck circle. "This is what we do here." "This is what we do going up to the plate as far as looking at the coaches and getting the sign is concerned." They talked about every play, offensively and defensively, around the home plate area. Same thing between home and first, how to run the bases. First base, breaks and leads. Offensive and defensive plays at first, second, short, third. Same thing in the outfield. All phases of the game. It used to take Richards about three days to get around the whole park, doing it for about two hours at a time. Bragan did the same thing. It's like going back to kindergarten, so to speak.

I don't know what the players thought of my approach. They

probably thought I was crazy as a loon. But, hell, I had a one-year contract. So if I was crazy, I was going to be crazy all year and give it the best I had. Frankly, I didn't make too many friends among the players that year. I was called a lot of things. But I don't have to be friends with them; I don't have to go out to dinner with them. I don't care if they like me or not. I am concerned, though, about them respecting my knowledge of the game. If they do, they'll play for me, and they'll play to the top of their ability. So they may not have liked me, but I do know that every one of them accepted their money when they cashed their World Series checks at the end of the year.

I was always a great believer in conditioning—in watching your weight. George Scott, who I think is just a tremendous ballplayer, had a tendency to get a little heavy. Well, I had a weight maximum for him, and I weighed him in each day. Once we had an off-day in Anaheim, and how he did it I don't know, but he put on seven pounds between our last game in Oakland and our first game in Anaheim. So I benched him. I told him I wasn't going to play him until his weight was down to where it was supposed to be. This is '67, mind you, and we're in the heat of a pennant race. We ended up losing all three games in Anaheim—with George sitting on the bench. When that little episode got around, it led Jim Fregosi to say, "We have nine managers in the league and one dietitian." Well, at the end of the season I sent Fregosi a note that read, "The dietitian won."

Sure, my attitude came from the old school. I'm definitely from the old school. But I'm not inflexible. I've gone along with certain things. I think it's a mistake for a manager not to go with the times. You can't stand alone against a new wave. It'll break you. That's why, when the Oakland ball club went to the long hair and mustaches, I went with them. When I managed the Red Sox, I had a butch haircut; with Oakland I was as hairy as the rest of them.

I made up my mind when I took over the Red Sox that the left field wall in Fenway Park was not going to be a factor in the way I ran the game. I'd played there in '63 and '64 and saw too many good hitters ruining themselves taking shots at that wall. I didn't

Jim Lonborg

want that to happen with my club. We didn't gear ourselves to try
to hit the wall. We bunted, we squeezed, we hit to the right side to
move a guy from second to third, we stole, and we hit-and-run.
We didn't lay back and wait for the big inning.

As far as our pitching was concerned, we pitched in on the
right-handed hitters. They always came up there looking for the
ball away, figuring we'd try to keep them from pulling. But I
think the way to pitch in Fenway Park is inside. Keep doing that
and gradually you'll back them up a little—then go outside with
it, and it'll be very effective. Jim Lonborg did that beautifully for
us all year; so did Jose Santiago.

You see, for years the Red Sox had had great teams, but still they had won only one pennant in twenty-one years. They always won at home but traditionally were a poor road club. That's because their game was always geared for Fenway Park, for that wall. What good was that right-handed home run swing in old Griffith Stadium or Yankee Stadium with those long, long left fields? I was determined to play one sound fundamental game wherever I was, and I stuck with it all the way. We had a winning record on the road in 1967, and that's where we won the pennant. Won it by one game. You can't get any thinner than that, can you?

It was one hell of a race. With a week to go there were still four teams in it—the Red Sox, White Sox, Tigers, and Twins. All bunched up. We played Cleveland on Tuesday and Wednesday that last week, and Cleveland beat us both ball games. So it looked like we were completely out of it. The White Sox were playing a doubleheader in Kansas City, and they're starting Joel Horlen and Gary Peters, their two best pitchers. I was sitting home in Massachusetts that day trying to pick the games up on radio. I finally had to go out to my car and was able to pick the games up on the radio there. I sat in my car all day and listened to the White Sox lose a doubleheader. That put them on the skids and us right back in the thick of things.

We had Thursday and Friday off; then we have the Twins coming into town. Meanwhile, the Tigers are playing the Angels—a doubleheader Friday and single games Saturday and Sunday. Well, they get rained out of the doubleheader Friday, meaning they've got back-to-back doubleheaders to play. The situation was this: We have to beat the Twins both games on Saturday and Sunday, and the Tigers have to split their four games for us to win it.

Well, on Saturday the Tigers split their doubleheader and we beat the Twins, putting us in a tie with them and a half game ahead of the Tigers. In that Saturday game we got a break. We were down 2–0 to Jim Kaat when he came up with a bad arm. He had to come out. They brought in Jim Perry, and we got to him and won that ball game.

On Sunday we pitch Lonborg. We're down 2–0 on unearned runs going into the last of the sixth. Dean Chance is pitching against us, and he's a hell of a pitcher. Lonborg leads off the bottom of the sixth, and he beats out a bunt. We went on from there to score five runs and won it, 5–3.

Carl Yastrzemski. You can't say enough about the job he did in those last two games. It was just unbelievable. He went seven for eight, under the most extreme pressure a ballplayer can experience. The other players felt that if they could get on base and give Yaz a shot, he was going to come through, and he certainly did. In fact, he did that all year. I've never seen a ballplayer have a year like Yaz had in '67, and I mean in all phases of the game—running, throwing, fielding, hitting, hitting with power.

Meanwhile, the Tigers win their first game. So now we're all in the clubhouse listening to that game in Detroit. If the Tigers win, there's going to be a play-off; if they lose, we win it all. The beer and champagne are on ice, but we can't celebrate yet. So there's the whole ball club sitting around the clubhouse listening to that game on the radio. Well, the Tigers lost it, and all hell broke loose in that clubhouse. You can imagine.

That kind of pennant race is hard on the manager, but I'd have to say it's rougher on his wife and kids because he's so engrossed in what he's doing. The more the pressure builds, the further the outside world drifts away from you. I don't mean you yell at your wife and use the kids for footballs; it's just that you're centered on that one thing and you can't even hear anything else. The family never has a chance to relax because you're never relaxed; you're too wound up for any recreational activities. That shell gradually builds up around you, gets thicker and thicker, and no one can penetrate it.

I would say that going into a World Series after a finish like that was definitely a disadvantage for us. The Series, as much as you'd love to win it, has to be anticlimactic. Still, we carried the Cardinals to seven games. I had to start Lonborg with two days' rest that last game. He'd pitched a one-hitter in the second game and a three-hitter in the fifth game. In the seventh game he just got tired and they beat us. Of course Bob Gibson had something on the ball, too, that Series—he beat us three times.

Late in the year in '69 we'd just come back from a road trip, and

Carl Yastrzemski in 1964
"I've never seen a
ballplayer have a year like
Yaz had in '67."

I went to see Dick O'Connell, as I always did after every trip. I was interested in hiring a certain guy for the coaching staff the following season and asked Dick what he was doing about getting this particular guy.

"I can't give you an answer," he said.

There was something in the way he said it that prompted me to ask, "Well, my coaches and I are coming back next year, aren't we?"

"Dick," he said, "I'm afraid not."

Why? Well, I heard that Tom Yawkey had said I was too tough on the players. Maybe so, but I was also pretty tough on the turnstiles too—the Red Sox had three of the biggest attendance years in their history the three years I was there. If you will recall, the Boston Red Sox organization was always known as "The Country Club." That's why they went through a lot of managers. And they hadn't won in twenty-one years. Well, I don't think you can win it with lollipops and candy for the players. So I had to have a firm hand. I had no other choice. I was getting my first shot at managing, and I believed I knew how the game was supposed to be played. I had to enforce my ideas, and if I had to step on a few toes, that wasn't going to bother me.

After leaving Boston, I went up to Montreal and coached a year for Gene Mauch. And I learned a lot from him—I learned an awful lot from him. Going back to coaching that one year was like a refresher course. Mauch employed some innovations as a manager that I'm using today. Certain defenses in bunt situations, for instance, and certain maneuvers offensively on fake bunts, like teaching the batter to slap the ball past a charging third baseman. Little extra advantages that can add to your game. I also learned from him a lot about pickoff plays, rundowns, relays, cutoffs. I believe that if you take all the major league managers and have them go to a clinic, Gene Mauch should run that clinic. He knows his baseball inside out.

Gene told me during the year that I'd be back managing soon. During the season there were all sorts of rumors about things opening up here and there. Once I heard that they were going to let Harry Walker go at Houston and offer me the job. That one was so persistent that I started getting calls from guys asking about coaching jobs. But that one didn't materialize; they signed Harry for another year.

Then we were winding up the season in Philadelphia. I went out to dinner after one of the final games and got back to my hotel

around 1:00 A.M. There were some messages in my box. They
were from Charlie Finley. The last one said he'd call again at
seven o'clock in the morning.

Seven o'clock, right on the dot, he called. He wanted me to
manage the Oakland ball club. Was I interested? I told him yes.
We talked for a while and came to terms on the phone. That's how
I got the Oakland job.

Finley? Probably the best businessman connected with baseball I've ever known. But a very dominating man. I believe that if
you hire a guy to do something, let him do it. If he can't do it, then
get rid of him. But Finley is also his own general manager, you
see. When you're talking with him, you're talking with the
general manager, not necessarily the owner. He's both.

Dick Williams
"When I managed the Red Sox,
I had a butch haircut . . ."

One thing he didn't interfere with, and couldn't, was the operation of the ball game on the field. He might have made suggestions about who to play, and sometimes I followed them and sometimes I didn't. And when I didn't, we'd have a confrontation. Of course when you're winning, it's a lot different; the ground you're standing on is a hell of a lot firmer. But did you ever manage a ball game and after winning it have somebody say to you that you could have won it easier if you would have done this or that?

I was the only manager to last past one full year with Finley, until Dark recently did. And I stayed for three. But finally I had enough. There were a number of things that entered into it during the course of the three years, but the final straw was the Mike

Dick Williams
". . . with Oakland I was as
hairy as the rest of them."

Andrews incident in the '73 Series. If you'll recall, Finley humiliated him after Mike had had a bad game in the field. Well, that did it. I told my players in Shea Stadium during the Series that win or lose I was resigning as soon as it was over.

I don't dislike Charlie, and I don't think he dislikes me, although I'm the only guy that ever quit him. I never gave him the chance to fire me.

But I'll tell you one thing about Finley—if you needed a player, he'd make every effort to go out and get that player, and he'd usually succeed. He's made some outstanding moves. And he's had some fresh ideas. Playing night games in the World Series to get that big television audience. Night baseball in the All-Star Game. Finley's ideas. The designated hitter—that was a combined idea of Finley's and Calvin Griffith's, though probably more Charlie's than Calvin's. And he's certainly been exciting for baseball; you can't say he hasn't. I had just had enough of working for him.

I guess winning the '72 Series was my biggest thrill in baseball. Winning the pennant in '67 was great, but there's nothing like taking everything. The win in '73 was spoiled for me by the Andrews incident. So I've got to look back on 1972 as my own personal highlight, up to the present time. That was the Series where we faked Johnny Bench on the supposed intentional walk. I had that play in the back of my mind in case the situation came up. I was talking to one of my coaches, Bill Posedel, about it before the game.

"If the count goes to three and two on Bench," I said, "and the situation is right, I'm going to play like we're going to put him on, and then try to strike him out."

Well, the situation came up. Johnny was at bat with men on second and third and one out. The count went to three and two. I called time and went out to the mound, going through all the theatrics, pointing to Bench, pointing to first base. Rollie Fingers was pitching and Gene Tenace was catching. When I got out to the mound, I told Gene to stand aside like the pitch was going to be intentionally wide and then just as Rollie delivered, to drop back behind the plate. Now, you also have to have a breaking ball, not a fastball; in case Bench does get set, you still have a chance of fooling him with the breaking ball.

So we set it up. I went back to the dugout and held my breath. Somebody's going to look bad here, and it's going to be either me or Bench. Fingers went into his stretch and delivered. Well, Bench was completely fooled. You see, with men on second and third and one out, there was logic to putting him on. An intentional walk seemed the right thing to do, and that's how we got away with it.

After the game the writers come into the clubhouse and want to know about the play. Tenace says he's never heard about it before. And of course I'm strutting around because I'm a managerial genius for thinking of it. Then Fingers pipes up.

"Oh," he says, "I've known about the play for years. Our Little League coach taught it to us."

GEORGE BRACE PHOTO

Roger Peckinpaugh

11

ROGER PECKINPAUGH

ROGER THORPE PECKINPAUGH
Born: February 5, 1891, Wooster, Ohio
Managerial career: New York Yankees, 1914; Cleveland
    Indians, 1928–33, 1941

Managing the New York Yankees for 17 games in 1914 at
the age of twenty-three made Roger Peckinpaugh the youngest manager in major league history. After a long and distin-
guished playing career with the Yankees, Cleveland Indians,
Washington Senators, and Chicago White Sox, Peckinpaugh
returned to managing.

When I was a kid growing up on Hough Avenue in Cleveland, I lived right across the street from Napoleon Lajoie. I
used to sit out in front of my house just to watch him come home.
He was my idol. I might even have become an infielder because
he was, though he was a second baseman and I was a shortstop.

Sure I played ball when I was a kid. There were a lot of vacant
lots around in those days, and that's all you need to produce
ballplayers. We had a gang of kids, and we'd play every day after
school and keep playing until either it got dark or we'd lost the
ball. It wasn't a real ball either, just a lot of stuffings that we
bound together and wrapped tape over.

When I got further along, I played on the semipro teams. One
day a scout from the Cleveland ball club came over during a game
and asked me if I'd like to sign up to play professional ball. I
wanted to play, all right, but wasn't too sure what I should do. You
see, in those days professional ballplayers didn't have very good

reputations; people thought they just hung around barrooms all the time and played baseball as an excuse for not working.

So I talked it over with my old high school principal, and he said he didn't see anything wrong with the idea if I could make good in three years. He said I shouldn't spend more than three years in the minor leagues. Well, I made it to the top in two years.

That was in 1909. In 1910 I was playing with the Indians. Can you believe that? I played the last fifteen games or so after having been farmed out to New Haven. New Haven's season closed Labor Day, and that's when the Indians brought me up to finish the season. I'll say it was a thrill. But the biggest thrill was playing alongside Nap Lajoie, my boyhood idol.

Lajoie was one of the greatest. Fine fellow, too. Big, good-hearted Frenchman. During the game sometimes I couldn't help but glance over at him from shortstop, just like I was still a kid sitting up in the stands—that same kind of feeling. He was a graceful fielder, could pick up anything, and of course the glove that he wore—the gloves that we all wore back then—was little more than the glove you wear today when you're driving a car. He was a line-drive hitter; he'd send that ball all over the lot like rifle shots.

Addie Joss was on that team too. It was his last year. He died the next spring; I think he was around thirty years old. He was a great pitcher, that fellow. He would turn his back toward the batter as he wound up, hiding the ball all the while, and then whip around and fire it in. He threw the good fastball and the good curve. Very tough to hit.

I never batted against Joss, but I did against Smoky Joe Wood, Walter Johnson, and Lefty Grove, and I managed Bob Feller in his heyday. Who was the fastest? That's the million-dollar question, isn't it? I would say Walter Johnson. Now Bobby was fast all right, but he had that great big curveball to go along with it. Walter only threw a fastball. No curve to speak of. When he threw his curve, he'd come up over his head with it and everybody in the ball park knew what was coming—otherwise he always fired that thing in sidearm. But he was fast—just pure speed—and that ball was alive. I'll tell you another thing about his ball—you

Ed Walsh, left, *and Addie Joss in 1908*

could hear it go by you with a *swish!* I never heard that from anybody else. And you know, my first game in the major leagues was against Washington, and Walter was pitching. He was the guy I broke in against. Can you imagine that! A year before I was in high school, and now here's Walter Johnson staring down at me. I fouled out twice and was tickled to death for it.

Joe Jackson was on that Cleveland team too. He was a great hitter, one of the best I ever saw in my life. He used a big black bat and swung it right from the end, and he could hit a ball further than anybody, until the Babe came along.

Jackson couldn't read or write, you know. He was a big, likable country boy from South Carolina. We'd go in for breakfast and the waitress would hand him a menu. Well, he knew they always had ham and eggs and that's what he would order. But we'd go in for dinner and if the waitress went to him first for his order, he'd say, "I haven't made up my mind yet. See what they want." Then he'd listen to what the rest of us were ordering and he'd pick out something we said. That's how he got by in the dining room.

It was a pity what happened to him, getting mixed up in that World Series scandal. That was in 1919. You know, in 1920, when I was with the Yankees, we finished three games out of first place, and I'll never know whether we should have won it or not. The White Sox—they call that team the Black Sox today, don't they?— were monkeying around so much during the year you could never be sure. The scandal didn't come full bloom until near the end of the season. We'd play them one series and they would look terrible; we'd play them the next time and they'd look like the best club in the world. That's the way they set themselves up that year.

I remember one time we went into Chicago and little Nemo Leibold came up to me. He was on the White Sox but wasn't part of the shenanigans, but he smelled a mouse.

"Listen," he said, "something screwy is going on here. I don't know what it is, but it's something screwy all right. You guys bear down and you ought to take all four games."

You just never knew when they were going to go out there and beat your brains out or roll over and play dead. Somebody was betting on those games, that's a cinch. When they wanted to play, you had a hard time beating them, that's how good they were.

Eight of them were kicked out of baseball. Let's see, there was Happy Felsch, Buck Weaver, Chick Gandil, Joe Jackson, Eddie Cicotte, Swede Risberg, Fred McMullin, and Lefty Williams. I knew them all. Gee, I haven't thought of them for a long time. They're all dead now, I believe. That Happy Felsch was a hell of a ballplayer. And Eddie Cicotte was some pitcher. He had one of those phony pitches, a shine ball.

You know, when they barred the spitball, it wasn't the spitball exactly they wanted to bar. They wanted to get rid of all those phony pitches. All of those pitches were in the disguise of the

Walter Johnson

Smoky Joe Wood

Lefty Grove

"Who was the fastest? That's the million-dollar question, isn't it?"

Joe DiMaggio and Bob Feller

spitter. You see, the pitchers went to their mouths, but then they might throw you a shine ball or a mud ball or an emery ball. Russell Ford, the old Yankee pitcher, was the originator of the emery ball. His own teammates didn't know what he was throwing. They thought it was a spitter. But it was an emery ball. He'd rough up the cover and get it to sail. He had a hole in his glove and under it was a piece of emery paper. Then he wore a ring on his finger with a piece of emery paper wrapped around it. The ring was on a rubber band, and when he pulled it off, it went up his sleeve. Nobody knew what he'd been doing until he went out of the league, and then his catcher, big Ed Sweeney, told us. Sweeney was the only one who'd known.

So, as I understand it, the only way they could stop them fooling with that baseball was to bar the spitter, not let the pitcher go to his mouth. If a pitcher didn't go to his mouth and still threw one of those freak pitches, the umpire would know damn well that guy was doctoring the ball. That's how they stopped it.

You know, when I first came to the big leagues they never threw a ball out of the game. It could be black as ink and the cover could be soft, but they still kept it in. The only time a ball went out of play was when it was fouled into the stands. Many a time if I was leading off an inning and there was a ball that had been in the game two or three innings, it was my job to try and foul it into the stands to get rid of it. Today, if there's a spot on the ball, they holler and throw it right out.

Cobb was the greatest of all, in my book. In addition to everything else, he was a smart ballplayer. He never had one spot where he stood in the batter's box. He stood in different places for different pitchers, according to what they had and how they pitched him. I never saw another hitter do that. They have one spot and that's it. I'll tell you, they never threw at Cobb very much. If they did, he'd step out and warn them. "Don't do that again," he'd say. And if they did, he would drag a bunt down to first, and if the pitcher covered, Ty would knock him for a loop. So they seldom threw at him. He was a tough monkey, that guy. A real tough monkey. He played a slashing game out there. You could be behind ten runs, and he'd still come into second base and bat you around.

Nobody liked Cobb, including his own teammates. He was sort of a loner. Didn't get along with anybody. And I can tell you how deep those feelings went. We were in New York for an old-timers game once. A group of us were sitting around a table. Cobb wanted to buy the boys a drink, but they wouldn't take one from him.

I can tell you another story about how people felt about Cobb. This happened in 1910, my first year up. We were finishing out the season with a doubleheader in St. Louis. The Chalmers automobile people were giving away a car to the leading hitter in the league. Cobb and Nap Lajoie had been battling for the title all year. On that last day Cobb was hitting .385 and Lajoie was seven or eight points behind him. Cobb took himself out of the lineup that last day, so it meant Nap had to get something like eight hits in the doubleheader to catch him and win that car.

Here's how much they disliked Cobb: The manager of the Browns, Jack O'Connor, told his third baseman to play way back on the grass for Lajoie. The first time up Nap socked a triple, but after that he noticed where the third baseman was playing him. So he began dropping down bunts and beating them out. He went four for four in the first game. We all knew what was going on, but it was none of our business. Lajoie didn't say anything. If they wanted to give him base hits, he would take them.

The second game was the same thing—Nap got four for four again and I think three of them were bunts. He went eight for eight in the doubleheader and everybody figured he'd won the title. But when it was all over and the statistics came out, he was still a fraction of a point behind Cobb. When word got around what had happened, Ban Johnson, who was president of the American League, saw to it that Jack O'Connor lost his job.

In 1913 they traded me to the Yankees. You see, they had Ray Chapman coming along, and he had a tremendous amount of promise. And of course he turned out to be a wonderful ballplayer. You know, I was at shortstop for the Yankees when Ray got hit

Nap Lajoie
"He was my idol."

in the head with a pitched ball and was killed. That was in 1920. Carl Mays was the pitcher, and I'd say that pitch was almost a strike. Chapman crowded the plate more than anybody in the league; in fact he hit with his head practically in the strike zone. What happened was at the last second he turned his head and got hit right in back of the ear. The ball hit so solidly that it went out toward third base in fair ground, and Mays fielded it and threw it to first base—he couldn't tell from the sound whether it had hit the bat or not. That's how hard Chapman got smacked.

I managed the Yankees the last few weeks of the season in 1914. I was only twenty-three years old then, so I guess I'm the youngest man ever to manage a big league club. Sometimes I look at some of these twenty-three-year old kids today, and I have to laugh and think to myself, "Gee, when I was that age, I was managing the New York Yankees."

Frank Chance was the manager; he'd had a hassle with the owners and quit. He came to me and said, "I've recommended they put you in charge of the club the rest of the season." They went along with Frank's recommendation and I ran the club for those few weeks, got my first experience managing, and picked up a few extra bucks in the bargain.

Frank was a good manager and got along okay with the players. He'd managed the Cubs earlier and had some great years there, winning a few pennants. They had some wonderful ball clubs in Chicago. Tinker to Evers to Chance. Three-Finger Brown. Johnny Kling. I don't recall if Frank talked about those teams very much. It's getting to be a long while back. That's sixty years ago!

Of course, the Yankees at that time were what we used to call a joy club. Lots of joy and lots of losing. Nobody thought we could win and most of the time we didn't. But it didn't seem to bother the boys too much. They would start singing songs in the infield right in the middle of a game. There wasn't much managing to do outside of selecting the starting pitcher and hoping we didn't get beat too badly.

I don't think there was a great deal of difference in the game then as compared to today. The home run is the biggest difference, I'd say. Today pretty near anybody in the lineup can hit the ball out of the park. In my day, before they started feeding that baseball Wheaties, you had two or three fellows who could do that, and that was all.

I think today the manager has a little tougher job than when I was there because, I would guess, at least, a third of the players that are in the major leagues today should not be there. They should still be playing minor league ball. But the scarcity of players makes it necessary to bring these kids up when they show signs of anything at all. Watching them out there now and then, I see them making a lot of mistakes that they should be making in

Ray Chapman
"What happened was at the last
second he turned his head and got
hit right in back of the ear."

the minor leagues. You see, back when I was playing and managing, there were only sixteen big league clubs and barely enough players to fill a roster. Today you've got twenty-four clubs. Where are you going to get that many players from? So I would say a manager today has a lot more on his hands because he has so many inexperienced players.

When I broke in, a rookie had a hard time of it. You didn't get much cooperation from anybody because they didn't want you coming along and taking their jobs. That's the way it was most of the time. Anyway, they only had one coach on a club, and he generally had enough to do without bothering with a rookie. They had only one umpire, too. He worked in back of the plate until a man got on first, then he went in back of the pitcher and called balls and strikes from there. Even so, he couldn't watch everything. There was a lot of cheating in a ball game then; the smart runners were chopping off three or four feet when they went around second base on their way to third.

Hal Chase was first baseman when I joined the Yankees. Prince Hal. He later was suspected of betting on games. I was just a kid breaking in, and Hal Chase had the reputation of being the greatest fielding first baseman of all time. I remember a few times I threw a ball over to first base, and it went by him to the stands and a couple of runs scored. It really surprised me. I'd stand there looking, sighting the flight of that ball in my mind, and I'd think, "Geez, that throw wasn't that bad." Then I'd tell myself that he was the greatest there was, so maybe the throw was bad. Then later on when he got the smelly reputation, it came back to me, and I said, "Oh-oh." What he was doing, you see, was tangling up his feet and then making a fancy dive after the ball, making it look like it was a wild throw.

I don't know if anybody suspected anything at the time, but I do know they got rid of him later in the season.

Ballplayers weren't the celebrities then that they came to be later on, with a few exceptions of course, like Cobb and Walter Johnson. But the Babe changed that. He changed everything, that guy. So many, many people became interested in baseball because of him. Why, they would be drawing 1,500 a game in St. Louis. We'd go in there with the Babe and they'd be all over the ball park; there would be mounted policemen riding the crowd back. Thousands and thousands of people coming out to see that one guy. Whatever the owners paid him, it wasn't enough—it couldn't be enough.

Miller Huggins took over the Yankees in 1918, and then they got Ruth from Boston and the Yankees began to move. Huggins was a fine manager, one of the best I ever played for. He understood men, and he got along all right with everybody but the Babe. Babe was going to throw him off the train one night coming back from Boston. Huggins hadn't handled the pitching the way Mr. Ruth thought it should have been handled. So Babe had a few drinks and then went looking for Hug with the intention of throwing him off the train. He meant it, too. He was storming around looking for Hug. Finally three of us wrestled him down to the floor and held him there until he simmered down.

I had two very good years with the Yankees in 1920 and '21, but after the '21 season I was traded to Washington. I can tell you just how that happened to come about. Babe and Huggins were feuding all the time, and then Babe started openly announcing that they should get rid of Huggins and appoint me manager. Well, it turned out just the opposite—they got rid of me and kept Huggins. Babe thought he was doing me a favor, I guess, but it didn't work out that way.

I'll tell you what upset me about that trade. I was home trimming the Christmas tree when the phone rang. I picked it up and there was a reporter on the other end of the line.

"Hey," he said, "what do you think of the trade?"

"What trade do you mean?" I asked.

"Oh," he said, "didn't you hear? You've been traded to Boston."

It was a three-way deal, you see. I went from New York to Boston to Washington in one big swap. But that's the way I learned about it—from a reporter calling me up.

Bucky Harris took over the Washington club in 1924, and we won two pennants under Bucky, in '24 and '25. He was a tough, aggressive ballplayer, but I wouldn't call him a hard-driving manager. As far as I'm concerned, that kind of manager seldom made good. You take Rogers Hornsby. He was made manager of the Cardinals. So what does he do? He makes rules for the clubhouse that nobody likes. You had to check in by the clock. No smoking in the clubhouse, no eating, no card-playing. The players were unhappy, which is the last thing you want. I don't say you should cater to them, but for heaven's sake, you don't want to antagonize them.

I've often said that a bad manager can ruin a good ball club. But you put an ordinary manager in charge of a good club and they're going to win. Don't saddle them with too many rules; don't make them unhappy. That's the secret. Managing might make the difference of one or two games over the whole season. The third-base coach probably has more to say about winning or losing a ball game than the manager. He's the one who's got to send those runners in, or not send them. His good judgment can be crucial.

People talk about a good manager. Well, what's a good manager? It's somebody who can get the most out of his players. Strategy? There's nothing mysterious about that, is there? Geez,

ROGER PECKINPAUGH

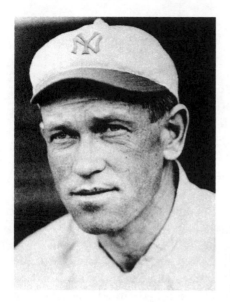

Hal Chase
*"I remember a few times I threw
a ball over to first base and it
went by him to the stands and a
couple of runs scored."*

don't I know what you're going to do, and don't you know what I'm going to do? I'm talking about most of the time. Give a manager those old Yankee teams like McCarthy and Stengel had, and it's hard for him to make a mistake. The ability is all there. The players can do practically anything the manager asks them to do. It's got to turn out right. All you have to remember is not to do anything to make them hate your guts.

We won the Series against the Giants in '24, then lost it the next year to Pittsburgh. That was the Series where Sam Rice made his great catch on a ball hit by Earl Smith. Boy, I'll never forget that one. Sam dove into the bleachers for the ball, just left his feet and disappeared with the ball in his glove, and when he came out, he still had it. There was a loud argument about it, the Pirates claiming he'd lost the ball in the bleachers and then picked it up again. That controversy went on for a long time. Then just before Sam died, he said he'd written a letter to be opened after his death which would tell the truth about that catch. Well, after he died, that letter was opened and in it Sam said that it had been a fair catch all the way. Under those circumstances, a man talking practically from his deathbed, you've got to believe him. I'll tell you, it was a whale of a catch.

Did I ever want to become a big league manager? Well, I hadn't thought about it too much, to tell you the truth. I was finishing out my playing career with the White Sox in 1927, which was around the time the Cleveland ball club was purchased by Alva Bradley and his associates. He hired Billy Evans as the general manager and me as field manager. I was from Cleveland and so was Billy, which made it nice.

I took over in 1928. Managing was all new to me, of course, but I'd had seventeen years' experience under some pretty good managers and had an idea of what it was all about.

That first year I was there Billy Evans made a trip out to the Coast League to look at an outfielder named Roy Johnson. When Billy got there, he learned that Johnson had already been sold to Detroit. But in talking with the players out there, he kept hearing that the best ballplayer in the league was a fellow named Earl Averill. So he wound up buying Averill, who became one of the all-time Cleveland greats. Then we got Dick Porter, and we had Eddie Morgan and Johnny Hodapp and Joe and Luke Sewell. We had plenty of hitting but were a little shy on the good pitching. We did have Mel Harder and Willis Hudlin and Wes Ferrell, but it wasn't enough. Wes was one of the best but very temperamental. He'd get mad at himself if anybody got a base hit off of him, and if they got two in a row, he was liable to fly right off the top.

But it was a tough time to be in that league. We were up against two great ball clubs. On the one hand you had Connie Mack's Athletics, with Foxx, Simmons, Grove, Cochrane. And on the other hand there were the Yankees, with Ruth, Gehrig, Lazzeri, Dickey, Combs, and those fellows. It was discouraging. You knew you were doomed the day the season opened, with those two monsters in the league.

I was let out of the job in the middle of the season in 1933. I got in Dutch with the newspapers, which is very easy to do if you don't keep your mouth shut. Some of the Cleveland writers got on me and just rode me unmercifully. I remember a story Ed Bang had. We got beat 1–0 one day. The next day Bang had a big story about the game. The other team had got a man on and they bunted him down and that led to the winning run. Apparently somewhere along the line I'd had a man on, and Bang thought I should have bunted him down. So he wrote that the other manager was not afraid to have his men sacrifice, and then he went on to give me hell.

I went up to the team office and checked the records, just for the hell of it. Well, I found out that the Cleveland club was leading the league by far in sacrifice hits. I cut that out and went up to the paper the next morning to see Bang.

"Ed," I said, "that story you wrote about me—did you ever look up to see what you're writing about?"

"Why?" he said. "What's wrong?"

"Take a look at this," I said and showed him the records.

He looked at the figures and said, "That's very interesting."

"You're goddamned right that's interesting," I said.

He was apologetic. Or chagrined—I think that's the better word for it. "What do you want me to do?" he asked.

"It's too late to do anything," I said. "The fans have got the other story fixed in their heads now. Anytime I don't bunt, they're going to give me hell." Which they did.

That's how some of these things get started—one guy not knowing the figures and everybody else believing what he writes.

How do you get a man out of a slump? There's no set way, really. Very often those slumps are mental. A fellow gets it into his head that he's not going to hit the ball, and consequently he doesn't hit it. What happens is you go up to the plate and look around and all you see are fielders. There's no room for you to hit it anyplace. I'll tell you what happened one time with Averill. He was having tough going, which was unusual for him. One day somebody gave me a bat that was a little burned. It had been given some kind of special heat treatment. I looked at that bat and had an idea. I brought it over to Averill.

"Look, Earl," I said, speaking in a very confidential way. "See

Frank Chance

what I have here. I want you to try this bat out. But just once. I
don't want to take a chance on you breaking it; otherwise we'll
both be in the soup. And for heaven's sake, don't tell any of the
other boys about it."

So he goes up to the plate with that bat and *whack!* A line shot
for a base hit. He came back to the bench later all smiles.

"Remember," I said. "Not a word to anyone about it."

You know, that snapped him out of it and he started hitting like
hell. What kind of bat was it? Just an ordinary bat that somebody
had put in an oven and burned a little. No different from any

other bat, except that Earl thought it was different. You see, that slump had become a mental thing with him, and all he needed to break out of it was some oddball notion.

You can have slumps in the field, too, you know. In 1925 I had that lousy Series against Pittsburgh. I made eight errors, though some of them were stinko calls by the scorer. And if you don't think ballplayers have long and stubborn memories, listen to this. Some of those calls were on balls hit by Max Carey. Well, whenever I run into Max in Florida, he still raises the devil about them, claiming they should have been base hits.

"For goodness sakes, Max," I tell him, "that's fifty years ago."

"All the same," he says, "they should have been base hits."

I still hold that darned record of eight errors by a shortstop in a World Series. But up to that time, as I understand it, Honus Wagner had the record with six. So I tell people that I once broke one of Honus Wagner's records, but I don't tell them what it was!

12

MAYO SMITH

EDWARD MAYO SMITH
Born: January 15, 1915, New London, Missouri
Managerial career: Philadelphia Phillies, 1955–58; Cincinnati Reds, 1959; Detroit Tigers, 1967–70

After losing the pennant to the Red Sox on the last day of the 1967 season, Mayo Smith led his Tigers the next year to the pennant and World Championship. Smith spent many years in the minor leagues as a player and as a manager and one year, 1945, in the big leagues with the Philadelphia Athletics, where he played for Connie Mack.

In 1967, my first year managing the Tigers, we lost the pennant to the Red Sox on the last day of the season. That made for an awfully long winter. You couldn't help thinking from time to time of that one thing you might have done to turn a ball game around, or that one thing you shouldn't have done.

Sometimes a tough loss like that can take you right out of the race the next year. I was determined not to let that happen, so when spring training came around, I changed the format a little. The pattern is to bring the pitchers and catchers down a week or so ahead of the rest of the club. Well, I decided to bring everybody down at the same time and get us all started off together. The theme was to generate that motivation just a little more, to start right off from scratch getting each and every man to believe that all he had to do was play just a little harder and we'd win it.

So we started off on a very positive note and went on to win the pennant fairly easily, clinching it sometime around the middle of September.

That was the year Denny McLain won 31 games and lost only six. He was as fine a pitcher that season as I've ever seen. Denny possessed great pitching know-how. He seemed to have a sixth sense out there. It was almost as if he always knew what the batter was thinking.

It wasn't publicized, but all during the '68 season he was getting cortisone shots in his arm. He had a type of tendonitis, and they had to keep shooting this stuff in. The doctors told me the cortisone would help him for only so long and then it was going to be rough on Denny. He came back the next year and won 24 ball games for me, but from then on it was downhill. The tendonitis got worse and worse and he just couldn't throw the ball. It was heartbreaking to see what was happening. A lot of people thought his suspension and forced layoff had something to do with his loss of effectiveness, but it didn't.

Denny was sort of a Peck's bad boy. He'd be hitting fungoes and would start putting them in the stands so the kids could get baseballs. I would have to remind him those balls cost money and that if he wanted the kids to have them, he could buy a few dozen and hand them out. So we got that stopped.

Another time he's pitching against Chicago. It's a hot, hot day. Denny doesn't have his good stuff, but going into the eighth inning he's beating them by a run. This, by the way, is the test of great pitchers—if they can still win with less than their best stuff. We come into the top of the ninth, there's one man out and Denny is up. I tell him to take three strikes and come back and sit down. I don't want him to move that bat. Everybody on the bench heard me tell him that. He walks up there and on the second pitch hits a ground ball to the shortstop, and he has to run. He comes back to the bench and the sweat is pouring off of him. I don't say anything.

He goes out there in the ninth inning and gets in trouble. I've got to go and get him. The relief pitcher comes in and holds them and we win it by the one run. I go into the clubhouse and tell the

Denny McLain
"He seemed to have a sixth sense out there."

clubhouse man I want to see McLain. A minute later Denny sticks his head in.

"You want to see me?"

"Yeah," I said. "That little episode cost you two hundred."

"What?" he yells.

"What did I tell you about going up there and taking three strikes?"

"I didn't think you were serious," he says.

"You'll see how serious I was when that two hundred comes out," I said.

That's the kind of guy he was. But a top competitor—and if he hadn't come up with that arm problem, there's no telling to what heights he would have gone.

Just before the Series started, I did something that a lot of people thought was very daring—I moved my center fielder, Mickey Stanley, in to play shortstop. I did this even though Mickey had virtually no experience anywhere but in the outfield. Why did I do that? Well, in the course of the season I had Willie Horton in left field, Al Kaline in right, and Jim Northrup and Stanley alternating in center. Then Kaline got hit on the hand by a pitched ball and was out for about five weeks. So the outfield had to become fixed—Horton in left, Stanley in center, Northrup in right. And all three of them started playing great ball, both in the field and up at bat. So when Kaline came back to where he could play, the best I could do was alternate him with Norm Cash at first base. I couldn't take any of those other fellows out because they'd played too well.

Then it came down to where I saw we were going to win the pennant, and I had to start thinking about the World Series. Now, Al Kaline was a great, great ballplayer; he'd been in the big leagues for many years and had never played in a World Series. He deserved to be in there, I wanted him in there, and we needed him in there. The problem was how to get him into the lineup. So I called him into my office.

"Al," I said, "I'll tell you what. I'm going to do everything I can to get you into the Series. I've got an idea, but I've got to talk to another guy to see if he'll be agreeable to making a move."

"Mayo," he said, "anything you want to do is fine with me."

Now I call in Mickey Stanley. He's a great outfielder. But before a game you never saw him out there shagging balls; he was always in the infield taking ground balls. He used to kid around a lot, telling the guys what a great infielder he could be. And maybe so. I'd watched him out there. He had good hands, a good arm. So I called him in.

"Say," I said, "you're always popping off to me how you can play shortstop, second base, third base. Well, how would you like to play shortstop?"

He didn't know what the devil I was getting at.

"Well, look," I said, "if you can play shortstop, I can put Kaline in the outfield when we go into the Series. I think our ball club would be better offensively than it's ever been."

None of this was to take anything away from our regular shortstop Ray Oyler, who was a great defensive ballplayer, though a bit weak at the plate. What I was interested in doing was getting Al Kaline into the World Series.

Mickey's got an impish grin anyway, and he gave me that grin and said, "When do I start?"

I didn't want anybody to know what I was planning, so what I did was bring Mickey and my second baseman, Dick McAuliffe, out to the ball park early each day before anybody was around. And they worked out around second base, very much in earnest.

Then I started Mickey in a game at short, against Baltimore. This is after the pennant's been clinched. I'll never forget that game. The leadoff man gets on and don't you know that the next ball is hit slowly to McAuliffe. He feeds it to Stanley, who has no chance in the world for the double play but throws it anyway—up into the stands.

But I didn't get discouraged and neither did Mickey. I knew these mistakes were going to happen, and I kept them working at it.

Finally I called McAuliffe in and said, "Hey, what do you think? Can he do the job?"

"Mayo," he said, "you've got to be kidding."

"Well," I said, "let's keep working."

Mayo Smith

They kept at it and Mickey kept getting better. By the time the Series opened, I felt confident enough to go ahead with it. I'll never forget when they announced the lineup for that first game against the Cardinals. Pee Wee Reese came to me and said, "Mayo, you're not serious, are you? You're not going to do it."

"The hell I'm not," I said.

So the game started and the best thing that could possibly have happened, happened. First man up for the Cardinals is Lou Brock. Well, he hit the nicest ground ball to Stanley, who threw him out. From then on Mickey made some nice plays. But getting that very first ball hit to him was just what I'd been hoping for.

So that worked out all right for us. Otherwise things weren't going so well. Bob Gibson shut us out in the first game and struck out 17, which set a new World Series record.

The Cardinals won three of the first four games and things were looking pretty bleak for us. In fact, going into the bottom of the seventh inning in the fifth game, we were losing 3–2. We're just three innings away from being out of it completely. Mickey Lolich was coming to bat for us and I let him hit for himself. Why? Well, he was pitching a very strong game and I wanted to keep him in there. But before I get into that, I have to go back to something else, something that occurred in the fifth inning that was to prove to be the key play. With one out Brock doubled. Then Julian Javier singled to left and Brock tried to score. It took two good plays to get him—a strong throw from Horton and a great job of blocking the plate by Bill Freehan. Also there was a sharp piece of umpiring by Doug Harvey. It was a close play. He was right on top of it, he took his time, and he called it correctly—the replays verified that later.

Now, if that run had scored and I'd been down two runs in the bottom of the seventh, then I've got to pinch-hit for Lolich. But I figured I've got a couple more innings to get a run, and I want to keep my good pitcher in there. So what does Lolich do? Fortunately he bloops a ball into right field for a hit. That starts the inning and we end up scoring three runs and win it, 5–3, with Lolich pitching good ball all the way. And do you know who got the base hit that drove in the fourth and fifth runs? Mr. Al Kaline.

Mickey Lolich pitching in the 1968 World Series

We were still down, three games to two. Going into game six, it looked like I might be stuck for a pitcher. You see, McLain's arm was bothering him. The Cardinals had beat him twice and Denny just didn't have it. In the fourth game his arm was hurting so bad he could barely get the ball up to the plate. But he came to me after that game and said, "Mayo, don't count me out. I'm going to the hospital for a shot." All right, I wasn't counting him out, but I certainly wasn't counting him in.

We had an off-day after the fifth game and were working out. McLain was throwing under the stands. I'm on the field surrounded by reporters wanting to know who I'm going to pitch in the sixth game. They're all figuring McLain is out.

"I'm not sure," I'm saying. "Maybe Earl Wilson."

Just then McLain comes walking by and winks at me. Doesn't say anything, just keeps on going. I watched him go. I didn't say anything to the reporters, but I thought to myself, "By God, there's my pitcher."

Sure enough, he went out the next day and beat them. We made it easy for him by getting 10 runs in the third inning and clobbered them 13–1.

That set up the seventh game, and I brought Lolich back with two days' rest. No, there was never any question in my mind that he would work that game. I had Johnny Sain, my pitching coach, talk to him, and Johnny came to me and said that Mickey felt all right, that he could pitch. He had already given me two complete games in the Series, and the last one, two days ago, had been a rough one for him; he'd thrown a lot of pitches. His arm was still a little tired, naturally, but you know, you find sometimes with pitchers that when their arms are a little tired, the ball moves better. I don't know if that was the case with Mickey, but I do know his ball sank all through the game. He had tremendous stuff. I didn't have to ask him if he was getting tired because I could see that movement on the ball.

Lolich hooked up with Gibson and they went into the seventh inning with a scoreless game. Then we got a break. Two men on and Northrup hit a shot out to Curt Flood in center. Curt took one step in, then saw it was going over his head and it was too late for him to get back. Two runs came in and we went on from there and won it, 4–1.

It was a nice comeback for us after having been down three games to one. It sure took the sting out of last year's near-miss.

Billy Herman in 1947

240

13

BILLY HERMAN

WILLIAM JENNINGS BRYAN HERMAN
Born: July 7, 1909, New Albany, Indiana
Managerial career: Pittsburgh Pirates, 1947; Boston Red Sox,
 1965–66

One of the greatest second basemen of all time, Hall of
Famer Billy Herman has spent nearly fifty years in baseball
as player, coach, manager, and scout. Remembered as one of
the most intelligent ballplayers of his era, Herman managed
in both the National and American Leagues.

The last few years I played I kind of had an idea I'd get a
managing job. It had been rumored around. That happens
with certain players, and I think I had that label. In fact, I always
suspected that the reason Jimmie Wilson traded me from the
Cubs to the Dodgers in 1941 was because he thought the Cubs
might be thinking of me as a potential manager. Nobody on the
Cubs ever said anything to me about it, but that's what I always
thought.

In 1946 I was traded from the Dodgers to the Boston Braves,
where I played for Billy Southworth. Southworth was a really
sound baseball technician and a fine gentleman, and we got along
great. A few weeks before the close of the season, he came to me
and asked if I was interested in managing. I told him I was.

"Well," he said, "I think you're going to manage the Pittsburgh
club next year."

Not long after, he sat down next to me on the bench toward the
end of a ball game and said, "As soon as this game is over, you get
dressed and go over to the Kenmore Hotel." He gave me a room

number and told me to go on up to that room. Frank McKinney, who had just bought the Pirates, and several other people were going to have a meeting, and they wanted me there.

So after the game I went to the Kenmore and went up to that room. McKinney was there and so was Lou Perini, who owned the Braves, and a few other men. I shook hands with everybody and sat down, and the next thing I know they're trying to negotiate a deal to get me to Pittsburgh to manage.

I guess you'd call that a unique experience, wouldn't you? I'm probably the only player in history to sit in on his own deal. McKinney was really determined to have me manage his ball club the next season, and they started negotiating to get me from Boston to Pittsburgh. Various deals were discussed back and forth, and meanwhile I'm just sitting there, still a player with the Boston Braves.

Finally they wrote a deal on paper. It was me and a few other players, none of whom had great stature, for Bob Elliott and another player. McKinney handed me the piece of paper and asked me what I thought of the deal. Now, I knew I was going to be the manager of the Pirates, and Bob Elliott was probably the best ballplayer they had at that moment.

"Mr. McKinney," I said, "that's a terrible deal."

"You think it is?" he asked.

"I sure do," I said. "I'm over the hill as a player, and these other fellows you're getting aren't going to help you very much. You can't give up Bob Elliott for us."

He thought it over for a few moments, and then said, "Well, I don't care. I want you to manage the ball club, so that's the deal."

And that was the deal.

Talk about a guy being in a peculiar situation. I wanted to manage the Pirates, and the minute I get the job, I lose Bob Elliott. But McKinney had the last word, of course, and that was what he wanted. I don't know why he was so intent on getting me—I'd never had any experience managing.

You know who was Most Valuable Player in the league the next year, don't you? Bob Elliott.

But I'll tell you something now. I was not a good manager with
Pittsburgh. In fact, I was terrible. I was stupid. I don't mean
about running the ball game. I could run the ball game as well as
anybody. But I was terrible with the men. I was too easy with
them, letting them have too much latitude. All I ever asked of
them was to play hard on the field, which they did. Every man
gave me a hundred percent. But I wanted to treat my players the
way I'd always wanted to be treated, and it didn't work.

When I played for Billy Southworth, I didn't even have any
signs. I played the way I wanted to play. I bunted when I wanted
to, I hit-and-run when I wanted to. He told me when I first joined
the club, "Hell, you know just as much about baseball as I do.

Billy Southworth and teammates at the 1926 World Series
Left to right: *Taylor Douthit, Southworth, Les Bell, Jim Bottomley,*
Chick Hafey, Bob O'Farrell

You know when you should bunt, when you should take a pitch, when you should hit. You're on your own."

Southworth trusted me, you see. He'd seen me play for years, and he trusted my judgment. Then when I was managing Pittsburgh, I got the screwy idea that everybody knew how to play. We had signs, of course, and I ran the game, but at the same time I wanted the players to have certain liberties out there because that was the way *I* had played best. So I gave them a lot of leeway on the field. But I realized later that you just have to run it yourself, for better or for worse.

I gave them the same leeway off the field as well, and that was another mistake. A bigger mistake. Some of those boys moved pretty fast, and I let them get away with it. You have to exert discipline, there's no two ways about it. You always have a few on every club who are going to cause problems no matter what. If you let them have their head and do what they want to do, by the end of the season you've only got a few who are behaving themselves. It's contagious. They see a guy going out and having fifteen or twenty beers and not getting as much sleep as he should, and they say, "Well, he's not playing so bad. I guess I'll try that." The first thing you know the whole club is out of hand. That's exactly what happened.

When it was announced I was taking over the Pirates, a few guys said to me, "Well, you've got to change now. It's going to be different." They were right, but I didn't think so at the time. Any person who's managing for the first time has to change. It's an altogether different situation for you on a ball club. For years you were friendly with everybody and were one of the boys. Suddenly that's changed. You're not one of the boys anymore—you're the boss. But I was determined not to change, and that's where I was wrong. I had some great friends on that team, like Kirby Higbe, and we buddied together a lot. I found out later that some of the other players resented it. I was naive about the psychology of a ball club. I shouldn't have been, but I was.

Once a ball club gets out of hand, it's too late to put on the brakes. By mid-season I could see what was happening and I got sore and tried to crack down, but by that time the front office had lost confidence in me, and I wasn't getting the cooperation I needed. They were probably thinking, "Well, this guy has let the team get out of hand. We'll be making a change anyway, so let it go." So when I did try to reverse the trend, there wasn't any backing from the front office. But I'm not blaming anybody for what happened. It was my fault. I should have taken charge from the beginning, made my rules, and seen that they were enforced.

I'd played for a lot of managers, of course, and each one was a different personality. Rogers Hornsby, Charlie Grimm, Leo Durocher, Southworth.

I broke in with the Cubs under Hornsby in 1931. He ignored me completely, and I figured it was because I was a rookie. But then I saw he ignored everybody. He was a very cold man. He would stare at you with the coldest eyes I ever saw. If you did something wrong, he'd jump all over you. He was a perfectionist and had a very low tolerance for mistakes. He was one of the greatest hitters that ever lived—maybe the greatest—but he never talked hitting with us. He just expected you to go up there and do it. In fact, in those days nobody taught you much of anything. You usually spent four or five years in the minor leagues, and when you came up, they expected you to know how to play ball. And if you couldn't, back you went. The best way to learn was from other players, sometimes on another team. You'd watch them, ask them questions. There was very little instruction given.

Hornsby tried to have discipline on the club, but he had some bad actors and couldn't control them—fellows like Pat Malone and Hack Wilson. They'd get drunk and get into fights and sometimes end up tossed into jail someplace. He'd fine them, but it didn't make any difference. There are some guys you just can't stop. I always believed in getting rid of guys like that, no matter how talented they are, because over the long haul they're not going to do the club any good.

Hornsby didn't smoke, didn't drink. And he wouldn't go to the movies or even read a newspaper because he said it was bad for the eyes. He wouldn't let you eat in the clubhouse, not even between games of a doubleheader. Couldn't even have a soft drink. Can you imagine a manager today trying to get away with rules like that in the clubhouse? I don't know what would happen. But Hornsby got away with it. He was the boss and there was nothing we could do about it. I guess there was greater respect for authority in those days, be it right or wrong.

I'll tell you a funny thing about Hornsby though. He was against smoking and drinking, but he did have a pinball machine in the clubhouse. He was a great gambler and he'd gamble against the boys on that pinball machine. So you couldn't say that in being against smoking and drinking, Hornsby was being moralistic, since he was such a heavy gambler. It was a case of a manager imposing his own prejudices on the players, and I think a lot of managers are like that. Hell, I guess a lot of people are like that, period.

Charlie Grimm followed Hornsby with the Cubs, and he did things pretty much the way I later did with Pittsburgh. He just let everybody go their way—no rules, no curfew. He ran the game on the field, of course, but away from it he was just a happy-go-lucky guy. He'd sing and dance in the clubhouse and play his banjo. One of the boys. And yet it all worked for him; we had winning teams with Charlie.

When I was with the Cubs, our best pitcher was Lon Warneke. He was the natural leader of the pitchers. Well, that son of a gun used to sit on the bench with a baseball during a game and he would keep spinning it, spinning it, spinning it. He could do that by the hour, just sit there and spin that ball. Well, he's the best pitcher on the team and he's always working on that rotation. The other pitchers saw that and fell in line; they all began looking for little things to do to improve themselves. So what's a guy like Warneke worth to his manager? His value doesn't show up just in the box scores. But of course he's got to be one of your stars. A .220 hitter can have all the fire in the world, but who's he going to inspire?

I coached the Milwaukee Braves for two years, in the late fifties, when they had their really fine teams. I'll tell you something interesting about that team, and I think you can apply it to

Babe Ruth and Rogers Hornsby at the 1926 World Series
Hornsby "was a perfectionist and had a very low tolerance for mis-
takes."

most any team. There were three leaders there—Spahn, Burdette,
and Mathews. All the other players followed those three guys.
They were going to set the standard, no matter what it was going
to be. Well, it so happened that those three guys went out every
day and worked their tails off. Spahn and Burdette would run and
run and run, and Mathews would always be a-fieldin' and
a-hittin' and in a pepper game. They were stars and they set a
great example. That makes it a hell of a lot easier for the manager.

I can tell you exactly where the manager makes his biggest
contribution to the winning and losing of ball games—in his
knowledge of the fundamentals and his insistence upon his
players' knowing them. If he's sound in his run-down plays and
his pick-off plays and in hitting cutoff men and throwing to the
right base and things like that, he's going to win as many games as
his team's ability can possibly win for him. If he loses, it's going
to be because of errors, bad pitches, strikeouts, and things like
that—things he had no control over. But if your fundamentals are
sound and you insist upon your players' sticking to them, you're

*"Those kids, Reese and
Reiser, idolized Leo and
played their hearts out for
him." Pete Reiser, left, and
Pee Wee Reese in 1941*

going to get every bit of mileage out of the talent you have. Hell, you see a game lost because a pitcher doesn't back up a play or a guy throws to the wrong base, that's the manager's fault; he's responsible for those things. And if he hasn't worked on them enough, then he's got to work on them some more and keep at it until those mistakes stop being made. And he can't be afraid to work his players hard or give a damn what they think of him.

A manager can never allow personal popularity to be a factor in running the club. Leo was great that way. He didn't give a damn whether you liked him or not as long as you put out for him on that field. And you'd be surprised how many guys there were who hated Leo's guts but who still went out there and broke their necks for him because they respected his baseball know-how. Those kids, Reese and Reiser, idolized Leo and played their hearts out for him.

Durocher, of course, was not just a good baseball man; he was also an outstanding personality. With a tremendous ego. That's all right, but it can get in the way sometimes. I can tell you about that. When I was playing for him on the Dodgers in 1941, we had a club that was notorious for stealing the catcher's signs. I'd say that almost half the time we played, we knew what the pitcher was going to throw. That can help some players tremendously; others it doesn't help at all because if they know a fastball is coming, they get set for it and swing at it no matter where it is. But we did have those signs. Our ace sign stealer was Charlie Dressen, our third base coach.

But here's where Leo's ego would get in the way. He couldn't help but rub it into the other team that we'd stolen their signs. He would start acting up and they'd find out about it. Just couldn't resist letting them know he'd outsmarted them. That happened a few times. Naturally once the other team knew what was happening, they'd start running new sequences, and we'd have to start all over again trying to steal them. It got so that if we picked up a team's signs, we would hide the fact from Durocher.

Dressen was kind of an egotistical man himself, but he had a lot of warmth and sincerity along with it. I liked him enormously as a person and respected him as a baseball man. He simply was the

finest baseball man I ever knew. Very sharp. And he lived
baseball, absolutely lived it, twenty-four hours a day.

I had gone up to Boston when Billy Jurges took over the club in
1960. Billy was there only a short time, but when they let him go,
I remained as a coach, working for Mike Higgins. When Mike
moved up to become general manager, they hired Johnny Pesky
to manage, and I continued on as a coach. When they let Pesky go,
Mike called me and asked me if I was interested in managing the
Red Sox. I told him I was.

Mike and I had become very close. He was one of the finest
men I ever worked for in baseball. We liked each other and we
trusted each other, and I was never treated better by anyone. So I
took over the Red Sox in 1965. Then, toward the end of '65, I
don't know what happened, but they let Higgins go. Well, I knew
from that time on that my days in Boston were numbered. They
probably would have let me out with Mike, except that I had a
year to go on my contract. But in my mind I feel I did a real fine
job in Boston because when I left, those young ballplayers had
begun to jell. Dick Williams took them the next year. He did a
first-rate job and won the pennant with them.

So as far as the Red Sox are concerned, I was satisfied with the
job I did, especially the second year. The first year I managed
there, I had a team similar to the Pittsburgh Pirates. There were a
few bad actors, and we had a lot of age on the team and very little
ability. We had a bad year. Now the second year we made a few
deals over the winter and decided to go with a lot of younger
players.

When we opened up the season in 1965, I had Joe Foy and
George Scott and Rico Petrocelli in the lineup, all of them very
young then. We started out poorly and for most of the first half of
the season stayed that way. But I didn't have anybody better to
put in, and these kids were hustling and starting to show a little
improvement, so I just kept them in there. Then they started
putting it together. As a matter of fact, that club won more games
in the second half of 1966 than the pennant-winning club won in
the first half a year later. The only team that played better ball

Chicago Cub infield in 1932
Left to right: *Billy Herman, Charlie Grimm, Stan Hack, Billy Jurges.*
All four managed in the major leagues.

than we did in the last half of '66 was Baltimore—and they were
World Champs that year. In other words, that Red Sox ball club
was starting to move.

How did I get along with Yastrzemski? Like everybody else
did. By that I mean nobody ever got along with Yastrzemski.
Every manager has trouble with him, and some of them had it by
the ton. He plays only as hard as he wants to play, and any
manager is going to resent that, I don't give a damn who it is,
because his job depends upon the players producing.

One time we're playing in Washington, a twi-night doubleheader. Something was bothering Yastrzemski, and I didn't think

he was giving me a hundred percent. I remember one ball in particular. Frank Howard hit it down the left-field line and it barely reached the wall; Yastrzemski trotted after it and Howard got three bases.

After the doubleheader was over, I was so goddamned mad I could hardly see. I went into my office and told the trainer to send Yastrzemski in. When he came in, I got up and closed and locked the door. Then I told him what I thought of his performance that night. Very frankly. I've never talked like that to any man in my life, before or since. I called him everything. It got to the point where I kind of got on guard because I thought for sure he was going to swing at me at any second. But he didn't say a damned word, just sat there with his head down and never even looked at me.

What gets you so mad is that the guy has as much ability as anybody in the game. If he gave you a hundred percent every time he walked out on the field, if he had the attitude of, say, a Pete Reiser or an Enos Slaughter or a Pete Rose, you'd never hear about another player, he'd be so outstanding. He's a great outfielder and his arm is absolutely deadly. He can hit with power to all fields. And listen to this. When I was coaching with the Red Sox, they had a second baseman named Chuck Schilling. This fellow could pick that ball up as well as anybody I ever saw. As an old-time second baseman, I really appreciated the way he did things out there. He and Yastrzemski were roommates and good buddies. One day in spring training Yastrzemski comes up to me and says, "Hey, this guy Schilling thinks he's pretty good out there. Well, we're going to have a contest." I took a fungo bat and started hitting the ball to them. I hit it harder and harder, until I was hitting just plain bullets at those guys. Schilling was good, he was great. But Yastrzemski played rings around him. At second base. As good a pair of hands as anybody who ever lived.

I'll tell you though, the easiest job in baseball would be managing—if you had twenty-five guys giving you a hundred percent. But it doesn't happen; it can't happen, not with twenty-five different personalities. You have to go out every day and try to convince them all that that extra bit of hustle can turn a ball game

around and a ball game can turn a team around. There's no way
you can really measure it, but at a guess I'd say that if every man
hustled on every play, it could mean an extra ten games a year for
the team.

I saw something of that in 1942, when I was with the Dodgers
and the Cardinals beat us out for the pennant. That Cardinal team
never stopped hustling, not for one minute. Hell, we won 104
games and they won 106. They just never stopped, that's all.
When a team has got that kind of fire, you can just feel it in the
clubhouse before a game. It's like electricity. And all it takes to
turn it off is just one key man not hustling. I've seen that too.

I remember one year when I was with the Cubs, we ran off a
21-game winning streak. I can't explain it, but something had
gotten into everybody's blood to the extent that we *knew* we were
going to win. It was all very matter-of-fact. We'd come to the ball
park in the morning, and it was in the air. We were going to win,
that's all there was to it.

The opposite can happen too, of course. There are times when
you go out there and just wait for something to go wrong. I've
played ball games where we had a five-run lead in the sixth
inning and you just knew something was going to happen and
you were not going to win that ball game, and often it did happen
and you didn't win.

The manager can help a little in those situations. He can sense
what's happening, and the big thing for him to do is use some
psychology, to say the right thing and try to get the guys loose
again. If a manager gets down, the whole team is gone; they'll go
right with him. He's got to keep them sparking. Durocher was
good at that. I don't know if it was his theory or not, but he always
got the team worked up by causing some kind of controversy, a
fight or an argument with the other team. He'd get them mad at us
and us mad at them. Of course, that can work against you, too.
You can wake up the old sleeping dog and turn it into a lion.

You know, I came close to having the opportunity to manage
the Yankees right after the war. When I was in the navy, I met a
guy named Jack White. He was the ticket manager at Yankee

Stadium for years after the war. He was a great friend with Dan Topping, who became the big wheel with the Yankees around that time. In December, 1945, just before I was to be separated from the navy, Jack White called me and said they wanted me to get my release from the Brooklyn club and then they would send me over to manage the Newark team in the International League. Newark was the Yankees' top farm club at that time.

"We're going to make a change," he said, referring to Joe McCarthy. "It's liable to be before the season, or it's liable to be in the middle of the season."

So I called Branch Rickey to ask for my release. I decided to give him a little bullshit. I told him he had all these young kids coming up, that I was over the hill as a player and didn't want to be in the way. Well, he smelled a mouse.

"Who's made you an offer?" he asked.

I couldn't very well tell him somebody had contacted me. Anyway, he wouldn't give me my release, and I went to spring training with the Dodgers in '46. I felt that a real opportunity had been lost. The Yankees did let McCarthy go late in the year, and I'm sure I would have gotten the job. The things that might have been, huh?

Billy Herman in 1932

14

LUKE SEWELL

James Luther Sewell
Born: January 5, 1901, Titus, Alabama
Managerial career: St. Louis Browns, 1941–46; Cincinnati
  Reds, 1950–52

Before they became the Baltimore Orioles in 1954, the St.
Louis Browns won only one pennant in their history. The
manager that year, 1944, was Luke Sewell, who had spent
twenty years as a catcher in the American League, playing
with the Cleveland Indians, Washington Senators, and Chicago White Sox.

That's right, I'm the only man that ever won a pennant with the
St. Louis Browns. I guess that's one record that'll never be
broken.

In almost thirty-five years in the big leagues as player, coach,
and manager, I was on only two winners—as manager of the 1944
Browns and as catcher on the 1933 Senators. That might not be so
much to show for so many years, but it makes those pennants all
the sweeter to remember. You know, if somebody would have
told me when I was in college that I was going to be in the big
leagues that many years, I never would have believed him.

I guess I got into baseball more or less by accident. My father
was a country doctor down in Titus, Alabama, where I grew up,
and my first ambition was to follow in his footsteps. Back in those
days a country doctor was quite an important man. He had the
respect of everybody. My brother Joe and I both decided we were
going to be doctors. We knew all about pills and adhesive tape
and a lot of other things before we even thought about going to

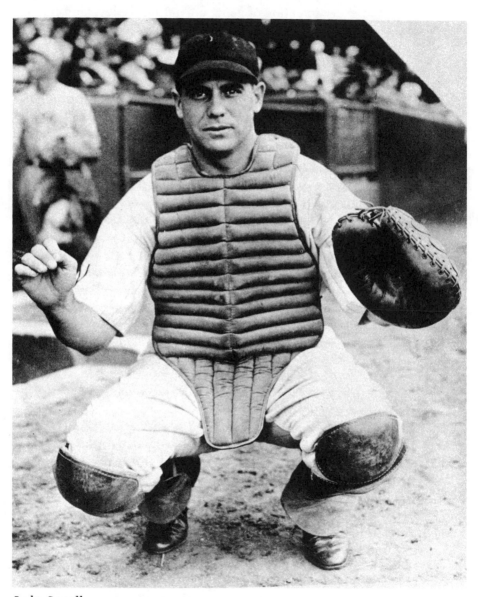

Luke Sewell

school. Baseball kind of was a second choice with us. As a matter of fact, I took premedical courses at the University of Alabama and had every intention of going on, until the Cleveland Indians came along.

Joe had already signed with Cleveland in 1920. I didn't play much baseball as a young man, but he did. He played quite a bit of semipro ball. He got to the majors after less than a year in the minors. They brought him up in August 1920, when their regular shortstop, Ray Chapman, died after being hit by a pitched ball.

Cleveland had a scout working out of Mobile named Patsy Flaherty who used to scout the schools down there. The first time I ran into him was in Atlanta when I was with the University of Alabama. We were there to play Oglethorpe College. He came around one night to the hotel where we were staying, and I'll never forget this. I was walking through the lobby when all of a sudden I heard myself being paged. I thought it was some kind of practical joke—you know, a bunch of college boys sitting around together, somebody's going to come up with something. So I ignored it, but the paging continued. Finally I walked up to the bellboy and introduced myself. He took me to another part of the lobby, over to a fellow who was leaning against a column. This was Patsy Flaherty. He told me who he was. He'd watched me play that day, and he wanted me to go up to Cleveland. I laughed.

"What kind of a joke is this?" I asked.

"It's not a joke," he said. "I'm recommending you to the Indians as a catcher."

The funny part about that was I wasn't a catcher. I was an infielder. But I had happened to be behind the plate that day because our regular catcher was hurt. I threw out a couple of runners, and I guess I looked pretty good to him. I told him that; I told him I was a shortstop.

"No you're not," he said. "You're a catcher."

"But I don't even own a catcher's mitt," I said.

"You will," he said.

So I went up to Cleveland as a catcher, and they got my name on a contract. This was in 1921. I had planned on going to medical school that September, but the Indians were battling the

Yankees for the pennant and they wanted me to stick around. Tris
Speaker, the manager, said to me, "If you'll just stay here and not
go back to school, you'll make yourself a minimum of two or three
thousand dollars." Now, that was a lot of money in those days.
Well, that kept me out of school. But when the race was over, we
hadn't won it, and by that time it was too late in the season to go
back to school.

The next year I shouldn't have been in the major leagues
because all I did was sit on the bench. All year. Steve O'Neill was
the regular catcher. Then that fall I took a trip to Japan with one
of those baseball tours, and that kept me out of school again. One
thing led to another, and I never did get back.

Tris Speaker was a great ballplayer, just great, but I never
thought he was an outstanding manager. He was a very person-
able man. He made friends easily, or I should say acquaintances—
you never know when you're making a friend, do you? He didn't
seem to have much patience with a young player. That was the
way it was in those days. A young player had to take his place
on the sidelines until he had a chance to prove himself. It was a different day and age. Young players weren't given much instruction,
and I think the reason for this lay in the fact that managers had a
greater number of experienced players to work with when I broke
in than they had later on. We had only one coach, and he had too
many things to do to have time for the young players. I didn't get
to take batting practice in spring training until my third year
with the club. That's right. They knew I wasn't going to play,
so they didn't want to waste any time with me.

I sat on the bench again in 1923. I would have been far better
off if I had started out in the minors, where I could have played.
Outside of a few games with Columbus in 1921, I never played
minor league ball.

Joe, of course, was the regular shortstop from the moment he
started. In fact, he played 1,103 consecutive games over one
stretch, which was the record until Gehrig broke it. But Joe still
holds the record for fewest strikeouts in a full season—four, and
he did that twice. Over his whole career, fourteen years, he struck
out only 114 times. He had a great eye up at the plate and a very

Joe Sewell
"He could take a pitch a
quarter of an inch off the
plate."

compact swing, and he had some power, too. He'd knock in 90 or 100 runs a year.

When we were together on the Indians, I used to accuse him of being the umpire's pet. You know how brothers kid around. But he would take pitches that looked great to me, and they would be called balls. I'd kid him about it, and he would say, "No, Luke, you don't look at them carefully enough. Those are balls." Then he went over to the Yankees and I had a chance to catch behind him, and, honestly, he could take a pitch a quarter of an inch off the plate. He simply had superb judgment of the strike zone, same as Cobb and Williams did. Those fellows would only swing at good balls, and when they swung the bat, they hit that ball. You seldom saw them foul one off.

Stanley Coveleski was our ace pitcher. He threw a spitball, and he had a good fastball, too. He could throw hard for a fellow who wasn't too big. We had George Uhle, too. He hurt his arm, had chipped bones or something in his elbow. But he was one of the finest pitchers I ever saw. He had a good assortment and sharp control. George was one of three pitchers I ever saw that I thought could pitch a ball game by themselves—in other words make their own selection at any stage of the game and go ahead and pitch without any trouble. The other two were Wes Ferrell and Alvin Crowder. Never bothered those fellows how many men might be on base.

We had another great pitcher on the club, except that he was an outfielder by the time I got there—Smoky Joe Wood. They say he was just about as fast as anybody until he hurt his arm. But he was a pretty good hitter and made a comeback as an outfielder. I'll tell you, he could still fire that ball, and he could throw the darndest knuckleball. He used to say to me, "Come on, I'll make a catcher out of you," and he'd take me down to the bull pen and throw that knuckler to me. I could hardly believe what I was seeing. I'd never seen a knuckleball before, and he could really make it dance.

In 1933 I was traded to Washington, and that was nice timing because they won the pennant that year. It was a darned good ball club. We had Heinie Manush, Goose Goslin, Joe Cronin, Ossie Bluege, Buddy Myer, Joe Kuhel; Earl Whitehill and Alvin Crowder each won over 20 games for us that season. I'll tell you something about that Bluege. He was the best third baseman that ever put a glove on. I never saw anybody that could compare with him, not Pie Traynor or Brooks Robinson either. Sometimes you just couldn't believe the plays he made.

I made a double play at home plate that year that I'll never forget. It was in New York. We were fighting the Yankees for the lead and wanted this ball game very badly. We were ahead a couple of runs in the bottom of the ninth. Gehrig got on and then Dixie Walker singled, putting men on first and second. Tony Lazzeri came up and sent a long drive out to right center. Goslin went after it, and it looked for a second like he might catch it, but the ball hit against the fence. Well, Gehrig thought it might be caught, and he was tagging up. But Walker was running hard, and he was down to second base. When Gehrig saw the ball bounce, he took off, with Dixie right behind him. Goslin picked it up and threw it to Cronin and Cronin threw it to me. A perfect throw. I took it and put the tag on Gehrig. Lou hit me so hard he spun me right around, and to my surprise there was Dixie right behind him, sliding in. I sat right down on top of him and put the ball on him for a double play.

I was with Washington for only two years, but they were memorable years. I'd say that anybody who missed playing at least a full year for Clark Griffith missed half his baseball life. Griff was a great character. He'd argue with you over five cents. In 1933 I caught 141 games for him and he wanted to cut me twenty-five hundred dollars the next year. I said to him, "Griff, I caught all of your ball games for you. What are you doing?"

"Well," he said, "you didn't win the World Series."

I couldn't help laughing. "You're right," I said. The Giants had beat us in six games.

We argued about salary, and I said I wasn't going to sign. A day or two before spring training opened in Biloxi, Mississippi, I got a wire from Griff telling me they were going to open the training camp on a certain day and that there was going to be a parade at nine o'clock in the morning. The fire department and the police department and everybody in town was going to be out for it. He said that if I was there in time to ride in the fire engine, he would give me the twenty-five hundred dollars back and a thousand-dollar bonus if I caught a certain number of games.

Well, I've got to tell you, I was sitting on that fire engine at nine o'clock in the morning when the parade started. So you see how Griff would handle things. He knew darned well he had to pay me that money, but in order to salve his pride, he made it look like he was getting something out of *me*. But he was a great fellow, one of a kind, and I liked him.

Around the time I joined the ball club, Cronin became engaged to Griff's daughter. That could have been one of the reasons Griff made Joe manager and put together such a good ball club for him. Anyway, we were playing the Yankees a doubleheader one day. We had them beat in the bottom of the ninth in the first game, but

Tris Speaker as a
naval aviation student in 1918

an error by Joe on what should have been the last out let in the tying and winning runs.

That put them within a game of us, so when we went out for the second game, we really wanted it. Griff was at the park, sitting in a box right next to our dugout, smoking one cigar after another. He was pretty gloomy after seeing his future son-in-law blow that first game for us. The second game was a close one, tied, I think, into the late innings. We got a couple of men on and darn if Cronin doesn't knock them in. Well, you should have seen Griff. He raised up in his seat and began waving his hat. Then I guess he just couldn't contain his excitement and jumped right over that low railing onto the field. Well, Griff had a bad back, and as he went over the railing, his back gave away and down he went, still yelling, still waving his hat, still smoking his cigar, as the runners were going around the bases.

Connie Mack and Clark Griffith

We all jumped out of the dugout, not knowing what to do. Here are men crossing the plate, and there's the club owner lying there howling with both pain and delight. You never saw so much confusion in your life. They finally had to get a stretcher to take him into the clubhouse. That's why I say, if you didn't play at least a year in Washington, you missed something. Griff really entered into the spirit of things.

I was a coach with Cleveland in 1940 when they had the rebellion there. The Cleveland ballplayers were unhappy with the way Oscar Vitt was running the team and asked Alva Bradley, the president, to get rid of him. Well, Bradley asked me three times if I would take over the club. I wouldn't do it. Why? Well, I was coaching for Vitt, he was in trouble, and I guess I felt some sense of loyalty.

So I wouldn't take it. But when the season was over and Vitt had been fired, Bradley never offered me the job. I would have taken it then. Instead he kept calling me up to ask my opinion of certain fellows who were after it, like Babe Ruth, Rogers Hornsby, and a few others.

In June of '41 the Browns let Fred Haney go and brought me in to manage. I actually didn't care about going to St. Louis, but Bradley told me to go over and talk to Don Barnes, who was running the Browns. Since I wasn't too enthusiastic about the idea, I figured I might as well make some demands. I told Barnes that one of the conditions of my taking the job was that I'd have absolute control of the personnel. I wanted to have the last word on who was on the club and who wasn't. I wanted the authority to make deals and a lot of other things. Barnes agreed to it and he lived up to it. We got along all right.

Managing was never a particular ambition of mine. If the opportunity hadn't come along, I would never have thought about it. In fact, at that time I was thinking about getting out of baseball and into some other business.

So if I was going to manage, then I wanted to have that authority. I felt then, back in those days, that I could take practically any ball club and, given the authority to do what I wanted, within three years make a winner out of it or at least get it into contention.

Too often when the scouts and the minor league managers in an organization get together, they have a tendency to formulate pretty much the same opinions. I don't know why that should happen, but it does. One thing we needed badly, among others, when I took over the Browns, was a shortstop. Well, we had Vern Stephens playing at Toledo. Fred Haney was managing there. That shows you the kind of shape the Browns were in then—they couldn't afford to pay Fred for not working, so after they fired him, they sent him to manage at Toledo and sent me the Toledo manager, Zack Taylor, as my pitching coach.

I saw Haney after the season and asked him what kind of ballplayer Stephens was.

"No good," he said.

"Can he play shortstop?"

"No," he said. "He'll never be a shortstop."

"Well," I said, "we'll take a look at him in spring training."

You know what Stephens's problem was? When he was in the field, he set his feet so they pointed out. Well, you get your feet in that position and you're locked. You can't break either way, right or left. So all he had to do was set those feet straight at the hitter. I worked with him all spring, wouldn't let anybody else near him. I finally got him to the point where he had a comfortable stance in the field. As far as his hitting was concerned, he couldn't hit a slow ball when he first came up. He was standing up there with his feet too close together, and all I did was spread him out. That's all I did for Stephens, and I went on to win a pennant with him. But that's why I wanted to have that authority, you see. If I hadn't had something to say about the personnel, we would never have had Stephens up.

Handling pitchers is the secret of managing. If a fellow can't do that, then I think they should have somebody else managing. When I was catching, I could tell you when a pitcher was losing his stuff, and sometimes an inning or two before he actually did. The secret of it is anytime a pitcher's fastball starts losing its break and straightening out, it won't be but a little bit before they'll start popping him.

There's an art to keeping a pitching staff in shape. You have to give them their proper rest and their proper work between starts. Naturally they're not all the same physically, and you have to know and allow for the differences. For instance, one of the great theories is to run pitchers with a fungo bat. Now, some fellows can't run as hard as others, so you don't hit the ball quite as far from them; otherwise you'll be tiring them out instead of giving them a useful workout. Some have to pitch batting practice between outings and some don't. They all have to be handled with the utmost care, and you'd better know how to do it because if you don't, then it's a good idea to keep your bags packed.

I did most of the coaching for my pitchers myself, with a few former catchers to help out. I had Zack Taylor with me on the Browns and Gus Mancuso when I was at Cincinnati. I always preferred a former catcher to handle the staff rather than a pitcher because I felt I could communicate better with a catcher, that he could more readily understand my thinking.

The idea of changing a pitcher's delivery is a real fallacy. Each pitcher has one angle that he can throw a fastball from better than he can from any other. It's natural with him and you have to find it. But you don't have to look too hard because he'll show it to you himself. Then what you do is work from that same angle in developing his curveball and a change of pace. But you never fool with that good fastball.

The only three pitches you need are the fastball, curveball, and change. A slider isn't worth two cents if you don't throw it through a knothole. Otherwise they'll hit it out of the park. I wish I had a dollar for every time I heard a pitcher say, "He hit my slider, but I got it in a bad spot." We used to call that pitch a nickel curve.

I don't think there's too much difference in the game as it was played when I broke in and the way it's played today. Of course, they livened the ball and shortened the fences, and hitters started going for distance more than they used to. You see, the bat changed. I don't know whether you ever thought of that. The structure of the bat changed. I've got one that Ty Cobb gave me years ago, and you can see the difference. Those bats didn't have the big ends on them; the weight was more evenly distributed, with bigger handles and smaller barrels than what you've got today. I believe George Sisler and Rogers Hornsby were the first ones to come out with the big-ended bats, putting the weight up on the end and giving them more driving power. Ruth used to hit with a slender stick. But when they put that weight at the end of

Lou Gehrig and Hank Greenberg

the bats and everybody started to use them, the ball began to fly further.

I'll tell you something else, and I'll bet it's going to be startling to you. The bat is round and tapered from top to bottom, right? Well, naturally the home-run hitter is going to hit it on the upper half to get the ball out of the park, isn't he? And the little ping hitter naturally would hit it on the bottom half because he's not elevating the ball. Right? Well, do you want to know something? The exact opposite is true. The home-run hitters bruise the bottom half of that bat and the little ping hitters the top half. If you don't believe that, you go look at the bats. From a scientific standpoint it's completely unexplainable. But it's true. I've seen those bats. Ruth, Gehrig, Greenberg, Foxx, York—all of those power hitters bruised the bottom half of their bats.

Night baseball has changed a lot of things. You wonder where all the high batting averages have gone. Well, night ball is the culprit, in my opinion. There's a terrific difference. When I was managing, I used to run records on what the hitters batted in daylight and what they batted at night. Well, the only two men that ever hit more at night than they did during the day, according to my records, were Ken Keltner and Al Zarilla. So there's no question in my mind that night ball has cut the averages. It's hard to pick up the spin of the ball at night, and since a lot of your timing and striding at the plate is determined by the spin of the ball, you can see why the averages have been cut.

We had a lot of free-swingers back then, but I'll tell you, when they had two strikes on them, they leveled off on their swing and cut back a little. The best two-strike hitter I ever saw was Charlie Gehringer. You might have thought you had an advantage when you had him two strikes; the truth was he became more dangerous in those situations. But today I see a lot of hitters still gunning from the end of the bat when they've got two strikes on them. That's not too smart. You're just giving the pitcher an extra advantage.

We got away to a fast start in 1944, winning our first nine

George McQuinn being congratulated at home plate by Mark Christ-
man (6) and Gene Moore (15) after hitting a home run in the first game
of the 1944 World Series. The catcher is Walker Cooper.

games, and kept on playing good ball. After about the middle of
the season, I thought we could win it, and I told the players that
and kept telling them. I never gave any thought to the fact that the
Browns had never won a pennant. If you start thinking about
history when you're trying to accomplish something, you can get
sidetracked.

It was a wartime ball club, of course, but we had some good
talent. Our pitching wasn't bad. We had Nelson Potter, Bob

Muncrief, Denny Galehouse, Jack Kramer, Sig Jakucki. Then we had George McQuinn, Stephens, Don Gutteridge, Mark Christman, Mike Kreevich, Chet Laabs, and Al Zarilla.

It was a four-way race for a while, but then the Red Sox and the Yankees fell out and we came down to the last day of the season tied with Detroit. They were playing Washington, and we were playing the Yankees. Well, we'd already beaten the Yankees three in a row and needed this one for at least a tie and maybe to win it all, depending on what Detroit did.

I wasn't too excited. I never got emotionally worked up over an athletic event. When I was at the University of Alabama, I was on the football team, and sometimes before a big game some of the alumni would come into the dressing room and give us those bloodcurdling speeches of inspiration. They'd give the yells and the team would yell back and run out on the field with murder in their eyes. All except me. I went out there wondering how I was going to keep myself in one piece, playing up against some of those big guys.

But I'd told the boys in July we were going to win it, and I still believed it. I believed it even more when Dutch Leonard beat the Tigers that last day. So all we had to do now was win our game and it was over. Sig Jakucki pitched for us and with a big lift from Chet Laabs, who hit two home runs, we won it.

People ask me what was the most memorable play I ever saw on a ball field. I tell them it was a play I saw George McQuinn make. There was a pop fly hit one day outside of first base in foul territory, and McQuinn caught it. "What was so great about that?" they'll ask. "It was the last out of the last game of the 1944 season," I tell them. Most memorable play I ever saw. It's hard to say that chills ran up and down your spine, but I believe I felt a few at that moment.

That was the year of the Trolley Car World Series because the Cardinals won in the National League. An all-St. Louis Series. The Cardinals had a pretty good ball club. They probably had lost fewer regulars to the service than anybody else. Some of them did go later on, but on that club they had Stan Musial, Marty Marion, Walker Cooper, Whitey Kurowski, Danny Litwhiler,

Johnny Hopp, and some real fine pitchers in Mort Cooper, Max Lanier, Ted Wilks, and Harry Brecheen.

The Cardinals were heavily favored, but I'll tell you, we came near to beating them. We beat them in the first and third games and should have won the second as well. It was a game we lost in eleven innings, 3–2. But there was a play early on in the game on which we made six misplays. That's right—six. Emil Verban got a single and Lanier bunted. He popped the ball up between the pitcher and the foul line. Potter and Christman ran over, looked at each other, and let it hit the ground. Either one could have caught it. That was the first misplay. Then Potter grabbed at the ball and it rolled up his arm. That's two misplays. When he threw it to first, he threw wild. That's three. Gutteridge was covering, and he tried to keep his foot on the bag as he reached for the ball instead of getting off and grabbing it. That's four. The ball went down into the corner, where Chet Laabs got after it. It hit the fence and bounced back between his legs. That's five. Then he picked it up and made a bad throw to second. That's six. Six misplays on one little pop bunt. It set up their first run. If it hadn't been for that, we would have beat them and then the next day had them down three games to none.

We still had them two games to one, but they took three in a row after that and beat us, four games to two.

I'll tell you an odd thing—it was the quietest World Series ever. I don't think the fans knew who to root for. They'd been waiting all their lives for this and when it finally came to be, they just sat and took it all in without too much cheering.

So I was in baseball for over thirty years and had only two winners. Of course, everybody wants to play on a winner. I can tell you a good story about that. This was around 1924, when I was with Cleveland. We weren't going too well; in fact, we were down in seventh place. A group of us were sitting around the lobby of the Ben Franklin Hotel in Philadelphia after dinner, reading the extras that came out at six o'clock. We were looking at the line scores. The Yankees had beaten somebody by about fifteen runs that day. One of the fellows said, "Boy, I'd sure like

to be on that Yankee team." "Wouldn't that be great?" somebody
else said. We all agreed. Everybody wanted to be on the Yankees.
Riggs Stephenson was sitting there, not saying anything. Finally
he spoke up. "Boys," he said, "it seems to me if we were all on the
Yankees, they'd be right down in seventh place."

15

JIMMY DYKES

James Joseph Dykes
Born: November 10, 1896, Philadelphia, Pennsylvania
Died: June 15, 1976
Managerial career: Chicago White Sox, 1934–46; Philadelphia Athletics, 1951–53; Baltimore Orioles, 1954; Cincinnati Reds, 1958; Detroit Tigers, 1959–60; Cleveland Indians, 1960–61

One of baseball's most colorful and engaging personalities, Jimmy Dykes spent twenty-two years as an active player in the American League and played for only three managers—Connie Mack, Lew Fonseca, and Jimmy Dykes. Dykes managed the Chicago White Sox for 12 full seasons, longer than anyone else in White Sox history. In 1951 he was Connie Mack's handpicked successor when the venerable Philadelphia legend stepped down after fifty-one years at the helm of the Athletics.

Connie Mack? To me he was one of the greatest managers that ever lived. He sat on that bench and moved his fielders around with a scorecard. He could be uncanny. We had Ty Cobb playing with us in '27 and '28, his last two years in baseball. One day he's in right field and Connie starts moving him over with that scorecard, keeps moving him and moving him. You could tell from the way Cobb was responding out there that he thought this was all very curious. But he went along with Connie. Well, the batter hit the ball right at him. He never had to move. When he came in to the bench at the end of the inning, Cobb said to Connie, "I've heard a lot about your scorecard, and from now on I'm going to believe in it."

Connie Mack exchanging
an autograph for a flower
as Jimmie Foxx watches

Mr. Mack was a wonderful man, a great guy to play for. Patience personified. He never lost his temper. Very seldom, if ever, used profanity. If he swore when he was talking to you, you knew you were in trouble. What I mean by swearing is he would use *Damn.* That was the extent of it. But coming from him, it carried great emphasis.

He had a lot of great ballplayers through the years and he had some brutes too; he had some terrible ballplayers. I remember the great teams he had through 1910–14. I was just a spectator then, but I had my hopes. He told me once that the best team he ever had was in 1912. Ironically, it was the only one that didn't win the pennant through that stretch. But he had some great players with him in those years, fellows like Eddie Collins, Frank Baker, Chief Bender, Eddie Plank, and Jack Coombs.

Rube Waddell
"I think Rube was one of his favorites."

Connie had seven last-place finishes in a row at one stretch. It didn't seem to bother him. Nothing ever seemed to bother him. He was the same man sitting on the bench all the time, whether he was in last place or in the World Series.

After 1914 he started to break the team up. I joined the A's in 1918, during the rebuilding era. At one point we used to say we had three teams: one playing that afternoon, one coming in that night, and one leaving the next morning. You think I'm kidding? One year we had over fifty guys coming and going. Sometimes when you shook hands with a guy you were saying hello and good-bye at the same time.

They used to call me Connie's boy. I could do no wrong. He liked me and I idolized him. If it wasn't for him, I probably wouldn't have been around because when I first came up I couldn't hit the side of a building. But he kept me around because I had a good arm and I was a good fielder. By the time we got up to those championship years—'29, '30, '31—I hit pretty good for him.

I used to sit and talk with him on those long train rides. He was very interesting, especially about the old days. He used to talk a lot about Rube Waddell, who pitched for him right after the turn of the century. I think Rube was one of his favorites. Waddell was kind of an eccentric, you know, a big overgrown kid who loved to chase after fire engines and ride on them. "But, Jimmy," Mr. Mack would say to me, "he could pitch. That fellow could really pitch. I didn't care whether he chased fire engines or not. The only thing I worried about was his falling off one of those engines and getting hurt."

He liked Waddell, but I think Grove was the best pitcher he ever had. And he had some good ones, too, like Waddell, Plank, Coombs, and Bender. But as far as Grove was concerned, I don't think there was anybody better. He could fire. And he didn't have a curveball. When they went up to hit against him, they knew all they were going to see was the fastball. You'd figure they'd hit him. But they didn't. He threw it right by them.

I remember one time the Libbey Owens Company made a nonshatterable glass which they were very proud of and wanted to demonstrate. So they came out to the ball park one morning and set up a sheet of that glass and asked Grove to throw at it. Well, you can see this coming a mile away, can't you? He wound up and threw one pitch and that ball shot right through the glass like a bullet. Nothing shattered; there was just this hole the size of a baseball in it, just as neat as could be.

Naturally all the executives were embarrassed.

"Listen," they said to Lefty, "this time don't throw it so hard." They brought out another sheet of that glass and set it up. Lefty wound up and fired again. He didn't throw it as hard this time. All the same, when the ball hit that glass, the pieces flew in a thousand different directions. That was the end of the nonshatterable glass.

Lefty could be a very temperamental fellow. Wouldn't have his picture taken the day he pitched. The photographers would come around, and he'd tell them to go away. They would go over to Mr. Mack and complain about it, but he would tell them, "If that's what he wants, then leave him alone. I'll see he's available tomorrow."

One day Connie put him in in the eighth inning against the White Sox in a 2–2 ball game. In the eleventh inning they beat him. Lefty stormed into the clubhouse and tore his locker apart. Then he left the ball park, got into his Pierce Arrow—one of those jobs with the lights on the sides, just the thing in those days—and drove all the way from Philadelphia back home to Lonaconing, Maryland. This was on a Tuesday. He stayed there; didn't come back until Saturday. Probably sat and fished the whole time, letting the steam out. When he showed up, nobody said anything—we were all familiar with Lefty's moods.

We were playing in Washington one time, and one of their guys got on me a little from the bench. I looked over and it was Joe Kuhel, just a rookie then. He played for me later in Chicago, and we became good friends. But he got me sore that day. Grove was pitching, and when Kuhel came up to hit, I walked over to Lefty and said, loud enough for Kuhel to hear, "Bore this guy in the back."

"All right," Lefty said.

He fired one high inside but missed Kuhel.

I'm over at third base and I holler, "What the hell's the matter with you? You losing control?"

Lefty hollered back to me, "I won't miss him this time."

And he didn't. He bored Kuhel right in the back. Joe went down to first base gritting his teeth. He told me afterwards, "Well, I learned my lesson. Keep your mouth shut."

As a rule, Lefty didn't throw at hitters. He might come in close, to drive them back off the plate, but he wouldn't throw at them to hurt them, which was just as well. Otherwise there would have been a lot of guys walking around with dents in them.

Connie wasn't strict with us. I can't ever remember him fining anybody. We had a midnight curfew—we only played afternoon ball in those days. If you were going to stay out late, he insisted you tell him about it beforehand. It was a good idea to tell him,

Lefty Grove
"When the ball hit that glass, the pieces flew in a thousand different directions."

too, because he'd find out about it. I don't know what his sources
of information were, but he always knew. If he accused you of
something and you were guilty, the thing to do was own up. Then
he'd say, "All right. I just wanted to let you know that I knew."
But if you denied something, if you tried to lie your way out of it,
then he'd lay you out. So we all got the idea pretty quick: Plead
guilty.

Connie could surprise you sometimes with his moves. Remember the '29 Series? We're playing the Cubs and we've got Grove,
George Earnshaw, and Rube Walberg—three of the best pitchers.
So who does he start? Howard Ehmke. Now, Howard was a fine
pitcher in his day, but he hadn't done much pitching for us that
year. Why did Connie do that? Well, Ehmke came from down
under with that ball. He could be tough on righties, and the Cubs
had a lot of good right-handed hitters in the lineup—Rogers
Hornsby, Kiki Cuyler, Hack Wilson, Riggs Stephenson.

Was I surprised when Ehmke went out to warm up? I'll say I
was. So was everybody else. When he saw Ehmke get up to start
throwing, Al Simmons said to Mr. Mack, "Is *he* pitching?" And
Mr. Mack said, "Yes. Don't you like him?" Simmons looked at
me, looked at Ehmke, and then looked back to Mr. Mack and
shrugged. "If it's all right with you, it's all right with me," he
said.

Ehmke pitched a hell of a game. Beat them 3–1 and struck out
13, which was a World Series record for a long time.

That was the Series when we had the 10-run inning. In the
fourth game we're down 8–0 in the bottom of the seventh. When
we came in to bat, Mr. Mack told some of the regulars to go to the
clubhouse after the inning, that he wanted to give a few of the
youngsters a chance to play in the World Series. He figured the
game was lost. But Simmons started off with a home run and one
hit led to another. I got two hits that inning. Second one was a
double that knocked in the ninth and tenth runs. Pat Malone
threw me a fastball. I can still see it. I really combed it.

We beat them again the next day with three runs in the bottom
of the ninth to end it. They had us down 2–0, but Mule Haas hit a
home run with a man on to tie it. Then Simmons doubled and

they walked Jimmie Foxx to get to Bing Miller. I was up next. Miller was as good a curveball hitter as I ever saw. Pat Malone was pitching, and he fired two fastballs for strikes. Miller stepped out to get some dirt on his hands.

"Come on," I told him. "Hit the damned thing."

"He's gonna throw me a curve and I'm gonna tear it," Bing said to me.

He stepped back in and, sure enough, Malone throws him the curve. Bing scorched it, and the World Series was over.

I'll tell you, that was a rough-going Series all the way. Talk about swearing! You should have heard the bench jockeying. What language! They poured it on us, and we gave it right back. It got so bad—hell, you could hear it all over the ball park—that before the last game, Judge Landis got Mr. Mack and Joe McCarthy together and laid down the law. No more profanity. If they couldn't control the ballplayers, then he would throw *them* out. So Mr. Mack came back to the bench and told us to cut it out. No more cussin'. When Cochrane went out to start the game, he yelled over to the Cub bench, "Come on out, boys. Put on your bib and tucker. We're serving tea and cookies today." After the game was over, Landis came into the clubhouse to congratulate us. When he came to Cochrane, he shook hands with him, put on a mock scowl, and said, "And we're not serving tea and cookies today, Mickey."

Cochrane laughed and said, "Did you hear me?"

"You said it loud enough," the Judge said.

That was a great ball club. The '29, '30, '31 Philadelphia Athletics. I always said that there may have been clubs as good, but there were never any better. The Yankees were good, but they weren't better. We beat them three years in a row.

It was a hell of a bunch of guys, too. Great gang. Anything could happen in the clubhouse. Shoes nailed to the floor. Sweat shirts tied into knots. Itching powder in your jockstrap. You're out there in front of thirty thousand people and dying to scratch. Christ. Limburger cheese smeared on your hatband on a hot day. You'd damn near pass out. But on the ball field, no fooling.

Simmons was one of the greatest right-handed hitters ever.

Judge Landis warning managers Joe McCarthy and Connie Mack about their players' profanity before the fifth game of the 1929 World Series

What a hitter! And he loved to rap that ball. If he didn't get a couple of hits in the game, he'd come storming into the club-house. Cochrane was the same way. My locker was set between those two, and if they'd had a bad day, I'd get the feeling sometimes my life wasn't worth two cents.

One day I saw Cobb giving Simmons batting lessons. How many guys do you know who could tell Simmons how to hit? Well, Cobb was, and Al was paying close attention. I figured, hell, if he can tell Simmons how to hit, then I ought to bend an ear there. So I edged up and listened. Cobb is showing him how to hit left-handers. He's telling Al to get up on the plate against them. The next day we're facing a lefty and I get up on the plate and go three for four. After the game I'm sitting in front of my locker all smiles. Cobb comes by, looks at me, and says, "Well, rockhead, you're finally learning, aren't you?" From then on I could hit left-handers real well.

But Cobb was the greatest all-around ballplayer of them all. I played against him for years. I'd have some fun with him now and then. He always had to tag second base on his way to and from the outfield. I'd get out there and stand on the middle of the bag. He'd come running up and have to stop and touch the edge of the bag with his foot; then he'd give me a little blast. He used to call me "H.S." I won't tell you what that means except that the *H* stands for "Hot."

Mr. Mack got Cobb and Tris Speaker at about the same time, in 1927. There's a story behind that. A pitcher named Hubert (Dutch) Leonard had accused Cobb and Speaker of betting on ball games. Both Ty and Tris were let go by their clubs and it looked like there might be a scandal. So in order to prevent any scandal from coming out, Mr. Mack signed them both. That stopped all the talk. That's what he wanted to do. He told me that himself. He knew that with his good reputation, if he took them on, the talk would stop. And it did. That's the kind of guy Connie Mack was.

I saw Walter Johnson after he'd slowed down somewhat. At least that's what they told me, but he looked pretty swift to me. He was the first major league pitcher I went up against. I don't know if Mr. Mack was trying to discourage me or what. Walter had great control, but wouldn't you know that the first pitch he throws to me gets away from him and knocks me down. Tommy Connolly was umpiring, and he says, "Lad, you'll have to move faster up here." I was white. I mean, I could *feel* myself turn white. I wasn't too crazy about staying in there, but according to the rules I had to. Then bang, bang, bang. Back to the bench. My first at bat in the big leagues. Didn't disturb anybody. I didn't

even disturb the air because I never swung. I could have
telephoned in that at bat! I went home that night and told my dad,
"If they're all like him, you'll be seeing a lot of me around here."

Still, Grove was faster than the Johnson that I saw. And Bob
Feller was fast. Plus he had that curveball. Great. For the longest
time he couldn't get it over. I used to tell my players, "Don't
swing at the curveball, even if you've got two strikes." "What if
it's a strike?" they'd ask. "Then come on back," I'd tell them,
"because you're not going to hit it anyway."

Best hitter I ever saw? No, not Cobb, not Joe Jackson, not Babe
Ruth. Teddy Williams. No question. He could do everything. He
would have established some beautiful records if he hadn't spent
five years in the service. He could hit. And what an eye! If he took
a pitch, the umpires called it a ball. They figured he knew the
strike zone better than they did.

In 1932 Mr. Mack sold Al Simmons, Mule Haas, and me to the
White Sox. You know, the funny thing about that is I wasn't going
to go. I was going to quit. I'd heard that Harry Grabiner, the
White Sox's general manager, was mean, that he didn't pay any
money. But Eddie Collins, who had played in Chicago, came to
me and said, "You go out there. Take my advice. Talk to Grabiner
and get to know him, and if you still don't like him, you can quit."
That's the best advice I ever got. Harry Grabiner was one of the
best guys I ever worked for. When I managed there, he never
asked me why I did this or why I did that.

Was I surprised when I was sold to the White Sox? I'll say I
was. Connie had just told me about four or five days before that
he would never let me go. And I believed him. Then I was in New
York at the World Series. I came back to the hotel after the game,
and George Earnshaw was standing out front.

"Hey, Jimmy," he says, "how are you going to like Chicago?"

"What do you mean?" I asked.

"You've been traded with Simmons and Haas."

"What!" I yelled.

I walked into the hotel and there's Mr. Mack standing in the
lobby. I walked up to him and asked him if it was true.

"Yes, Jimmy," he said. "It is. I'll explain to you later."

I didn't say any more. But, boy, was I burned up at him! It was the only time I was ever real mad at him. Later I went upstairs to his room, and we talked. The explanation was simple. He needed the money. And it turned out I was the key player in the deal. Not the best, but the key. The White Sox wouldn't take Simmons and Haas unless they got me, too. He said he'd been holding out on it since August but finally had to give in. The money was there, he needed it, and he had to get it. I think there was something like $150,000 involved, which was a king's ransom in those days.

So I went to the Sox in 1933. Lew Fonseca was managing, and he was a good friend of mine. In '34 we started off poorly. We

Jimmy Dykes scoring the first run ever in an All-Star Game, Comiskey Park, July 6, 1933

were in Washington, and I got a call from Lou Comiskey to come
up to his room. He owned the club. I went up to see him, and he
was there with Harry Grabiner. When I walked in, Comiskey
said, "How would you like to manage the White Sox?"

I said, "If you're asking as a point of information, I'd rather not
answer that."

"All right," he said. "Let's say this then. If you don't take it, I'm
going to give it to somebody else. Fonseca is out."

"Well," I said, "if you put it that way, I'll have to go along with
you. I'll take it."

The next day I went out to the ball park ready to start running
the ball club. First day as manager. I had my lineup set in my
mind, my starting pitcher picked out, and I'd set to memory a
little speech I was going to give the boys. Well, when I got out
there, I learned that Fonseca hadn't been notified of the change.
They had tried to reach him the night before but had been unable
to. I didn't say anything. Hell, *I* wasn't going to tell him. All I
know is that on my first day as manager of the White Sox, Lew
Fonseca managed the team.

I welcomed the opportunity to manage, but to tell you the truth,
I'd never given it a thought. Managing had never been one of my
burning ambitions. But I'll never forget what Mr. Mack told me
after I'd taken on the job. "You're now a player with authority,"
he said. "Don't ever let it get the best of you. Stay a player, think
of yourself as one of the boys, and you'll never have any trouble."
I tried to follow that advice.

As far as the ballplayers were concerned, I was friendly with
them all. I wasn't what you'd call a strict disciplinarian. I didn't
have many rules, but the ones I did have I wanted observed. One
thing I insisted upon was that my players never argue with me on
the bench. Even if I'm a hundred percent wrong, I told them,
don't argue with me. If there was something they didn't like, they
could come into the office later, and we could thrash it out there.

I'll never forget one incident. I got into an argument with one
of my pitchers on the bench. He said to me, "If you weren't the
manager, I'd punch you right in the nose." Well, he was a pretty
tough little rascal; I knew that.

"Is that so?" I said.

"Yeah," he said.

"All right," I said. "I'll give you a chance as soon as the game is over. You wait for me in the clubhouse."

Well, after the game I go up to the clubhouse, and I'm going with trepidation because I think he can lick me. In fact, I *know* he can lick me. I walk into the clubhouse and there he is, in front of his locker, waiting. I take a deep breath and walk over to him.

"Here I am," I said. "You ready?"

He looked at me and said, "Jim, I made a mistake. I shouldn't have said that to you. I'm sorry."

Those were the best words I'd heard in ages. We shook hands and forgot about it.

I was a playing manager for about six years, until June of '39. No, I didn't find any special problems with being a playing manager. I was playing third base and the only thing I had to be careful of was my pitcher. I always told them never to pitch until they'd looked around at me because I might be making a change. I'm in Cleveland one day and Clint Brown is pitching. I decide to make a change, and I'm waving to the bull pen. When I look around, there's the ball, rolling up the line and turning over so slowly you could count the seams. The batter had bunted it down to me. All I can do is pick it up. I walk over to Brown.

"You forget something?" I asked.

"I guess so," he says.

At that I was lucky—a line drive could have carried my head with it into left field.

I never had any problems with clubhouse lawyers. Once in a while there would be some bitching about salaries. This is after everybody has signed, mind you. Ballplayers talk a lot among themselves. You had a pretty good year and I had a pretty good year, but I'm a better businessman than you, so I got more money than you did. So you get sore, right? I heard this talk going on and it wasn't doing any good. Finally I got them all together. "Look," I said, "I want one thing understood around here. No more discussing salaries among yourselves. You signed, I signed, he

Mickey Cochrane

signed. When you signed, you all said the same thing to yourselves, 'I'm satisfied.' So stop comparing salaries. If the next guy
is smarter than you are and got a little more, give him credit and
forget about it." That stopped it.

I guess my most oft quoted wisecrack was the one when I
called Joe McCarthy a "push-button manager." Well, Joe and I
were always great friends and still are today. One night I was
sitting around during spring training with a writer from the
Associated Press, just shooting the breeze. He got to talking about
how great McCarthy was. Well, I'm a wisecracker at heart—
always have been—and I said, "What do you mean he's a great

manager? All he's got to do is push a button and a better ballplayer comes off the bench. If I had a club like that, I wouldn't even go out to the ball park. I'd just telephone in now and then."

So this sportswriter goes to the Yankee camp later on and tells McCarthy what I said. Joe hit the ceiling. The funny part of it was, that winter I went up to New York for the Baseball Writers dinner. They had some ceremony or other planned, and there was a delay of about fifteen minutes. Nobody knew what was going on. I found out later that the delay was caused by Joe—they wanted him to push a button to start the thing going and he didn't want to do it. He finally did it, but they had to talk him into it.

But if Joe was ever sore at me for that wisecrack, he never showed it to me. Never once did he ever mention push-button manager to me. And I'll tell you, when I said that, I had no intention of casting any reflections upon his ability. He was a good manager; he had to be or he wouldn't have been winning as often as he did. What I wanted to point out was that he had all

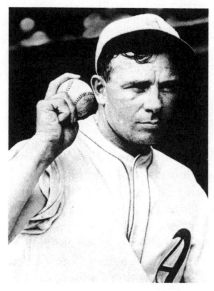

Jimmy Dykes

these good ballplayers sitting on the bench, each one bigger and stronger than the next guy. I never meant to be critical of Joe.

I made a great deal with Joe once. I had a ballplayer who didn't want to play for me, and I couldn't trade him. I went to the winter meetings that year, still trying to get rid of this guy. I got hold of Joe.

"Do you want this guy?" I asked him.

He shrugged. He wasn't too enthusiastic about the idea.

"Joe," I said, "you need a left-handed pitcher. This guy's got a chance. Not much, but he's got a chance."

"What do you want for him?" he asked.

"Give me a box of Coronas," I said.

"What?"

"Bring me a box of fifty Coronas tomorrow morning here in the lobby," I said.

Next morning I'm coming out of the dining room and here's Joe with the box of cigars.

"He's yours," I said.

Now I've got to go to Grabiner and explain the deal. I went up to his room and told him I'd just traded this pitcher to the Yankees.

"Fine," he said. "What did you get for him?"

"I'm holding it," I said.

"You mean to say you traded a pitcher for a box of cigars?"

"These are very fine cigars, Harry," I said.

He looked at me like I was crazy. Then he started to laugh.

"Christ," he said, "I don't even smoke. I don't get *anything* out of this deal, do I?"

"That's right, Harry," I said, lighting one up.

So when you have a pitcher who's only worth a box of cigars, you can see there are some problems with your ball club. I managed the White Sox for thirteen years and was in the second division most of the time. Never came close to a pennant. That wouldn't happen today, would it? I mean, today a guy is in the second division a few years and he's out of a job. The difference is I had a great general manager in Harry Grabiner. He knew I had second-division material to work with and that I was doing the

Mule Haas

best I could with it. Believe me, if I had ever had a contending team and finished in the second division with them, I would have been out of a job. I did have some good ballplayers along the way—Luke Appling, Ted Lyons, Mike Kreevich, Jackie Hayes, Thornton Lee, a few others. But never enough.

Appling was a great ballplayer and a wonderful, fun-loving guy. He could foul those balls off all day long up at the plate. You've heard those stories. One day he asked Grabiner for a dozen baseballs. Harry wouldn't give them to him. That was a mistake because Luke got piqued and went out in batting practice the next day and fouled two dozen into the stands. He could do it.

I don't think I'd want to manage today. You can have it. Too many clubhouse managers. Guys don't want to play. Don't feel good. Want a day off. I never wanted a ballplayer around who wasn't satisfied. I remember one day I overheard a guy in the clubhouse say to somebody, "I never want to play another game for him." I happened to be walking by, and I stopped and said to him, "Young man, you may never speak the truth again in your life, but you just spoke it then. You never will play for me again." I let him go. Waived him right out of the league. In those days if you had a disgruntled ballplayer, you'd ask waivers on him. If somebody claimed him, you'd call them up and say, "Waive on this guy. We want to send him to Shreveport. We'll do you a favor someday." So that's what would happen. He'd end up in Shreveport. It was different in those days.

It's a different game today in a lot of respects. Today they run pitchers in and out of there like rabbits. Righty, lefty, righty, lefty. It's that much rougher on the batters. They're always looking at different speeds, different motions. We used to leave our pitchers in. You got in a jam, you get yourself out. Don't be looking for any help from the bull pen, not till the eighth or ninth innings anyway.

I don't believe in platooning your hitters. That's a lot of crap, to me. If a guy can hit a left-hander, he can hit a right-hander. The pitch has got to come over the same plate, it's got to be a strike. Cobb used to say "If you can hit, you can hit from either side." The ball has got to come through the strike zone, right? Stay in there; don't pull away from a sidearmer. If you're going to pull back, that's different. But, hell, when I talk to some left-handed hitters today and I ask them if they can hit lefties, they say they don't know, they never get in there against them.

I had the same curfew rules as Connie—twelve o'clock, and if you're going to stay out later, let me know so I don't have to stay up and wait for you. One night in New York four guys are out. Four of my best ballplayers. Three o'clock in the morning I'm still sitting in the lobby of the New Yorker, really burned up because I liked to go to sleep around midnight. But I was determined to catch these guys. Finally, a few minutes after three o'clock in walk three of them.

"Good morning, boys," I said. "That'll cost you each five hundred dollars."

I didn't wait around for the other guy. The next morning I went out to the ball park and there he is jumping around, full of pep. Must have had a hell of a time. I walked over to him.

"Hey," I said, "what time did you come in last night? Make it after three o'clock."

"I didn't come in," he said.

"Five hundred dollars," I said.

Now, all four of these guys are married. So they're nervous because when momma finds out that money is missing out of their paychecks, she's going to want to know why. Every time they got a paycheck, they were waiting for that five hundred to be missing. But it never was. I never turned the fine in. It was something I held over them for the rest of the season. When they got their last paycheck in Chicago, all four of them came over and thanked me.

"Don't thank me," I said. "You made it yourselves. I fined you because you were guilty, but I didn't take your money because I wanted to make sure you didn't stay out again all year." That was the whip I held over them and it was a pretty good one. They behaved themselves all season after that. I never liked to take anybody's money.

In 1945 Grabiner was fired. I was his man and I knew I was going to go. I left early in the '46 season.

In '51 I replaced Mr. Mack as manager of the Athletics. He was eighty-five years old at the time, and he couldn't handle it any longer. The way I heard it, they had a big powwow in the office all day long, debating back and forth about who was going to be the new manager. Mr. Mack sat mum the whole time until finally they asked him if he had somebody in mind to take his place. And he spoke right up. "There's only one man," he said. "Jimmy Dykes." That sealed it. That was the biggest thrill of my life, replacing Mr. Mack.

Yeah, I had a reputation for being an umpire-baiter. But I don't know if that's true or not. Well, maybe a little bit. We were playing in Philadelphia one day and it's hot—and I mean hot. Close to a hundred degrees. Not a breath of air stirring. By the fourth inning everybody's wrung out. A play comes up at second base and Hank Soar calls my man out. Well, here's what I've been waiting for. I go charging onto the field.

I'm arguing with Soar and he's showing a lot of patience. Too

Jimmy Dykes explaining the situation to Cal Hubbard
"Yeah, I had a reputation for being an umpire-baiter. But I don't know
if that's true or not. Well, maybe a little bit."

much patience. I follow him around the infield, letting him have
it. And he's taking it. Finally I know I've got to use my ace in the
hole. I say, "Hank, you're just a lousy SOB." He wheels around
with his eyebrows shooting up.

"You're out of here, Dykes!" he yells.

I smiled at him. "Thanks," I said.

"What do you mean, 'thanks'?"

"You don't think I came all the way out here in this hot sun not
to get put out, do you? Now I'm going into an air-conditioned

clubhouse and have a cold beer and a nice ham sandwich and listen to the rest of the game on the radio. And you can stay out in this sun for the next five innings."

"Dykes," he says. "Dykes—I ought to make you stay in the game."

"You can't," I said. "You can throw me out. You can't throw me back in."

APPENDIX: STATISTICS

Major League Managing Career

Columns:

year	team	league	games managed	games won	games lost

games tied	no decision	winning pct.	standing*		

*standing. The figures in this column indicate the standing of the team at the end of the season and when there was a change in manager. Cases are as follows:

a. If there was only one manager for the team that year, it is shown by a single digit to the immediate right of the "Winning Pct." column.

b. If the manager started the season, but did not complete it, this is shown by two digits; the first shows the standing of the team when the manager left, and the second the final standing of the team that year.

c. If the manager finished the season, but did not begin it, the first digit shows the standing of the team when the manager began, and the second digit the standing at the season's end.

d. If the manager neither started nor finished the season, the first digit shows the standing of the team when the manager took over, the second the standing when the manager left, and the third indicates the final standing of the team that year.

e. The 1981 season was divided into two halves. Each half is listed separately; the digit in parentheses to the right of the "Standing" column indicates which record is for the first and second half-season. *See* Dick Williams.

year	team	league	games managed	games won

games lost	games tied	no decision	winning pct.	standing*

ALSTON, WALTER EMMONS (Smokey)
B. Dec. 1, 1911, Venice, Ohio
D. Oct. 1, 1984, Oxford, Ohio
Hall of Fame 1983

			G	W	L	T	N	PCT	Standing
1954	BKN	N	154	92	62	0	0	.597	2
1955			154	98	55	1	0	.641	1
1956			154	93	61	0	0	.604	1
1957			154	84	70	0	0	.545	3
1958	LA	N	154	71	83	0	0	.461	7
1959			156	88	68	0	0	.564	1
1960			154	82	72	0	0	.532	4
1961			154	89	65	0	0	.578	2
1962			165	102	63	0	0	.618	2
1963			163	99	63	1	0	.611	1
1964			164	80	82	2	0	.494	6
1965			162	97	65	0	0	.599	1
1966			162	95	67	0	0	.586	1
1967			162	73	89	0	0	.451	8
1968			162	76	86	0	0	.469	7
1969			162	85	77	0	0	.525	4
1970			161	87	74	0	0	.540	2
1971			162	89	73	0	0	.549	2
1972			155	85	70	0	0	.548	3
1973			162	95	66	1	0	.590	2
1974			162	102	60	0	0	.630	1
1975			162	88	74	0	0	.543	2
1976			158	90	68	0	0	.570	2 2
23 yrs.			3658	2040	1613	5	0	.558	

LEAGUE CHAMPIONSHIP SERIES

			G	W	L	T	N	PCT	Standing
1974	LA	N	4	3	1	0	0	.750	

WORLD SERIES

			G	W	L	T	N	PCT	Standing
1955	BKN	N	7	4	3	0	0	.571	
1956			7	3	4	0	0	.429	
1959	LA	N	6	4	2	0	0	.667	
1963			4	4	0	0	0	1.000	
1965			7	4	3	0	0	.571	
1966			4	0	4	0	0	.000	
1974			5	1	4	0	0	.200	
7 yrs.			40	20	20	0	0	.500	

Major League Playing Career

WALTER ALSTON   BR TR 6'2" 195 lbs.

year	team	league	games	B.Ave.	at bats	H	2B	3B	HR	Runs	RBIs	BB	SO	SB	PO	A	Fldg. Pct.	Games by position
1936	StL	N	1	.000	1	0	0	0	0	0	0	1	0	0	1	0	.500	1B-1

BLUEGE, OSWALD LOUIS
B. Oct. 24, 1900, Chicago, Ill.
D. Oct. 14, 1985, Edina, Minn.

			G	W	L	T	N	PCT	Standing
1943	WAS	A	153	84	69	0	0	.549	2
1944			154	64	90	0	0	.416	8
1945			156	87	67	2	0	.565	2
1946			155	76	78	1	0	.494	4
1947			154	64	90	0	0	.416	7
	5 yrs.		772	375	394	3	0	.488	

OSSIE BLUEGE

BR TR 5'11" 162 lbs.

year	team	league	games	B.Ave.	at bats	H	2B	3B	HR	Runs	RBIs	BB	SO	SB	PO	A	Fldg. Pct.	Games by position
1922	WAS	A	19	.197	61	12	1	0	0	5	2	7	7	1	18	33	.927	3B-17, SS-2
1923			109	.245	379	93	15	7	2	48	42	48	53	5	131	251	.939	3B-107, 2B-2
1924			117	.281	402	113	15	4	2	59	49	39	36	7	118	231	.946	3B-102, 2B-10, SS-4
1925			145	.287	522	150	27	4	4	77	79	59	56	16	160	290	.953	3B-144, SS-4
1926			139	.271	487	132	19	8	3	69	65	70	46	12	146	270	.950	3B-134, SS-8
1927			146	.274	503	138	21	10	1	71	66	57	47	15	185	337	.961	3B-146
1928			146	.297	518	154	33	7	2	78	75	46	27	18	150	330	.960	3B-144
1929			64	.295	220	65	6	1	5	35	31	19	15	6	74	145	.973	3B-34, 2B-14, SS-10
1930			134	.290	476	138	27	7	3	64	69	51	40	15	138	258	.964	3B-134
1931			152	.272	570	155	25	7	8	82	98	50	39	16	151	286	.960	3B-152, SS-1
1932			149	.258	507	131	22	4	5	64	64	84	41	9	158	295	.970	3B-149
1933			140	.261	501	131	14	0	6	63	71	55	34	6	116	247	.965	3B-138
1934			99	.246	285	70	9	2	0	39	11	23	15	2	114	202	.969	3B-41, SS-30, 2B-5, OF-5
1935			100	.263	320	84	14	3	0	44	34	37	21	2	148	238	.958	SS-58, 3B-25, 2B-4
1936			90	.288	319	92	12	1	1	43	55	38	16	5	177	258	.989	2B-52, SS-23, 3B-15
1937			42	.283	127	36	4	2	1	12	13	13	19	1	78	95	.956	SS-28, 1B-2, 3B-2
1938			58	.261	184	48	12	1	0	25	21	21	11	3	100	144	.980	2B-38, SS-10, 1B-1, 3B-1
1939			18	.153	59	9	0	0	0	5	3	7	2	1	103	22	.977	1B-11, 2B-2, 3B-2, SS-2
18 yrs.			1867	.272	6440	1751	276	68	43	883	848	724	525	140	2265	3932	.962	3B-1487, SS-180, 2B-127, 1B-14, OF-5
WORLD SERIES																		
1924	WAS	A	7	.192	26	5	0	0	0	2	3	3	4	1	8	24	.914	SS-5, 3B-4
1925			5	.278	18	5	1	0	0	2	2	1	4	0	1	14	1.000	3B-5
1933			5	.125	16	2	1	0	0	1	0	1	6	0	3	13	1.000	3B-5
3 yrs.			17	.200	60	12	2	0	0	5	5	5	14	1	12	51	.955	3B-14, SS-5

BRAGAN, ROBERT RANDALL
B. Oct. 30, 1917, Birmingham, Ala.

			G	W	L	T	N	PCT	Standing	
1956	PIT	N	157	66	88	3	0	.429	7	
1957			104	36	67	1	0	.350	8	7
1958	CLE	A	67	31	36	0	0	.463	5	4
1963	MIL	N	163	84	78	1	0	.519	6	
1964			162	88	74	0	0	.543	5	
1965			162	86	76	0	0	.531	5	
1966	ATL	N	112	52	59	1	0	.468	5	5
	7 yrs.		927	443	478	6	0	.481		

BOBBY BRAGAN

BR   TR   5'10 ½"   175 lbs.

year	team	league	games	B.Ave.	at bats	H	2B	3B	HR	Runs	RBIs	BB	SO	SB	PO	A	Fldg. Pct.	Games by position
1940	Phi	N	132	.222	474	105	14	1	7	36	44	28	34	2	268	443	.936	SS-132, 3B-2
1941			154	.251	557	140	19	3	4	37	69	26	29	7	324	438	.944	SS-154, 2B-2, 3B-1
1942			109	.218	335	73	12	2	2	17	15	20	21	0	242	263	.949	SS-78, C-22, 2B-4, 3B-3
1943			74	.264	220	58	7	2	2	17	24	15	16	0	264	55	.970	C-57, 3B-12, SS-5
1944	BKN	N	94	.267	266	71	8	4	0	26	17	13	14	2	207	130	.966	SS-51, C-35, 2B-1
1947			25	.194	36	7	2	0	0	3	3	7	3	1	56	5	1.000	C-24
1948			9	.167	12	2	0	0	0	0	0	1	0	0	11	1	1.000	C-5
			597	.240	1900	456	62	12	15	136	172	110	117	12	1372	1335	.950	SS-420, C-143, 3B-18, 2B-7

WORLD SERIES

year	team	league	games	B.Ave.	at bats	H	2B	3B	HR	Runs	RBIs	BB	SO	SB	PO	A	Fldg. Pct.	Games by position
1947	BKN	N	1	1.000	1	1	1	0	0	0	1	0	0	0	0	0	—	

DYKES, JAMES JOSEPH
B. Nov. 10, 1896, Philadelphia, Pa.
D. June 15, 1976, Philadelphia, Pa.

			G	W	L	T	N	PCT	Standing	
1934	CHI	A	138	49	88	1	0	.358	8	8
1935			153	74	78	1	0	.487	5	
1936			153	81	70	2	0	.536	3	
1937			154	86	68	0	0	.558	3	
1938			149	65	83	1	0	.439	6	
1939			155	85	69	0	1	.552	4	
1940			155	82	72	0	1	.532	4	
1941			156	77	77	2	0	.500	3	
1942			148	66	82	0	0	.446	6	
1943			155	82	72	1	0	.532	4	
1944			154	71	83	0	0	.461	7	
1945			150	71	78	1	0	.477	6	
1946			30	10	20	0	0	.333	7	5
1951	PHI	A	154	70	84	0	0	.455	6	
1952			155	79	75	1	0	.513	4	
1953			157	59	95	3	0	.383	7	
1954	BAL	A	154	54	100	0	0	.351	7	
1958	CIN	N	41	24	17	0	0	.585	7	4
1959	DET	A	137	74	63	0	0	.540	8	4
1960			96	44	52	0	0	.458	6	6
1960	CLE	A	58	26	32	0	0	.448	4	4
1961			160	77	83	0	0	.481	5	5
21 yrs.			2962	1406	1541	13	2	.477		

JIMMY DYKES

BR　TR　5'9"　185 lbs.

year	team	league games	B.Ave.	at bats	H	2B	3B	HR	Runs	RBIs	BB	SO	SB	PO	A	Fldg. Pct.	Games by position
1918 PHI	A	59	.188	186	35	3	3	0	13	13	19	32	3	139	190	.940	2B-56, 3B-1
1919		17	.184	49	9	1	0	0	4	1	7	11	0	28	58	.945	2B-16
1920		142	.256	546	140	25	4	8	81	35	52	73	6	363	457	.948	2B-108, 3B-36
1921		155	.274	613	168	32	13	17	88	77	60	75	6	434	522	.954	2B-155
1922		145	.275	501	138	23	7	12	66	68	55	98	6	193	307	.943	3B-140, 2B-5
1923		124	.252	416	105	28	1	4	50	43	35	40	6	285	366	.963	2B-102, SS-20, 3B-2
1924		110	.312	410	128	26	6	3	68	50	38	59	1	257	326	.957	2B-78, 3B-27, SS-4
1925		122	.323	465	150	32	11	5	93	55	46	49	3	225	302	.962	3B-64, 2B-58, SS-2
1926		124	.287	429	123	32	5	1	54	44	49	34	6	198	322	.963	3B-77, 2B-44, SS-1
1927		121	.324	417	135	33	6	3	61	60	44	23	2	864	112	.984	1B-82, 3B-25, SS-5, P-2
1928		85	.277	242	67	11	0	5	39	30	27	21	2	166	164	.973	2B-32, SS-23, 1B-8, OF-1
1929		119	.327	401	131	34	6	13	76	79	51	25	8	203	273	.935	SS-60, 3B-48, 2B-13
1930		125	.301	435	131	28	4	6	69	73	74	53	3	125	191	.960	3B-123, OF-1
1931		101	.273	355	97	28	2	3	48	46	48	47	1	136	188	.956	3B-87, SS-15
1932		153	.265	558	148	29	5	7	71	90	77	65	8	158	282	.976	3B-141, SS-10, 2B-1
1933 CHI	A	151	.260	554	144	22	6	1	49	68	69	37	3	132	296	.953	3B-151
1934		127	.268	456	122	17	4	7	52	82	64	28	1	383	252	.959	3B-74, 1B-27, 2B-27
1935		117	.288	403	116	24	2	4	45	61	59	28	4	290	185	.969	3B-98, 1B-16, 2B-3
1936		127	.267	435	116	16	3	7	62	60	61	36	1	108	240	.951	3B-125
1937		30	.306	85	26	5	0	1	10	23	9	7	0	152	27	.994	1B-15, 3B-11
1938		26	.303	89	27	4	2	2	9	13	10	8	0	75	72	.942	2B-23, 3B-1
1939		2	.000	1	0	0	0	0	0	0	0	0	0	2	0	.667	3B-2
22 yrs.		2282	.280	8046	2256	453	90	109	1108	1071	954	849	70	4916	5132	.959	3B-1253, 2B-726, 1B-148 SS-140, OF-7, P-2
WORLD SERIES																	
1929 PHI	A	5	.421	19	8	1	0	0	2	4	1	1	0	3	4	.778	3B-5
1930		6	.222	18	4	3	0	1	2	5	5	3	0	8	6	.933	3B-6
1931		7	.227	22	5	0	0	0	2	2	5	1	0	4	12	1.000	3B-7
3 yrs.		18	.288	59	17	4	0	1	6	11	11	5	0	15	22	.925	3B-18

GRIMES, BURLEIGH ARLAND
(Ol' Stubblebeard)
B. Aug. 18, 1893, Emerald, Wis.
D. Dec. 6, 1985, Clear Lake, Wis.
Hall of Fame 1964

			G	W	L	T	N	PCT	Standing
1937	BKN	N	155	62	91	2	0	.405	6
1938			151	69	80	2	0	.463	7
	2 yrs.		306	131	171	4	0	.434	

BURLEIGH GRIMES (Batting Record)   BR   TR   5'10"   175 lbs.

year	team	league	games	at bats	H	2B	3B	HR	Runs	RBIs	BB	SO	SB	BA	Games by position
1916	PIT	N	6	17	3	0	0	0	1	0	0	6	0	.176	P-6
1917			44	69	16	3	0	0	7	4	2	18	2	.232	P-37
1918	BKN	N	41	90	18	2	1	0	5	4	3	14	2	.200	P-41
1919			26	69	17	4	0	0	8	12	0	10	1	.246	P-25
1920			43	111	34	8	3	0	9	16	8	21	2	.306	P-40
1921			37	114	27	6	0	1	10	11	2	16	1	.237	P-37
1922			36	93	22	3	1	0	15	11	9	15	2	.237	P-36
1923			40	126	30	3	1	0	15	15	7	15	0	.238	P-39
1924			40	124	37	3	0	0	11	7	5	13	1	.298	P-38
1925			34	96	24	4	1	1	12	14	8	25	0	.250	P-33
1926			31	81	18	4	0	0	4	9	4	8	2	.222	P-30
1927	NY	N	39	96	18	4	0	0	10	6	5	16	0	.188	P-39
1928	PIT	N	48	131	42	8	1	0	17	16	4	15	1	.321	P-48
1929			33	91	26	3	3	0	11	12	4	10	0	.286	P-33
1930	2 teams	BOS N (11G–.188)		STL N (23G–.263)											
1930	total		34	73	18	5	0	0	12	13	6	14	0	.247	P-33
1931	STL	N	29	76	14	0	0	0	4	8	1	10	0	.184	P-29
1932	CHI	N	30	44	11	1	0	0	4	5	0	9	1	.250	P-30
1933	2 teams	CHI N (17G–.150)		STL N (4G–.200)											
1933	total		21	25	4	1	0	0	2	5	1	5	0	.160	P-21
1934	3 teams	NY A (10G–.000)		PIT N (8G–.143)	STL N (4G–.000)										
1934	total		22	9	1	0	0	0	0	0	0	1	0	.111	P-22
19 yrs.			634	1535	380	62	11	2	157	168	69	241	15	.248	P-617
WORLD SERIES															
1920	BKN	N	3	6	2	0	0	0	1	0	0	0	0	.333	P-3
1930	STL	N	2	5	2	0	0	0	0	0	0	1	0	.400	P-2
1931			2	7	2	0	0	0	0	2	0	2	0	.286	P-2
1932	CHI	N	2	1	0	0	0	0	0	0	0	1	0	.000	P-2
4 yrs.			9	19	6	0	0	0	1	2	0	4	0	.316	P-9

BURLEIGH GRIMES (Pitching Record)

BR TR 5'10" 175 lbs.

year	team	league	W	L	Pct	ERA	G	GS	GC	IP	H	BB	K	ShO	PO	A	E
1916	PIT	N	2	3	.400	2.36	6	5	4	45.2	40	10	20	0	1	16	3
1917			3	16	.158	3.53	37	17	8	194	186	70	72	1	9	62	6
1918	BKN	N	19	9	.679	2.14	41	28	19	269.2	210	76	113	7	12	94	5
1919			10	11	.476	3.47	25	21	13	181.1	179	60	82	1	12	50	3
1920			23	11	.676	2.22	40	33	25	303.2	271	67	131	5	17	95	7
1921			22	13	.629	2.83	37	35	30	302.1	313	76	136	2	17	89	2
1922			17	14	.548	4.76	36	34	18	259	324	84	99	1	12	79	6
1923			21	18	.538	3.58	39	38	33	327	356	100	119	2	16	101	10
1924			22	13	.629	3.82	38	36	30	310.2	351	91	135	1	25	91	4
1925			12	19	.387	5.04	33	31	19	246.2	305	102	73	0	18	92	7
1926			12	13	.480	3.71	30	29	18	225.1	238	88	64	1	4	72	3
1927	NY	N	19	8	.704	3.54	39	34	15	259.2	274	87	102	2	16	71	0
1928	PIT	N	25	14	.641	2.99	48	37	28	330.2	311	77	97	4	9	106	4
1929			17	7	.708	3.13	33	29	18	232.2	245	70	62	2	10	65	3
1930	2 teams	BOS N (11G 3-5)			STL N (22G 13-6)												
1930	total		16	11	.593	4.07	33	28	11	201.1	246	65	73	1	8	47	1
1931	STL	N	17	9	.654	3.65	29	28	17	212.1	240	59	67	3	16	57	4
1932	CHI	N	6	11	.353	4.78	30	18	5	141.1	174	50	36	1	12	33	2
1933	2 teams	CHI N (17G 3-6)			STL N (4G 0-1)												
1933	total		3	7	.300	3.78	21	10	3	83.1	86	37	16	1	6	16	1
1934	3 teams	STL N (4G 2-1)			PIT N (8G 1-2)	NY A (10G 1-2)											
1934	total		4	5	.444	6.11	22	4	0	53	63	26	15	0	5	16	0
19 yrs.			270	212	.560	3.53	617	495	314	4179.2	4412	1295	1512	35	225	1252	71

WORLD SERIES

1920	BKN N	1	2	.333	4.19	3	3	1	19.1	23	9	4	1	1	7	1
1930	STL N	0	2	.000	3.71	2	2	2	17	10	6	13	0	0	3	0
1931	N	2	0	1.000	2.04	2	2	1	17.2	9	9	11	0	0	3	0
1932	CHI N	0	0	—	23.63	2	0	0	2.2	7	2	0	0	0	0	0
4 yrs.		3	4	.429	4.29	9	7	4	56.2	49	26	28	1	1	13	1

HERMAN, WILLIAM JENNINGS BRYAN
B. July 7, 1909, New Albany, Ind.
D. Sept. 5, 1992, West Palm Beach, Fla.
Hall of Fame 1975

			G	W	L	T	N	PCT	Standing	
1947	PIT	N	155	61	92	2	0	.399	8	7
1964	BOS	A	2	2	0	0	0	1.000	8	8
1965			162	62	100	0	0	.383	9	
1966			146	64	82	0	0	.438	10	9
	4 yrs.		465	189	274	2	0	.408		

BILLY HERMAN

year	team league	games	B.Ave.	at bats	H	2B	3B	HR	Runs	RBIs	BB	SO	SB	PO	A	Fldg. Pct.	Games by position
1931	CHI N	25	.327	98	32	7	0	0	14	16	13	6	2	76	79	.939	2B-25
1932		154	.314	656	206	42	7	1	102	51	40	33	14	401	527	.961	2B-154
1933		153	.279	619	173	35	2	0	82	44	45	34	5	466	512	.956	2B-153
1934		113	.303	456	138	21	6	3	79	42	34	31	6	278	385	.975	2B-111
1935		154	.341	666	227	57	6	7	113	83	42	29	6	416	520	.964	2B-154
1936		153	.334	632	211	57	7	5	101	93	59	30	5	457	492	.975	2B-153
1937		138	.335	564	189	35	11	8	106	65	56	22	2	384	468	.954	2B-137
1938		152	.277	624	173	34	7	1	86	56	59	31	3	404	517	.981	2B-151
1939		156	.307	623	191	34	18	7	111	70	66	31	9	377	485	.967	2B-156
1940		135	.292	558	163	24	4	5	77	57	47	30	1	366	448	.974	2B-135
1941 2 teams	CHI N (11G-.194) BKN N (133G-.291)																
1941 total		144	.285	572	163	30	5	3	81	41	67	43	1	330	374	.964	2B-144
1942 BKN N		155	.256	571	146	34	2	2	76	65	72	52	6	412	404	.973	2B-153, 1B-3
1943		153	.330	585	193	41	2	2	76	100	66	25	4	345	390	.972	2B-117, 3B-37
1946 2 teams	BKN N (47G-.288) BOS N (75G-.306)																
1946 total		122	.298	436	130	31	5	3	56	50	69	23	3	352	207	.972	2B-76, 3B-63, 1B-22
1947 PIT N		15	.213	47	10	4	0	0	3	6	2	7	0	20	15	1.000	2B-10, 1B-2
15 yrs.		1922	.304	7707	2345	486	82	47	1163	839	737	428	67	5084	5823	.968	2B-1829, 3B-100, 1B-27
WORLD SERIES																	
1932 CHI N		4	.222	18	4	1	0	0	5	1	1	3	0	5	12	.944	2B-4
1935		6	.333	24	8	2	1	1	3	6	0	2	0	15	19	.971	2B-6
1938		4	.188	16	3	0	0	0	1	0	1	4	0	5	14	.905	2B-4
1941 BKN N		4	.125	8	1	0	0	0	0	0	2	0	0	4	13	1.000	2B-4
4 yrs.		18	.242	66	16	3	1	1	9	7	4	9	0	29	58	.956	2B-18

LOPEZ, ALFONSO RAYMOND
B. Aug. 20, 1908, Tampa, Fla.
Hall of Fame 1977

			G	W	L	T	N	PCT	Standing		
1951	CLE	A	155	93	61	1	0	.604	2		
1952			155	93	61	1	0	.604	2		
1953			155	92	62	1	0	.597	2		
1954			156	111	43	2	0	.721	1		
1955			154	93	61	0	0	.604	2		
1956			155	88	66	1	0	.571	2		
1957	CHI	A	155	90	64	1	0	.584	2		
1958			155	82	72	1	0	.532	2		
1959			156	94	60	2	0	.610	1		
1960			154	87	67	0	0	.565	3		
1961			163	86	76	1	0	.531	4		
1962			162	85	77	0	0	.525	5		
1963			162	94	68	0	0	.580	2		
1964			162	98	64	0	0	.605	2		
1965			162	95	67	0	0	.586	2		
1968			11	6	5	0	0	.545	9	9	8
1968			36	15	21	0	0	.417	9	8	
1969			17	8	9	0	0	.471	4	5	
17 yrs			2425	1410	1004	11	0	.584			
WORLD SERIES											
1954	CLE	A	4	0	4	0	0	.000			
1959	CHI	A	6	2	4	0	0	.333			
2 yrs.			10	2	8	0	0	.200			

AL LOPEZ

BR TR 5'11" 165 lbs.

year	team	league	games	B.Ave.	at bats	H	2B	3B	HR	Runs	RBIs	BB	SO	SB	PO	A	Fldg. Pct.	Games by position
1928	BKN	N	3	.000	12	0	0	0	0	0	0	0	0	0	9	0	1.000	C-3
1930			128	.309	421	130	20	4	6	60	57	33	35	3	465	66	.983	C-126
1931			111	.269	360	97	13	4	0	38	40	28	33	1	390	69	.977	C-105
1932			126	.275	404	111	18	6	1	44	43	34	35	3	456	82	.976	C-125
1933			126	.301	372	112	11	4	3	39	41	21	39	10	452	88	.991	C-124, 2B-1
1934			140	.273	439	120	23	2	7	55	54	49	44	2	548	68	.982	C-137, 2B-2, 3B-2
1935			128	.251	379	95	12	4	3	50	39	35	36	2	472	65	.980	C-126
1936	BOS	N	128	.242	426	103	12	4	8	46	50	41	41	1	448	107	.975	C-127, 1B-1
1937			105	.204	334	68	11	1	3	31	38	35	57	3	342	83	.984	C-102
1938			71	.267	236	63	6	1	1	19	14	11	24	5	240	42	.989	C-71
1939			131	.252	412	104	22	1	8	32	49	40	45	1	424	72	.986	C-129
1940	2 teams		BOS N (36G—.294)	PIT N (59G—.259)														
1940	total		95	.273	293	80	9	3	3	35	41	19	21	6	343	62	.990	C-95
1941	PIT	N	114	.265	317	84	9	1	5	33	43	31	23	0	345	54	.980	C-114
1942			103	.256	289	74	8	2	1	17	26	34	17	0	327	53	.995	C-99
1943			118	.263	372	98	9	4	1	40	39	49	25	2	378	67	.989	C-116, 3B-1
1944			115	.230	331	76	12	1	1	27	34	34	24	4	372	52	.984	C-115
1945			91	.218	243	53	8	0	0	22	18	35	12	1	326	38	.992	C-91
1946			56	.307	150	46	2	0	1	13	12	23	14	1	173	30	.985	C-56
1947	CLE	A	61	.262	126	33	1	0	0	9	14	9	13	1	144	28	1.000	C-57
19 yrs.			1950	.261	5916	1547	206	42	52	613	652	561	538	46	6654	1126	.984	C-1918, 2B-3, 3B-3, 1B-1

McCARTHY, JOSEPH VINCENT
(Marse Joe)
B. Apr. 21, 1887, Philadelphia, Pa.
D. Jan. 3, 1978, Buffalo, N. Y.
Hall of Fame 1957

			G	W	L	T	N	PCT	Standing	
1926	CHI	N	155	82	72	1	0	.532	4	
1927			153	85	68	0	0	.556	4	
1928			154	91	63	0	0	.591	3	
1929			156	98	54	4	0	.645	1	
1930			152	86	64	2	0	.573	2	2
1931	NY	A	155	94	59	2	0	.614	2	
1932			156	107	47	1	1	.695	1	
1933			152	91	59	2	0	.607	2	
1934			154	94	60	0	0	.610	2	
1935			149	89	60	0	0	.597	2	
1936			155	102	51	2	0	.667	1	
1937			157	102	52	2	1	.662	1	
1938			157	99	53	5	0	.651	1	
1939			152	106	45	1	0	.702	1	
1940			155	88	66	0	1	.571	3	
1941			156	101	53	2	0	.656	1	
1942			154	103	51	0	0	.669	1	
1943			155	98	56	1	0	.636	1	
1944			154	83	71	0	0	.539	3	
1945			152	81	71	0	0	.533	4	
1946			35	22	13	0	0	.629	2	3
1948	BOS	A	155	96	59	0	0	.619	2	
1949			155	96	58	1	0	.623	2	
1950			59	31	28	0	0	.525	4	3
	24 yrs		3487	2125	1333	26	3	.615		

			G	W	L	T	N	PCT	Standing
WORLD SERIES									
1929	CHI	N	5	1	4	0	0	.200	
1932	NY	A	4	4	0	0	0	1.000	
1936			6	4	2	0	0	.667	
1937			5	4	1	0	0	.800	
1938			4	4	0	0	0	1.000	
1939			4	4	0	0	0	1.000	
1941			5	4	1	0	0	.800	
1942			5	1	4	0	0	.200	
1943			5	4	1	0	0	.800	
	9 yrs.		43	30	13	0	0	.698	

**Joe McCarthy had no
major league playing career.**

PECKINPAUGH, ROGER THORPE
B. Feb. 5, 1891, Wooster, Ohio
D. Nov. 17, 1977, Cleveland, Ohio

			G	W	L	T	N	PCT	Standing	
1914	NY	A	20	10	10	0	0	.500	7	6
1928	CLE	A	155	62	92	1	0	.403	7	
1929			152	81	71	0	0	.533	3	
1930			154	81	73	0	0	.526	4	
1931			155	78	76	1	0	.506	4	
1932			153	87	65	1	0	.572	4	
1933			51	26	25	0	0	.510	5	4
1941			155	75	79	1	0	.487	4	
8 yrs.			995	500	491	4	0	.505		

ROGER PECKINPAUGH

year	team	league games	B.Ave.	at bats	H	2B	3B	HR	Runs	RBIs	BB	SO	SB	PO	A	Fldg. Pct.	Games by position
1910	CLE A	15	.200	45	9	0	0	0	1	6	1		3	20	38	.906	SS-14
1912		69	.212	236	50	4	1	1	18	22	16		11	127	188	.924	SS-67
1913	CLE A (1G--.000)																
1913	NY A (95G--.268)	96	.268	340	91	10	7	1	36	32	24	47	19	184	303	.931	SS-94
1914	NY A	157	.223	570	127	14	6	3	55	51	51	73	38	356	500	.956	SS-157
1915		142	.220	540	119	18	7	5	67	44	49	72	19	291	468	.942	SS-142
1916		146	.255	552	141	22	8	4	65	58	62	50	18	285	468	.946	SS-146
1917		148	.260	543	141	24	7	0	63	41	64	46	17	292	467	.934	SS-148
1918		122	.231	446	103	15	3	0	59	43	43	41	12	260	439	.961	SS-122
1919		122	.305	453	138	20	2	7	89	33	59	37	10	271	434	.943	SS-121
1920		139	.270	534	144	26	6	8	109	54	72	47	8	263	441	.962	SS-137
1921		149	.288	577	166	25	7	8	128	71	84	44	2	318	443	.948	SS-149
1922	WAS A	147	.254	520	132	14	4	2	62	48	55	36	11	265	524	.951	SS-147
1923		154	.264	568	150	18	4	2	73	62	64	30	10	311	510	.948	SS-154
1924		155	.272	523	142	20	5	2	72	73	72	45	11	278	487	.963	SS-155
1925		126	.294	422	124	16	4	4	67	64	49	23	13	219	346	.953	SS-124, 1B-1
1926		57	.238	147	35	4	1	1	19	14	28	12	3	89	109	.957	SS-46, 1B-1
1927	CHI A	68	.295	217	64	6	3	0	23	23	21	6	2	101	170	.964	SS-60
17 yrs.		2012	.259	7233	1876	256	75	48	1006	739	814	609	207	3930	6335	.949	SS-1983, 1B-2

WORLD SERIES

year	team	league games	B.Ave.	at bats	H	2B	3B	HR	Runs	RBIs	BB	SO	SB	PO	A	Fldg. Pct.	Games by position
1921	NY A	8	.179	28	5	1	0	0	2	0	4	3	0	18	28	.979	SS-8
1924	WAS A	4	.417	12	5	2	0	0	1	2	1	0	1	7	14	1.000	SS-4
1925		7	.250	24	6	1	0	1	1	2	1	2	1	10	22	.800	SS-7
3 yrs.		19	.250	64	16	4	0	1	4	4	6	5	2	35	64	.917	SS-19

RICHARDS, PAUL RAPIER
B. Nov. 21, 1908, Waxahachie, Tex.
D. May 4, 1986, Waxahachie, Tex.

			G	W	L	T	N	PCT	Standing	
1951	CHI	A	155	81	73	1	0	.526	4	
1952			156	81	73	2	0	.526	3	
1953			156	89	65	2	0	.578	3	
1954			146	91	54	1	0	.628	3	3
1955	BAL	A	156	57	97	2	0	.370	7	
1956			154	69	85	0	0	.448	6	
1957			154	76	76	2	0	.500	5	
1958			154	74	79	1	0	.484	6	
1959			155	74	80	1	0	.481	6	
1960			154	89	65	0	0	.578	2	
1961			136	78	57	1	0	.578	3	3
1976	CHI	A	161	164	94	0	0	.398	6	
12 yrs			1837	923	901	13	0	.506		

PAUL RICHARDS

BR TR 6'1½" 180 lbs.

year	team	league	games	B.Ave.	at bats	2B	3B	HR	Runs	RBIs	BB	SO	SB	PO	A	E	Fldg. Pct.	Games by position
1932	BKN	N	3	.000	8	0	0	0	0	0	0	0	2	0	21	3	1.000	C-3
1933	NY	N	51	.195	87	17	3	0	0	4	10	3	12	0	74	17	.989	C-36
1934			42	.160	75	12	1	0	0	10	3	13	8	0	86	15	1.000	C-37
1935 2 teams	NY N (7G--.250)	PHI A (85G--.245)																
1935 total			92	.245	261	64	10	1	4	31	29	26	13	0	300	42	.977	C-83
1943	DET	A	100	.220	313	69	7	1	5	32	33	38	35	1	537	86	.986	C-100
1944			95	.237	300	71	13	0	3	24	37	35	30	8	413	60	.979	C-90
1945			83	.256	234	60	12	1	3	26	32	19	31	4	361	44	.995	C-83
1946			57	.201	139	28	5	2	0	13	11	23	18	2	311	35	.997	C-54
8 yrs.			523	.227	1417	321	51	5	15	140	155	157	149	15	2103	302	.987	C-486
WORLD SERIES																		
1945	DET	A	7	.211	19	4	2	0	0	0	6	4	3	0	46	5	.981	C-7

SAWYER, EDWIN MILBY
B. Sept. 10, 1910, Westerly, R. I.

			G	W	L	T	N	PCT	Standing	
1948	PHI	N	63	23	40	0	0	.365	6	6
1949			154	81	73	0	0	.526	3	
1950			157	91	63	3	0	.591	1	
1951			154	73	81	0	0	.474	5	
1952			63	28	35	0	0	.444	6	4
1958			70	30	40	0	0	.429	7	8
1959			155	64	90	1	0	.416	8	
1960			1	0	1	0	0	.000	8	8
8 yrs			817	390	423	4	0	.480		

WORLD SERIES

| 1950 | PHI | N | 4 | 0 | 4 | 0 | 0 | .000 | | |

**Eddie Sawyer did not
have a major league career.**

SEWELL, JAMES LUTHER
B. Jan. 5, 1901, Titus, Ala.
D. May 14, 1987, Akron, Ohio

			G	W	L	T	N	PCT	Standing	
1941	STL	A	113	55	55	3	0	.500	7	6
1942			151	82	69	0	0	.543	3	
1943			153	72	80	1	0	.474	6	
1944			154	89	65	0	0	.578	1	
1945			154	81	70	3	0	.536	3	
1946			125	53	71	1	0	.427	7	7
1949	CIN	N	3	1	2	0	0	.333	7	7
1950			153	66	87	0	0	.431	6	
1951			155	68	86	1	0	.442	6	
1952			98	39	59	0	0	.398	7	6
10 yrs			1259	606	644	9	0	.485		

WORLD SERIES

			G	W	L	T	N	PCT
1944	STL	A	6	2	4	0	0	.333

LUKE SEWELL

BR TR 5'9" 160 lbs.

year	team	league	games	B.Ave.	at bats	2B	3B	HR	Runs	RBIs	BB	SO	SB	PO	A	E	Fldg. Pct.	Games by position
1921	CLE	A	3	.000	6	0	0	0	0	0	1	0	3	0	7	4	1.000	C-3
1922			41	.264	87	23	5	0	0	14	10	5	8	1	108	21	.963	C-38
1923			10	.200	10	2	0	1	0	2	1	1	0	0	5	5	.833	C-7
1924			63	.291	165	48	9	1	0	27	17	22	13	1	171	42	.959	C-56
1925			74	.232	220	51	10	2	0	30	18	33	18	6	222	54	.972	C-66,OF-2
1926			126	.238	433	103	16	4	0	41	46	36	27	9	437	91	.983	C-125
1927			128	.294	470	138	27	6	0	52	53	20	23	4	402	119	.963	C-126
1928			122	.270	411	111	16	9	3	52	52	26	27	3	430	117	.972	C-118
1929			124	.236	406	96	17	3	1	41	39	29	26	6	433	81	.966	C-124
1930			76	.257	292	75	21	2	1	40	43	14	9	5	283	49	.974	C-76
1931			108	.275	375	103	30	4	1	45	53	36	17	1	384	61	.980	C-105
1932			87	.253	300	75	20	2	2	36	52	38	24	4	306	50	.978	C-84
1933	WAS	A	141	.264	474	125	30	4	2	65	61	48	24	7	516	61	.990	C-141
1934			72	.237	207	49	7	3	2	21	21	22	10	0	215	30	.992	C-50, OF-7, 1B-6, 2B-1, 3B-1
1935	CHI	A	118	.285	421	120	19	3	2	52	67	32	18	3	399	83	.988	C-112
1936			128	.251	451	113	20	5	5	59	73	54	16	11	461	87	.984	C-126
1937			122	.269	412	111	21	6	1	51	61	46	18	4	502	72	.985	C-118
1938			65	.213	211	45	4	1	0	23	27	20	20	0	205	55	.985	C-65
1939	CLE	A	16	.150	20	3	1	0	0	1	1	3	1	0	24	4	.966	C-15, 1B-1
1942	STL	A	6	.083	12	1	0	0	0	1	0	1	5	0	12	5	.944	C-6
20 yrs.			1630	.259	5383	1393	273	56	20	653	696	486	307	65	5522	1091	.978	C-1561, OF-9, 1B-7, 2B-1, 3B-1

WORLD SERIES

year	team	league	games	B.Ave.	at bats	2B	3B	HR	Runs	RBIs	BB	SO	SB	PO	A	E	Fldg. Pct.	Games by position
1933	WAS	A	5	.176	17	3	0	0	0	1	1	2	0	1	23	2	1.000	C-5

SHAWKEY, JAMES ROBERT
B. Dec. 4, 1890, Siegel, Pa.
D. Dec. 31, 1980, Syracuse, N. Y.

			G	W	L	T	N	PCT	Standing
1930	NY	A	154	86	68	0	0	.558	3

BOB SHAWKEY (Pitching Record)

BR TR 5'11" 168 lbs.

year	team	league	W	L	Pct	ERA	G	GS	CG	IP	H	BB	K	ShO	PO	A	E
1913	PHI	A	6	5	.545	2.34	18	15	8	111.1	92	50	52	1	3	40	4
1914			16	8	.667	2.73	38	31	18	237	223	75	89	5	6	63	5
1915	2 teams	PHI A (17G 6-6) NY A (16G 4-7)															
1915	total		10	13	.435	3.68	33	22	12	185.2	181	73	87	2	5	49	3
1916	NY	A	24	14	.632	2.21	53	27	21	276.2	204	81	122	4	12	79	3
1917			13	15	.464	2.44	32	26	16	236.1	207	72	97	2	18	79	4
1918			1	1	.500	1.13	3	2	1	16	7	10	3	1	6	4	0
1919			20	11	.645	2.72	41	27	22	261.1	218	92	122	3	22	59	4
1920			20	13	.606	2.45	38	31	20	267.2	246	85	126	5	15	48	1
1921			18	12	.600	4.08	38	31	18	245	245	86	126	3	14	35	3
1922			20	12	.625	2.91	39	33	19	299.2	286	98	130	3	13	70	4
1923			16	11	.593	3.51	36	31	17	258.2	232	102	125	1	9	61	2
1924			16	11	.593	4.12	38	25	10	207.2	226	74	114	1	11	39	6
1925			6	14	.300	4.11	33	20	9	186	209	67	81	1	7	37	0
1926			8	7	.533	3.62	29	10	3	104.1	102	37	63	1	2	23	1
1927			2	3	.400	2.89	19	2	0	43.2	44	16	23	0	3	11	1
15 yrs.			196	150	.566	3.09	488	333	194	2937	2722	1018	1360	33	146	697	41

WORLD SERIES

year	team	league	W	L	Pct	ERA	G	GS	CG	IP	H	BB	K	ShO	PO	A	E
1914	PHI	A	0	1	.000	5.40	1	1	0	5	4	2	0	0	0	3	0
1921	NY	A	0	1	.000	7.00	2	1	0	9	13	6	5	0	0	0	0
1922			0	0	—	2.70	1	1	1	10	8	2	4	0	0	2	0
1923			1	0	1.000	3.52	1	1	0	7.2	12	4	2	0	1	2	0
1926			0	1	.000	5.40	3	1	0	10	8	2	7	0	0	1	0
5 yrs.			1	3	.250	4.75	8	5	1	41.2	45	16	18	0	1	8	0

BOB SHAWKEY (Batting Record)

year	team	league	games	at bats	H	2B	3B	HR	Runs	RBIs	BB	SO	SB	BA	Games by position
1913	PHI	A	18	44	6	1	0	0	3	5	1	10	0	.136	P-18
1914			38	83	17	3	0	0	6	5	4	22	0	.205	P-38
1915	2 teams	NY A (16G--.241)		PHI A (17G--.129)											
1915	total		33	60	11	5	1	0	3	3	3	21	0	.183	P-33
1916	NY	A	53	93	17	1	0	0	5	4	3	21	0	.183	P-53
1917			32	84	16	4	0	0	3	8	3	15	0	.190	P-32
1918			3	4	3	0	0	0	1	0	1	0	0	.750	P-3
1919			41	94	22	1	0	0	5	6	1	15	0	.234	P-41
1920			38	100	23	1	0	0	13	10	4	13	0	.230	P-38
1921			38	90	27	2	1	1	13	11	2	13	0	.300	P-38
1922			39	115	21	2	0	1	12	12	2	18	0	.183	P-39
1923			36	99	20	1	1	0	8	10	0	15	0	.202	P-36
1924			38	69	22	4	1	1	12	15	7	5	0	.319	P-38
1925			33	68	10	1	2	0	1	2	0	4	0	.147	P-33
1926			29	35	9	1	0	0	4	3	3	6	0	.257	P-29
1927			19	11	1	0	0	0	1	0	0	3	0	.091	P-19
15 yrs.			488	1049	225	26	6	3	90	94	34	181	0	.214	P-488

WORLD SERIES

Year	Team	Lg												AVG	
1914	PHI	A	1	2	1	1	0	0	0	1	0	1	0	.500	P-1
1921	NY	A	2	4	2	0	0	0	2	0	0	1	0	.500	P-2
1922			1	4	0	0	0	0	0	0	0	1	0	.000	P-1
1923			1	3	1	0	0	0	0	1	0	0	0	.333	P-1
1926			3	2	0	0	0	0	0	0	0	1	0	.000	P-3
5 yrs.			8	15	4	1	0	0	2	2	0	4	0	.267	P-8

SMITH, EDWARD MAYO

B. Jan. 17, 1915, New London, Mo.
D. Nov. 24, 1977, Boynton Beach, Fla.

			G	W	L	T	N	PCT	Standing
1955	PHI	N	154	77	77	0	0	.500	4
1956			154	71	83	0	0	.461	5
1957			156	77	77	2	0	.500	5
1958			84	39	45	0	0	.464	7 8
1959	CIN	N	80	35	45	0	0	.438	7 5
1967	DET	A	163	91	71	1	0	.562	2
1968			164	103	59	2	0	.636	1
1969			162	90	72	0	0	.556	2
1970			162	79	83	0	0	.488	4
	9 yrs		1279	662	612	5	0	.520	

WORLD SERIES

			G	W	L	T	N	PCT	Standing
1968	DET	A	7	4	3	0	0	.571	

MAYO SMITH

BL TR 6' 183 lbs.

year	team	league	games	B.Ave.	at bats	H	2B	3B	HR	Runs	RBIs	BB	SO	SB	PO	A	Fldg. Pct.	Games by position
1945	PHI	A	73	.212	203	43	5	0	0	18	11	36	13	0	120	4	.976	OF-65

WILLIAMS, RICHARD HIRSCHFELD
B. May 7, 1928, St. Louis, Mo.

			G	W	L	T	N	PCT	Standing	
1967	BOS	A	162	92	70	0	0	.568	1	
1968			162	86	76	0	0	.531	4	
1969			153	82	71	0	0	.536	3 3	
1971	OAK	A	161	101	60	0	0	.627	1	
1972			155	93	62	0	0	.600	1	
1973			162	94	68	0	0	.580	1	
1974	CAL	A	84	36	48	0	0	.429	6 6	
1975			161	72	89	0	0	.447	6	
1976			96	39	57	0	0	.406	4 4	
1977	MON	N	162	75	87	0	0	.463	5	
1978			162	76	86	0	0	.469	4	
1979			160	95	65	0	0	.594	2	
1980			162	90	72	0	0	.556	2	
1981			55	30	25	0	0	.545	3	(1st)
1981			26	14	12	0	0	.538	6 1	(2nd)
1982	SD	N	162	81	81	0	0	.500	4	
1983			163	81	81	1	0	.500	4	
1984			162	92	70	0	0	.568	1	
1985			162	83	79	0	0	.512	3	
1986	SEA	A	133	58	75	0	0	.436	6 7	
1987			162	78	84	0	0	.481	4	
1988			56	23	33	0	0	.411	6 7	
	21 yrs.		3023	1571	1451	1	0	.520		

LEAGUE CHAMPIONSHIP SERIES

			G	W	L	T	N	PCT		
1971	OAK	A	3	0	3	0	0	.000		
1972			5	3	2	0	0	.600		
1973			5	3	2	0	0	.600		
1984	SD	N	5	3	2	0	0	.600		
	4 yrs.		18	9	9	0	0	.500		

WORLD SERIES

			G	W	L	T	N	PCT		
1967	BOS	A	7	3	4	0	0	.429		
1972	OAK	A	7	4	3	0	0	.571		
1973			7	4	3	0	0	.571		
1984	SD	N	5	1	4	0	0	.200		
	4 yrs.		26	12	14	0	0	.462		

DICK WILLIAMS

BR TR 6' 190 lbs.

year	team league	games	B.Ave.	at bats	H	2B	3B	HR	Runs	RBIs	BB	SO	SB	PO	A	Fldg. Pct.	Games by position
1951	BKN N	23	.200	60	12	3	1	1	5	5	4	10	0	21	1	1.000	OF-15
1952		36	.309	68	21	4	1	0	13	11	2	10	0	51	3	1.000	OF-25, 1B-1, 3B-1
1953		30	.218	55	12	2	0	2	4	5	3	10	0	24	0	.923	OF-24
1954		16	.147	34	5	0	0	1	5	2	2	7	0	12	0	1.000	OF-14
1956	2 teams	BKN N (7G–.286)	BAL A (87G–.286)														
1956	total	94	.286	360	103	18	4	11	45	37	30	41	5	249	17	.985	OF-81, 1B-10, 2B-10, 3B-4
1957	2 teams	BAL A (47G–.234)	CLE A (67G–.283)														
1957	total	114	.261	372	97	17	2	7	49	34	26	40	3	244	72	.975	OF-63, 3B-34, 1B-12
1958	BAL A	128	.276	409	113	17	0	4	36	32	37	47	0	359	61	.981	OF-70, 3B-45, 1B-26, 2B-7
1959	KC A	130	.266	488	130	33	1	16	72	75	28	60	4	349	181	.976	3B-80, 1B-32, OF-23, 2B-3
1960		127	.288	420	121	31	0	12	47	65	39	68	0	376	131	.979	3B-57, 1B-34, OF-25
1961	BAL	103	.206	310	64	15	2	8	37	24	20	38	0	209	16	.987	OF-75, 1B-20, 3B-2
1962		82	.247	178	44	7	1	1	20	18	14	26	0	180	13	1.000	OF-29, 1B-21, 3B-4
1963	BOS A	79	.257	136	35	8	0	2	15	12	15	25	0	64	28	.989	3B-17, 1B-11, OF-7
1964		61	.159	69	11	2	0	5	10	11	7	10	0	50	21	.986	1B-21, 3B-13, OF-5
13 yrs.		1023	.260	2959	768	157	12	70	358	331	227	392	12	2188	544	.982	OF-456, 3B-257, 1B-188, 2B-20

WORLD SERIES

year	team league	games	B.Ave.	at bats	H	2B	3B	HR	Runs	RBIs	BB	SO	SB	PO	A	Fldg. Pct.	Games by position
1953	BKN N	3	.500	2	1	0	0	0	0	0	1	1	0	0	0	—	

INDEX

Italic numbers indicate pages on which there are photographs.